A Dissolving Dream

GW00762218

A Dissolving Dream

A New Zealander in Amin's Uganda

Heather Benson

First published in 1992 by Bridget Williams Books Limited
P.O. Box 11-294, Wellington New Zealand
Reprinted 1992, 1993

This edition first published 1993
Reprinted 1994, 1995

ISBN 0 908912 58 7

Cover design by Mission Hall Design Group
Typeset by Typocrafters Limited, Auckland
Printed by SRM Production Services, Malaysia

To Tanya, Joseph and Moira
For your enduring patience, *webale nnyo*

Author's Note

This book is based on actual events – or rather my interpretation of those events. Since much of what happened occurred twenty years ago, I trust I will be forgiven if a little imagination crept in when memory faded.

Apart from my immediate family and a number of public figures, every effort has been made to protect the identities of the people who touched my life.

I must acknowledge two valuable sources that assured the historical accuracy of this story. These are *General Amin* by David Martin and *State of Blood* by Henry Kyemba.

Finally I must say thank you to family, friends and colleagues for their love and support while I was writing this book.

Map of Uganda

Showing

MAIN TOWNS

MAJOR TRIBES

and the

FOUR TRADITIONAL KINGDOMS

Nubian/Sudanese Settlements   National Parks

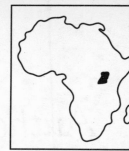

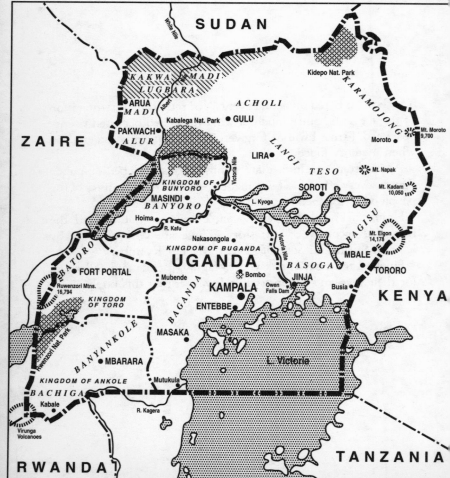

SUDAN

White Nile

KAKWA *MADI*
LUGBARA

Kidepo Nat. Park

KARAMOJONG

ARUA
MADI

ACHOLI

ZAIRE

Kabalega Nat. Park ● **GULU**

Albert

Mt. Moroto
9,700

PAKWACH
ALUR

● Moroto

Victoria Nile

● **LIRA**

LANGI

Mt. Napak

*KINGDOM OF
BUNYORO*

TESO

Mt. Kadam
10,050

● **MASINDI**

BANYORO

● **SOROTI**

● Hoima

L. Kyoga

BAGISU

R. Kafu

Mt. Elgon
14,178

BATORO

● Nakasongola

Victoria Nile

KINGDOM OF BUGANDA

● **MBALE**

FORT PORTAL ●

● Mubende

BASOGA

● **TORORO**

Ruwenzori Mtns.
16,794

UGANDA

Bombo

KAMPALA

JINJA

Rwenzori Nat. Park

*KINGDOM
OF TORO*

BAGANDA

ENTEBBE ●

Owen
Falls Dam

● Busia

KENYA

● **MASAKA**

BANYANKOLE

L. Victoria

● **MBARARA**

KINGDOM OF ANKOLE

● Mutukula

BACHIGA

● Kabale

R. Kagera

Virunga
Volcanoes

RWANDA

TANZANIA

Heaven smiles, and faiths and empires gleam,
Like wrecks of a dissolving dream.

Percy Bysshe Shelley
Hellas, *1822*

The Kingdom of Uganda is a fairy tale. You climb a railway instead of a beanstalk and at the end there is a wonderful new world. The scenery is different, the vegetation is different, the climate is different and, most of all, the people are different from anything elsewhere to be seen in the whole range of Africa.
Uganda . . . the pearl of Africa.

Sir Winston Churchill,
My African Journey, *1907*

Chapter 1

Midnight: December 1969.

Next stop Entebbe. I felt sick with apprehension.

The American woman next to me painstakingly painted her last fingernail and replaced the brush in the bottle. She held out her hands, surveying her blood-red talons. I had met her on a brief stopover in Mauritius and we had become acquainted; she was escaping from her third husband, I was about to join my first. The intercom crackled and announced: 'We are now approaching Entebbe Airport. Please return to your seats and fasten your seatbelts.'

'Jesus,' I whispered. 'We're there.'

Will he be waiting? Will his parents be there to lynch me? Do I look all right?

Designer jeans, a scanty silk top, tanned limbs, youth on my side – I should have been supremely confident. I wasn't.

The plane lurched in descent. For some minutes I stared out the window into the night. My reflection stared back at me from a very young, wide-eyed, slightly scared face. I tried to conjure up Joe's features. The strong dark contours that once came readily to mind were now vague and elusive, melting into the blackness outside. Far below me I could see the airport lights winking feebly. Africa looked cold and uninviting.

'God, I'm scared!' I said to the American.

'What for?' she said with a laugh. 'If you can come through Mauritius without getting laid by a Qantas pilot, you can come through anything!'

The plane screamed along the runway. I stood up. I was the only passenger getting off. The woman blew me a kiss from scarlet lips. I swung my bag over my shoulder and disembarked into the black African night.

The airport was dingy and old. It looked like an oversized barn that had been reluctantly converted into a third-rate bus terminus and then, even more reluctantly, into an airport. There were no elevators, conveyor belts or computerised machines. There were a number of people milling about – wide-bottomed, slow-moving women in voluminous gowns, Indian clerks, a handful of eager black students in spectacles and pinstripes about to leave on my plane for England. I felt conspicuous and alone.

I found my luggage and a barefoot youth came over and helped me carry it through Immigration (a jowly Indian with garlic-flavoured halitosis) and Customs (a short man with a startling Afro hairdo that suggested he was plugged into an electrical point beneath the counter). We then made our way through a pair of wooden doors to the lobby outside.

I saw Joe immediately, dropped my bags and ran to him. For a minute we embraced and laughed and clung to each other, and then, with his arm around my shoulders, he turned me towards three people – two Africans and a European.

'I want you to meet my friends. This is my cousin Byron who drinks Kampala dry every weekend.' I nodded at Byron who was plump, bespectacled and smiling. 'And this is John Musoke, a friend of mine from schooldays' – a broad solid man with a big, good-natured face.

'And this Muzungu,' he pulled over the European, 'is James. We came in his car. He's British. Teaches upcountry on an aid programme.' James had a boyish face overhung by a cowlick of lank, fair hair. He shook my hand and suggested we go upstairs for a drink before driving back to Kampala.

'Yes. Heather must sample our waragi,' said Byron beaming. He called the youth to follow us upstairs with the luggage.

'Waragi,' said James, in a Pommy voice in my ear as we sat down at a table, 'is a local alcoholic concoction made from bananas.'

A white-uniformed bar attendant brought our drinks and a dish of groundnuts. Although it was after midnight, the bar was still quite busy. A group of Sikhs at the next table snapped their fingers for service. I sipped my drink, which was not unlike gin, and gazed out of the windows. At the end of the runway my BOAC plane was taking off for London. I felt a stab of panic and clutched Joe's hand beneath the table.

'It's okay, darling,' he whispered, and squeezed my hand.

I stared down at the table, feeling homesick already. Beside me James was babbling happily. 'Marvellous country, this. Varied as hell – lakes, mountains, bush that goes on forever. We're in Buganda here, you know. Terrifically fertile place. Drop a groundnut and it'll sprout from the soil before your eyes.'

Under the table Joe caressed my fingers. I longed to be alone with him.

Musoke, with the big face and kind eyes, told me about his family and invited us to spend the following Sunday with them. He also promised to tell me stories of Joe's escapades at school.

'I always thought he was a studious type,' I said with a smile and Musoke laughed and shook his head. I decided I liked Musoke a lot.

After our drinks we descended to the main lobby. Joe informed me that there was a state of emergency since the recent attempt on President Obote's life and that we might strike army roadblocks on the way to Kampala. Musoke and James followed us downstairs, with Byron and a porter struggling in the rear with my luggage. They were held up by a group of Indians who had congregated at the foot of the stairs and I heard Byron muttering angrily.

'We have tons of Indians in Uganda,' said Joe as we crossed the carpark. 'Although they make a real contribution to the country they've never been popular.' He told me that much of their unpopularity was caused by their unwillingness to mix with the Africans and by the stranglehold they had on the commercial sector.

We got into the car, James and Byron in the front and Joe, Musoke and me in the back. Joe's arm came round me.

'I've missed you so much, Heather,' he whispered and his lips felt warm on my neck. I snuggled close to him.

We sped through the sleeping town of Entebbe.

'Kampala is twenty miles further on,' said James behind the wheel. 'Look to the right. There's Lake Victoria.'

Victoria Nyanza, source of the Nile! I had read so much about it. The lake shimmered in the moonlight, calm and beautiful, coming almost to the road and fringed with dark trees.

'Beautiful, but not for swimming,' said Joe, as if reading my thoughts. 'It's full of a parasite called bilharzia. It affects the bloodstream.'

'What a terrible waste,' I murmured. Suddenly the car screeched to a halt. Three armed soldiers opened the doors and began pulling us all out. My arm was seized and I was hauled to the side of the road. Byron was dragged from the front seat and flung at me with such force that his shoulder struck me in the mouth, splitting my lip. Joe, James and Musoke were shoved over to join us. Two hurricane lanterns cast eerie shadows across the road and I watched, frightened and angry, as my suitcases were thrown on the road along with the contents of James's car. A tall, skinny soldier approached, his rifle pointed at us.

'Who owns the suitcases?' he said in laborious English.

'They're mine!' I said indignantly.

He barked that he needed to search them. I handed over the keys, which he tossed to his two cronies who immediately opened my bags and began rummaging through my things. A white lacy nightgown, a wedding present from my sister, was tossed carelessly in the air, floating to the ground like an injured swan. The contents of my sponge bag were emptied gleefully on to the road, the soldiers snickering like a pair of hyenas. The skinny soldier informed me that they were conducting an arms search.

'There are no guns in my cases,' I informed him.

Joe nudged me to keep quiet. The soldier shouted at me for my insolence; I thought he would strike me. He then demanded my passport. With shaking hands I scrabbled in my bag for my passport. As I held it out to him blood from my lip dripped on to my arm.

'Muzungu! Why have you a Kiganda name?' he barked at me.

4

He stared again at the passport and then his voice rose in mounting disbelief. 'Surely you're not married to one of these!' He gestured at Joe and his friends.

I nodded.

'Shauri yako,' he muttered, shaking his head. Then he pointed to James. 'Why aren't you married to her?'

'Me? Marry a Kiwi?' James's voice broke with astonishment. Even his cowlick looked surprised. He looked at me, flustered, and as our eyes met we became aware of the idiocy of the situation. Simultaneously we burst out laughing, the noise pealing into the night. The soldiers rummaging through my belongings slowly straightened up and stared at us in amazement. The skinny soldier screamed, 'Stop!'

We stopped.

'You're not permitted to laugh at a roadblock.' The soldier shut my passport and tossed it to me. 'You can go now.'

We walked to the car in silence. Joe helped me gather up my scattered belongings while the soldiers waylaid James for cigarettes. Eventually we all got back in the car. As we were about to leave the skinny soldier suddenly beamed down at me through the car window.

'Uganda nice country. Very nice country.'

I nodded and dabbed my bleeding lip.

Once we were on the road again Joe turned to me, stiff with repressed anger. 'You could have been shot for laughing like that, or at least beaten up! This isn't New Zealand where the army is a pack of civil nursemaids!'

'Me, marry a Kiwi?' James hooted with laughter.

Joe turned on him furiously. 'It's all very well for you Bazungu to laugh,' he said. 'You don't have to stand by and watch your people suffer! It's all a bit of an adventure to you!'

There was silence. I looked at Joe. The wide beautifully boned face that I loved so much was tight with fury. I, who had known him for four years, had never guessed he was capable of such anger. I felt I did not know this angry, bitter man.

Uncomfortable and apprehensive, I sat miserably with a tissue pressed to my lip. For the first time I began to realise the depth of unrest in this country.

'Don't worry,' whispered Musoke beside me. 'He's angry and

ashamed that you were introduced to Uganda this way.' I was glad Musoke was with us.

As we drove on into the blackness I took Joe's indifferent hand between mine and tried to rub away the tension. The fingers gradually responded and I could feel his body relaxing. He squeezed my hand.

'God, I'm sorry, darling. I haven't even asked about the cut on your lip. Let me look.' It was not deep and had already stopped bleeding. He kissed it softly and drew me tight against him. 'This is a crazy country. I so much wanted you to like it.'

James took us past the Kabaka's former palace. The car lights shone on the massive battle-scarred walls, a legacy from the battle that ousted the Kabaka, the traditional king of the Baganda, Joe's people.

'One day Obote will pay for this,' said Joe quietly.

We finally reached the outskirts of Kampala, James calling out the suburbs as we passed – Mengo, Old Kampala, Nakivubo. The area, poorly lit, seemed old and worn. We headed upward and arrived on Kampala Road, the city's main thoroughfare. It was long, wide, well lit and lined with modern shops. Guards – askaris, Joe called them – sat in shop doorways in shapeless, greatcoated bundles. Joe said that the country was experiencing an enormous crime wave and askaris were in big demand. Since most of them appeared to be sleeping, they didn't seem to represent any great threat to would-be criminals.

I looked about me with growing interest. Kampala lay across a series of gentle hills pinpricked with hazy lights. From a nearby hill rose the majestic Apolo Hotel with its rows of shining windows. For a minute I thought it was our destination, but we plunged down a side road where the surroundings deteriorated rapidly into small alleys, mean little stores or dukkas, and shabby tenements. There was a huge, flat, concreted area to our left.

'That's the Shauri Yako Market. Deserted now, but busy as hell in the daytime.' Joe smiled at me. 'Shauri yako is Swahili for "your problem". That's what that soldier said to you when he discovered you were married to me.'

To my surprise the car slowed to a halt near the market. Across the road was a seedy hotel set back from the road. My heart sank and I looked back across the city to where the Apolo sparkled on the hillside. As we got out, the smell of mouldering vegetation from the market hit us. The Shauri Yako Hotel looked squat and rundown, with little dukkas clinging to its sides like clumps of parasites. Its miserable neon sign had long since given up the ghost.

'It's not so bad inside,' whispered Joe.

James took my luggage from the boot and deposited it on the ground. 'See you round, old girl,' he said and patted my shoulder.

There was a round of goodbyes before they drove off. Joe crossed the road to rouse the hotel askari who lay semi-comatose in the doorway. I stood alone, baggage at my feet, watching the car disappear.

The askari who tottered towards me on creaking legs looked at least a hundred years old. A wooden baton hung from his waist, flapping limply at his groin like a tired sex organ. We divided up the luggage and followed him back to the hotel.

At that moment the hotel door burst open and a short, fat Greek in a white safari suit flew out towards us with outstretched arms. 'Welcome, welcome,' he panted, taking the bag from me. 'I am Dimitrios. This is my hotel. We have been waiting so anxiously for your arrival, eh Joe?'

Dimitrios hurried me into the dimly lit foyer. To the left a somewhat shaky staircase climbed steeply skyward. On the right was a reception desk on which sat a black telephone, a vase of dusty plastic flowers, and a girlie magazine. The Greek dispatched Joe and the askari upstairs with the luggage, telling Joe to join us in his parlour when he had finished. Dimitrios then plunged through a private door behind the reception desk, urging me to follow. Feeling rather like Alice chasing the White Rabbit, I pursued him through a warren of passages until we landed suddenly in a brightly lit room with overstuffed chairs and brilliant floral curtains. He sat me down and called loudly for tea.

Several seconds later a sleepy black woman in a bathrobe entered, carrying a tray. Taking this from her, he dismissed her curtly. He poured the tea, talking all the time.

'She's my wife. A mistake. You'll find out, my dear, that Africans are just not like us.' He leaned towards me conspiratorially, his words like effluvium dropping from thick, glistening lips. 'They are lazy, childish and stupid.'

I could hardly believe my ears. 'Marriages like yours and mine never last because the African is inferior to us.'

'What a load of bullshit!'

He threw back his head and laughed at me, the cavernous nostrils showing hairy bristles. 'You wait and see, my little one.'

'You've just maligned an entire race of people out of hand,' I said angrily. 'You're arrogant and intolerant and you treat your wife like a serf in her own country.'

Now he'll kick us out.

Joe appeared suddenly at the door. Standing up with relief and without finishing my tea, I allowed him to escort me from the room. Dimitrios wished us goodnight, holding me back by the arm as I passed. His breath was foetid as he whispered, 'One day you'll find that all I told you is true.'

And on that auspicious note I went upstairs to bed.

Chapter 2

Dawn broke with the muezzin calling Kampala's Moslems to prayer. Market noises drifted in with the light. I lay with my head on Joe's chest, listening to the boom-boom-boom of his heart.

'Don't go to work. Throw a sickie.'

'I have to go, darling.'

'Oh, stuff your work!' I tried to keep him beneath the sheets but he kissed me and pulled away to sit on the edge of the bed. I clasped him around the waist, burying my face in the small of his back. Beneath my lips his skin was damp and salty. He gently unclasped my arms and went to the window. He had a new job at a United Nations-sponsored management training and advisory centre, a position almost tailor-made for his interests and qualifications, and he was eager to prove himself.

I sat up and sighed. Our night together was over, the demands of a new life already upon us. In a creaking bed in a stuffy room in a seedy hotel our reunion had been one of unforgettable passion – warm lips, clasping limbs, hot, wet bodies and the bittersweet smell of our mingling. I recalled the endless whispered declarations of love and the quiet aftermath when I was filled with peace and warm security. I wondered crossly why Joe's work had to intrude.

Joe stood at the window, alone with his thoughts. There was something vulnerable about his stance, something childlike in the droop of his neck, the softness of his ear, the roundness of his cheek. I longed to gather him in my arms again. He seemed worried about how I would pass the day without him and suggested I visit some real estate agents and go flat-hunting.

Breakfast was brought to our room by a pixie-ish, barefoot lad called Innocent, which I suspected was a misnomer as I watched him, eyes downcast, slyly waiting for a tip. Over breakfast Joe and I caught up on news of our families and friends and discussed my proposed visit to the village to meet his parents. We moved on to politics and Joe told me in low tones about the problems under Uganda's President Obote.

'He has always disliked the Baganda and his government discriminates against us wherever possible. Most people feel that the Kabaka's death in England was engineered by Obote.'

It was a disquieting thought and for some time after Joe left I mulled over the situation in this strange country. After showering in the depressing bathroom down the hall, I dressed and wandered downstairs, stepping around the ancient askari, who was drinking tea from a tin mug on the bottom step.

'Jambo, memsahib,' he greeted me, revealing withered gums.

'Jambo,' I replied in self-conscious Swahili, instantly disliking his use of the title.

From the adjoining dining room came the smell of fresh coffee and, recalling the lukewarm brew on our breakfast tray, I decided to have some. The dining room was deserted except for Innocent, who sat chatting to a morose-looking Asian bartender. I ordered coffee and sat down at a table. The Asian, whose name was Musa, brought it to me with a shy smile and I asked for directions to the main road and the post office. For the next few minutes he and Innocent, in a mixture of Swahili and English, proceeded to give me thoroughly contradictory instructions. The door opened and Dimitrios walked in. Innocent fled on silent feet while Musa hastily repositioned himself behind the bar where he energetically applied himself to the counter with a wet cloth.

'Did you have a good night?' asked Dimitrios in a silken voice – the ordinary question sounded dirty in his mouth.

I told him that I had slept soundly, thank you, and tried to ignore him. He invited me to his parlour, smiling over cratered teeth as he told me of a new liqueur he thought I would like.

10

I declined his offer and left as quickly as I could, to find myself on the hotel doorstep, looking out on the busy street and blinking in the bright sunlight.

There were people everywhere. Men in impeccable British suits walked briskly up towards Kampala Road. Women swayed across to the market in voluminous basutis, gowns fashioned for them in the Victorian era. Modern bewigged girls tottered along the pavement in high heels and mini-skirts, several of them with faces cosmetically bleached to a peculiar shade of amber. I watched, fascinated, as bicycles overloaded with bananas, cloth and crates of squawking chickens made their way precariously to the market, where fruit and vegetables were heaped high on the stalls and small boys ran about on dusty legs drumming up business. Mothers, wide-faced black madonnas, glided through the produce with babes on their backs, making purchases that went into large grass baskets.

Set up on the footpaths were shoe repairers, peanut sellers, hairdressers. One sign on a table near me read 'Doctor of Watches'. Behind it sat a dim-witted individual in bifocals who looked scarcely able to comprehend time. There were tailors seated at old sewing machines, talking and laughing as they treadled their way through acres of material.

I hesitated on the doorstep, suddenly a little shy about going out among them. Feeling alone and conspicuous, I wandered into the market and bought a bunch of short, plump bananas. Munching, I made my way up to Kampala Road.

Here it was quite different. There were modern, well-maintained buildings, and shrubs and flowers growing in carefully tended plots. Beside the wide footpaths airy shops were stocked to capacity with imported appliances, foodstuffs and fashions, and I noticed interesting indoor-outdoor restaurants offering Italian, Indian and Chinese cuisine. Still munching, I looked up beyond the city confines. The hills around me were a profusion of lush, green bush and bright flowers. The vegetation seemed poised, ready to repossess the city at the first opportunity.

The shops, almost without exception, were owned by Asians who thronged the pavements in all shades and castes – turbaned Sikhs, saried Hindus, bejewelled and handsome Ismailis and dark-eyed Goans. I remembered the caustic remarks that Joe had made about them the night before.

I lounged against the window of a curio shop, observing the carvings and leather goods and longing to do some shopping for my family back home. Such thoughts only served to remind me of our precarious financial state. Years as students had left Joe and me with no savings and I had arrived in Uganda broke. Joe, although he had returned four months earlier, had spent most of that time receiving job rejections, thanks to Obote's discriminatory recruitment practices. He had landed his present job only a week before my arrival and his first pay cheque was not due for three weeks, since wages here were paid only at the end of each month. I wondered suddenly if we would be trapped into staying with Dimitrios for a month until we could afford to pay up and leave.

I found the post office, checked our box and, with the handful of change Joe had left me earlier, bought aerograms and stamps. I wandered into several real estate offices and discussed our requirements with the staff. Since we lacked ready cash, our prospects for renting a flat immediately were not promising. It was after midday when I returned despondently to the hotel. Not feeling like lunch, I ensconced myself with a Coke at a window table in the dining room and began a letter home.

I was halfway through the first page when all hell broke loose in the market opposite. Voices rose in a roaring crescendo and askaris converged from all sides of the square, blowing whistles and laying about them with batons.

'Mubi! Mubi!' shouted Innocent, running to the window.

'They've caught a mubi or thief,' explained Musa, as we looked out on the confusion. 'Unless the askaris get to him first, the people could beat him to death.'

A man extricated himself from the mob and ran past our window, an onlooker tripped him up and the crowd caught up with him. He was kicked and punched, someone threw a stone at his head, blood spurted. Askaris, whistles blowing ineffectually, tried to pull the crowd off him. A police siren wailed in the distance. People began to disperse, muttering. When the police arrived, no one appeared to know anything. Even the askaris shook their heads. The police, apparently used to such things, threw the body in the Landrover and drove away.

Innocent went back to the kitchen, Musa to the bar, the diners to their tables. I sat down to finish my letter but found myself staring blankly at the page.

Shocked and horrified, I relayed the story to Joe when he returned that evening.

'People are tired of robbery,' he said. 'Obote's law and order are ineffectual. The army itself commits a lot of the crime. People can only protect themselves by meting out their own justice.'

I pointed out bitterly that he appeared to be justifying the murder of someone who had probably only stolen a cabbage. His face hardened and he told me to stop analysing Uganda's problems through Western eyes.

Hurt, I turned from him and went to the window. I felt hemmed in by the grubby walls of our room, oppressed by the tattered curtains, sagging bed and fly-specked mirror. I heard Dimitrios roaring for Innocent deep within the bowels of the hotel. Outside a large vulture wheeled in the sky over the market. Below a peanut seller spat into the gutter.

I thought suddenly of home – its clean, sandy beaches and glistening shorelines where old ladies paddled on translucent legs. It seemed on another planet. In a wave of homesickness I turned back to Joe but his face was still grim and unyielding.

I sank wearily on to the bed reflecting, for the second time in twenty-four hours, that I did not know this strange new Joe. I longed for the Joe I had known in New Zealand.

Chapter 3

March 1966.

I first became aware of the African in English class. He had a dark, handsome face and a quick, intelligent way about him. He wrote pages of notes during lectures and when he was not writing he was alert and attentive. He always sat in the same place on the far side of the room.

One cool autumn morning, as our English lecturer droned on about John Donne, my friend Jane, red-haired and gipsyish, nudged me.

'Othello's looking,' she whispered.

I looked up and saw the bronze face of the African man. His dark eyes held mine for a second before they turned away in confusion. He took up his pen and began to write furiously. I, too, turned away and tried to concentrate on the lecture but for some reason I found this difficult and I wanted to look at the man again.

Jane passed me a note in her urgent scrawl. DO YOU THINK HE FANCIES YOU? *No, you twit!* I wrote beneath it. The note was shoved back under my nose. WELL I THINK HE JOLLY WELL DOES! I screwed it up and put it in my pocket as Jane turned to Pam on her other side to begin a whispered discussion about the situation. I decided to ignore them.

The next day I passed the African in a busy corridor. Our eyes met for an instant and flicked away. A day or so later he entered the same lift as me and, a little flustered, I got out on the wrong floor. In English after that I studiously avoided looking to the far side of the room.

It was an eventful year for me. I was enrolled for an arts degree at Victoria University in Wellington, with plans to major in psychology and anthropology. Freed from the stultifying atmosphere of a private Anglican school I had loathed, I now revelled in a freedom that I had never before experienced. I grew my hair, wore jeans to lectures and joined the anti-Vietnam War movement. I made new and exciting friends, vastly different from the aspiring debutantes of my schooldays. We were hippies and socialists and freedom fighters all at once. Fired with idealism and determination, we stood in the rain and chanted messages of love and tolerance to a violent, muddled world. My parents watched from afar with growing trepidation.

It was at the Plunket Street party that the African and I exchanged our first words, me spattered in mud and minus a shoe, him immaculate in suit and tie.

The party had been noisy and overcrowded, with Jefferson Airplane and the Beatles belting out into the cool Wellington night. There had been a drug raid and Jane, Pam and I, completely innocent but intent on avoiding the police, had leapt from a balcony into the bush below. The drop was further than we expected and we had floundered blindly in the mud and undergrowth. I had lost a shoe.

'Shit, there's Othello!' said Jane, scarf askew, staring up through the vegetation. Sure enough, on the road above us, clearly visible beneath a streetlight, was the African, staring down at us. Behind him were the flashing lights of police cars and a swelling crowd of onlookers.

We made our way up the bank to the road, where Jane and Pam left me to see who was being hauled into the paddy wagons. I remained in the shadows at the side of the road, pulling twigs from my hair.

'That was quite some jump.' The African materialised beside me. His voice was soft and well modulated. I nodded in agreement and, conscious of my dishevelled state, sank further into the shadows, embarrassed.

'At least you won't be taken in for questioning,' he said, as angry shouting erupted from the paddy wagons.

'Thank God.'

'Yes. Thank God.'

Our eyes met and this time neither of us turned away. He smiled and I found myself telling him about my lost shoe down in the bush.

'They were my favourite pair,' I said, sighing heavily.

'"When thou sigh'st, thou sigh'st not wind . . .",' he laughed, quoting from John Donne. I asked him how the rest of it went but he said he had forgotten. I had a feeling he hadn't – conscientious students like him did not forget quotes.

Later that night, as I curled up to sleep in my hostel bed, the rest of the quotation from Donne came to me.

'When thou sigh'st, thou sigh'st not wind,
But sigh'st my heart away.'

In English Jane told me she had found out that his name was Joseph – Joe to his friends – and that he was from Uganda. *Uganda!* I wondered why someone from Uganda needed to study John Donne.

My eyes strayed to the other side of the room. He looked up suddenly. We both started, then smiled.

The note was not long in coming. HE'S LOOKING AT YOU AS THOUGH HE COULD EAT YOU!! ARE UGANDANS CANNIBALS???

Jane, in her inimitable way, had arranged for us to have coffee with Joe and his friends after the lecture. As we entered the cafeteria we spotted Joe at a nearby table with two friends. He smiled and rose to his feet as we approached. The wide, handsome face suggested both intelligence and strength. He was at least six feet tall, with broad shoulders narrowing to his waist, neatly clad in sports jacket and good trousers.

As we sat down he introduced us to his two friends. Paul, the one sitting beside me, asked what we would drink.

'Three coffees, please,' said Jane quickly. 'Pam and I take

white' – her eyes twinkled and she kicked me under the table – 'and Heather likes hers black.' I kicked her back hard and for a moment she forgot about coffee, white, black or otherwise.

Over coffee we discussed our studies and current political issues. It was a stimulating conversation and no one noticed the time until Paul looked at his watch and hurriedly departed. The rest followed suit, leaving only Joe and me. There was an uncomfortable silence for a moment and then he asked politely if I came from Wellington. Telling him I came from Marton, a little town about a hundred miles north, I briefly described my upbringing. When I asked him about his home, I heard about a childhood that was light years away from mine. We were soon chatting like old friends. It was impossible not to respond to his warmth and sensitivity. I began to share with him my interest in anthropology.

'You should come to Uganda. There's a host of things to interest an anthropologist,' he said.

'Maybe I will,' I replied laughing.

'If I ever come across you in the field studying us, I'll take you out to lunch. Do you like bananas?' He smiled at me then, a delightful smile that seemed to bring every feature alive.

I looked at my watch and reluctantly began to gather up my books.

'I've noticed you for a long time now.' His voice was quiet.

'Oh?' I said and kept stacking.

'I look at you in English. You have a very interesting and very attractive face.' There was no flattery in his words and I was covered in confusion.

'You would do better to listen to the lecturer and his opinions on English poets,' I said primly, getting up to go.

'Now I've offended you. I'm sorry.'

'Don't be. I'm hopeless with compliments. And I did enjoy our talk.'

He asked me to have dinner with him, promising it would not be bananas. I hesitated, then accepted and we settled on the following Saturday. He gave me his address and stood up beside me.

'There are five more days until Saturday,' he said quietly. 'May they pass quickly.'

He held out his hand and my palm was lost in his huge gentle clasp.

He occupied comfortable rooms on The Terrace and I was nervous as I knocked at his door. I shivered in the cold, wishing I was back in the bright hostel kitchen eating steamed pudding and custard with my friends. The door opened and Joe stood before me, smiling in welcome. Any apprehensions I had quickly disappeared in the warmth of his presence. He led me into his living room, which overlooked the harbour. The moonlight glistened on the calm water and lights like drops of amber dotted the edge of Oriental Bay.

Over dinner he told me about Uganda. I sat, fascinated. He told me about his tribe, the Baganda, the largest and most progressive in Uganda, and about its king or Kabaka. It became clear that the Kabaka, the thirty-fifth ruler of a five hundred-year-old dynasty, was regarded by his people as something between monarch and deity.

'There's mounting conflict between Prime Minister Obote and our Kabaka, who is also the President. The Baganda are one of the four great kingdoms in the south of Uganda. Obote's tribe, the Langi, are from the north, where the people are completely different and far less politically sophisticated. There's not much common ground between King Freddie, as the West calls the Kabaka, and Obote.'

He went on to explain the tensions. Buganda, the kingdom of the Baganda people, had always been the most powerful and prosperous region in Uganda. With its industrious people and its modern towns of Entebbe, Masaka and Kampala, Buganda had considerable political clout. Joe feared that Obote, wary of Buganda's power, was now filling up the army with his northerners, particularly Langi and Acholi people who could one day oust the Kabaka and thus destroy Buganda's power.

'Why can't the Baganda rise up?'

'They don't have the guns. They don't have the military training. Our people were always more interested in educating their children than enlisting them in the army. It was a mistake that we may have to pay for.'

18

After dinner we sat at the window, talking a little more about Uganda, and I was entranced by Joe's great love for his country. He put on a Billie Holiday album and the plaintive bluesy music filled the room with sadness. For a while we sat in silence, Joe gazing out at the harbour lost in thought, his eyes sad, his head with its crisp black hair leaning against the window. He seemed lonely and vulnerable, and evoked in me a feeling of intense tenderness.

Around ten o'clock Joe's friend Paul called in on his way home from the library. He had a lean, bony face and an infectious sense of humour and I warmed to him. While Joe was in the kitchen preparing coffee Paul sprawled on the sofa to chat. I learned during the course of our conversation that Joe was a first-class boxer, that he had a conservative Roman Catholic background and that he was twenty-seven years old. Paul made me laugh as he described Joe's early attempts to find out more about me.

When Joe returned with coffee, his reflective mood had disappeared and he laughed heartily with us as we gossiped about the personal lives of some of our lecturers.

Paul left at eleven and Joe put on more music, blues again. He leaned back in his chair and closed his eyes. I felt an inexplicable desire to rise, put my arms about him and offer him comfort. Abruptly he opened his eyes.

'Do you know why I asked you to come here?'

'To have dinner with you, which I've enjoyed.'

'And my company?'

I felt I was on dangerous ground. He half-smiled but there was no change in the dark eyes, which were still serious as they regarded me.

'I enjoyed your company,' I said lightly but I was uneasy. There was no doubt now of the growing attraction between us. Like a lazy tide it swirled about us, its gentle pull unmistakable.

It was nearly midnight when I left. He walked me back to the hostel gates. A light a few paces away cast a reluctant glow on his face.

'Thanks, Joe, for a lovely evening.'

'Come here, Heather,' he whispered and, taking me in his arms, he kissed me gently. My arms went round his neck; I felt warm and safe. When he released me he asked if I would like to see him again.

'Yes,' I replied truthfully.

'Then I shall sleep happy tonight.' He lifted both my hands to his lips. 'Goodnight,' he whispered and vanished into the darkness.

And so began a relationship with Joe that was to change the course of my life. I often wondered what he saw in me – not yet out of my teens, a long-haired borderline hippy in beads and flowers, who did not share his interest in academic achievement or political debate or his masters thesis in public administration, who laughed at his well-tailored suits and looked with disdain on his boxing. And yet he loved me, as I did him, and made me feel clever and worthwhile and important.

'How does he do it?' I asked Jane one night.

'Black magic!' and she screamed with laughter and woke the matron.

The months passed and one year turned into another. There was only one little blot on an otherwise perfect horizon – my family. I knew that somehow my future would be closely bound up with Joe, and my family in Marton still knew nothing about him.

Chapter 4

On Sunday Musoke picked us up from the hotel to spend the day with his family at Tank Hill. His was a typical Muganda household – a gentle, softly spoken wife called Sarah, a number of children, one or two relatives and a couple of servants. Musoke was a company accountant and lived in a middle-class, predominantly African area. He had an airy bungalow set in a lovely garden of bougainvillea, hibiscus and jacaranda. After a week in the Shauri Yako Hotel it was a relief to be in pleasant surroundings.

Byron and James arrived after us, tooting loudly in a car almost awash with bottles of beer. We had lunch under the trees and, as the beer flowed, there was much laughter and storytelling. As the afternoon grew warm, the fragrance of a flowering bush wafted across to us on the soft lake breezes. For the first time since I had come to Uganda I felt completely relaxed. Around me the others had lapsed into Luganda. I told Sarah that I wanted to learn the language and she went inside to get her Luganda manual. James and I flicked through it with interest. It looked complicated but I was determined to persevere.

As evening approached Musoke and the houseboy lit up two sigilis – small charcoal stoves – and put on meat to roast while Sarah brought out bowls of rice, matoke and beans. The night was warm and pleasant with the aroma of flowers, charcoal and food, and I felt content in the companionship of Joe's friends.

It was dark when we said goodbye. I didn't want to go back to the miserable hotel. The smell of rotting vegetables in the market greeted us on our return and we had to step over the drunken body of the askari in the hotel doorway.

The days were passing. I filled in the hours by flat-hunting, job-hunting and exploring the town. I wrote to Jane and to Paul. 'It's a bit of a joke,' I said. 'We're so broke we can't leave this bloody hotel.'

Some mornings I walked with Joe to his office, returning to the hotel along narrow streets where pyjamaed Asian men sat on shop doorsteps drinking tea. I became familiar with the shrill, Gujerat-chattering children, oiled and braided, as they hurried to school. I enjoyed watching the little dukkas come to life – iron grilles rolled back from doors and windows, merchandise of all descriptions hung high in doorways, early morning greetings called across counters.

But time weighed heavily. I wrote letters and read newspapers. I joined the library at the other end of town and started learning Luganda from Sarah's book, trying it out on everyone I could. Sometimes I sat at the bar drinking Coke with Musa; at other times, out of sheer desperation, I played cards with Dimitrios and his Greek cronies. One of them once showed me a lump of gold he had smuggled in from Zaire.

'Congolese gold! Beautiful! I brought it out in the body of my dead brother,' he explained and I looked vacuously at the gold in my palm, deposited there by means of a Greek rectum.

One day Dimitrios asked us to clear our bill. Joe explained that he would settle the account when he got paid at the end of the month. Dimitrios was not happy about this and his attitude became distinctly unfriendly. He watched our movements closely, as if expecting us to do a moonlight flit at any time. Our breakfast no longer came up on a tray and I was no longer invited to join him and his friends at cards. He stared as we ate, begrudging us every mouthful, and I was convinced that he had ordered the cook to decrease our portions at mealtimes.

Musa's cousin Osman wandered into the bar one day, looking

as if he had lost his way to a fifties fancy dress party. He was a James Dean clone in black leathers and sideburns. His huge new motor bike, a gleaming red and silver monster, sat on the pavement outside, attracting attention. He asked if I wanted a ride. He seemed a nice enough chap but I hesitated. Dimitrios, counting money at the till, looked up and stared at me balefully. Suddenly the prospect of a spin in the fresh air seemed wonderful.

We zoomed through the narrow streets of Nakivubo and into the green hills beyond the city. In the shambas, or yards, there were hens, goats, toddling children and women bent over buckets of soapy water. Their laundry, like flags, lay about on bushes to dry. I waved to a group of naked children eating mangoes.

'This is the real Uganda!' I shouted joyfully at Osman's immaculatey coiffed duck's arse.

We cruised around Makerere University and then roared up Kampala Road, almost collecting two old men on bicycles outside the Bank of Uganda. We entered the suburbs on the other side of the city, stopping just past Bugolobi to look at a huge construction site.

'It looks like a space station. What is it?'

Osman explained that it was a housing estate being built by the Israelis. I had heard that Israel was providing considerable aid to Uganda, particularly in military training. I could understand Israel's wish to have an ally in black Africa, particularly in Uganda where they could keep an eye on the civil war in Sudan between the African southerners and Arab northerners.

'People say that Uganda and Israel are actually arming the southern Sudanese,' I mused. 'I suppose the Israelis want to occupy the Arabs on as many fronts as possible.'

But Osman didn't know, didn't care and was eager to be off so we burned down Port Bell Road and drew up at Silver Springs, a modest little hotel with thatched cottages and a swimming pool. Ordering Pepsis, we sat at a poolside table. It was warm and Osman looked moist and uncomfortable in his leathers. I asked if he were a Ugandan citizen.

'All my family are,' he said. 'We are as Ugandan as any African here.' I took in the swept-up coiffure, the studded jacket, the expensive Swiss watch at his wrist, and found it a little hard to believe.

We watched a European man determinedly doing lengths in the pool. On the far side two large Russian women in dowdy swimsuits sat on the edge of the water, trailing pale hairy legs. Sipping his Pepsi, Osman chatted about his hopes to go to California and break into the movies.

It was after five when we headed back to Kampala. Maribou storks on the roof of the Meat Packers building fled in fright as we zoomed by. Joe was waiting outside the hotel when we pulled up. His face furious, he grabbed Osman by the collar and dragged him off the bike. A few people gathered. Musa peered anxiously through the dining room window. Joe shoved Osman up against the wall.

My God! He's going to fight him!

Joe shook Osman vigorously and then suddenly released him. Terrified, Osman slid down the wall, his careful hairdo dismantling by the minute. I tried to intervene but Joe turned on me.

'And you! Where have you been?' he said in a voice of terrible quietness. 'Gallivanting, si bwe keri? With a Muyindi on a motor bike!'

'He's going to beat her! He's going to beat her!' cried Innocent, dancing excitedly on the footpath.

Here is the other Joe again. The one I don't know. The one that lay dormant all those years.

Joe forced me into the hotel and up to our room. To my surprise, when he shut the door behind us, he flung his arms around me, cried, 'Don't ever do that again!' and buried his face in my neck.

'You've made a fool of yourself, me and Osman,' I said coldly.

'I had you murdered and buried by that highway cowboy! This is Uganda. Anything could happen to you. Please, please behave more responsibly. He's a total, total stranger!'

'So were you when I first met you.' But his eyes were dark and pleading and they melted away the anger within me.

'Berali fulu,' I grumbled. 'We're a laughing stock now.'

It was Musa who finally found us a flat. It belonged to his Uncle Karim and although it was not nice, it was the only place that had come our way in nearly a month so we had to take it. Joe paid the deposit and Karim handed over the keys. We decided to move in at the weekend.

On Friday morning I began packing. The hotel was almost empty. The kitchen staff were shopping at the market, Dimitrios's wife was in Jinja with relatives and the Greek smugglers were back in Zaire. I prowled about the deserted corridors. I took soap from the bathroom, tinned jam from the store. I lifted matches, cups and sugar, sped back to my room and packed them among Joe's underwear.

On my second foray I banged into Dimitrios. 'Come and have a drink with me in my parlour,' he said. 'You know me only as a proprietor, not as a man.'

'That is sufficient, thank you very much.' I sounded like my aunts at the dinner table.

'Ah, the things I could show you,' he sighed.

I laughed.

'"Won't you come into my parlour," said the spider to the fly;
"It's the sweetest little parlour that ever you did spy.
The way into my parlour is up a winding stair,
And I have many a curious thing to show you when you're
    there."'

Now that we were leaving I could afford to be rude.

'One day you'll discover there's more to life than a black prick and nursery rhymes,' he cautioned. I watched him walk away, tears of anger smarting my eyes. He spent the rest of the day closeted in his room with two plump schoolgirls. In his absence I carried out my second foray with a vengeance.

The flat was on William Street, at the top of a dismal apartment block in what appeared to be downtown Bombay. Our building consisted of twelve apartments housing large families of Asians, who seemed as unenthusiastic as we were about our moving in.

A rickety fire escape running up the outside of the building was the most congenial access to our third floor flat. The internal access smelt of stale urine and cats. The fire escape passed by everyone else's doors and windows and as we climbed to the top floor with our luggage, we were aware of eyes watching us from behind curtains.

We stood mournfully in the doorway, surveying the dusty concrete floors and grubby walls. There was a bedroom, a living room, a kitchen and a bathroom – bare concrete cells with small windows. The kitchen had a solitary cold tap hanging over a leaking sink, with two mildewed cupboards beneath. The bathroom consisted of a rank, discoloured lavatory with a cranky pull chain and a rusty shower-head sticking out from the wall about seven feet up. Again, there was only cold water. The shower hung directly over a hole in the floor, which one presumably straddled when showering. The water was supposed to escape through this hole but, as we found out later, it flowed across the room and encircled the lavatory because the floor was on a slant.

'Curtains, bed, stove,' I murmured, listing the essentials on paper.

'Fridge, table, broom . . .' said Joe dolefully. 'We'll need to scour this place completely . . . God, there's so much we need. Where do we start?'

'Right here,' I said, dropping to my knees, opening the largest suitcase and bringing out some cutlery and crockery. 'And here's sheets, towels, toilet paper. Courtesy of Dimitrios although he doesn't know.' I flung them on the floor, laughing. 'Jam, tomato sauce, soap. Oh, salt and pepper too. And look, sugar in a dear little sugar bowl.'

'You'll take it all back! Now!'

But I refused. I reminded Joe how Dimitrios had overcharged us by several hundred shillings, treating our protestations with contempt. I had also acquired detergent and cleaning powder and for the next few hours we scrubbed the floors, washed the windows and walls and scoured out the kitchen and bathroom. We killed dozens of giant cockroaches in the kitchen, which left me feeling slightly sick. Then, exhausted, we showered, huddling together under the cold water. Somewhat revived, we dressed and went out to do our shopping.

We struggled up the stairs some hours later laden with goods. The box I carried contained groceries and several lengths of cheap local sheeting for curtains. Joe had a primus stove, two sufurias – local cooking pots – and a plastic bucket full of paraphernalia. Two market boys humped in a lumpy double mattress and deposited it on the bedroom floor. They stared curiously about them until Joe shooed them away with a tip. We put the groceries away in the scrubbed cupboards and began to organise the flat.

We made makeshift curtains by fixing the sheeting to lengths of cord and hanging them above the windows. We made up our bed on the mattress with Dimitrios's sheets and two local blankets. As there was no wardrobe, our clothes had to remain in suitcases and these we stowed neatly in one corner, covering them with a tablecloth. An upturned box camouflaged with a kitenge – a local fabric – made a solid little bedside table. I stood back. The room seemed a little more inviting already.

'Come here, darling,' said Joe and caught me round the waist. 'No. I've got a headache,' I giggled, but he pulled me down on the mattress and, laughing, we broke in our new bed.

Afterwards I lay with my head on his chest, looking at the patterns on the wall made by the afternoon sun.

'It's not so bad here,' said Joe. 'And our wedding presents will make a difference.'

I thought of the presents – the electric frypan, the toaster, the iron, all the kitchenware and linen that my mother had packed so carefully – ploughing their way through the seas somewhere between New Zealand and Africa. We dozed a little and woke up around four. I put on Joe's shirt and padded out to the kitchen to make tea.

'How do you work this silly little stove thing?' I jerked open a cupboard to get out the tea and a mass of cockroaches scattered in all directions.

'They're here for keeps,' said Joe, when I had stopped screaming.

In the evening we met up with Byron and Musoke to have dinner at the Speke Hotel. It was late when we tiredly climbed the stairs to our flat. A curtain in a dimly lit window parted slightly as we passed.

'A spying Patel,' said Joe and tapped sharply on the window. The curtain dropped back hastily. We doubled up with laughter. We were still laughing as we stumbled up the remaining stairs and entered our flat. We had forgotten to buy lightbulbs, so we groped our way in the darkness to our room. Joe tripped over the mattress and pulled me down with him. Blind and giggling, we prepared for our first night in William Street.

That night I dreamed of a lovely land of hills and rivers and bird-filled bush. It was my home in the Rangitikei. So clear and beautiful was the dream that when I awoke I could not let it go, but lay there in the early dawn piecing together the road that led from home to Joe.

Chapter 5

My parents arrived in the Rangitikei in a battered old Ford during the latter stages of the Second World War. They were newlyweds from Dunedin, where they had married in local tearooms.

'Tearooms!' exclaimed my sister Janet when she found out. 'We must never tell anyone!'

The reason for the wedding in the tearooms was straightforward enough. Dad was Jewish and Mum Anglican. Their families were determined that the marriage be performed in the presence of God, but Dad's family refused to have the wedding in a church and Mum's refused to have it in a synagogue. The rabbi and the vicar, equally unco-operative, refused to officiate at any ceremony that was not held on their respective premises. After some searching, and a few tears, a Presbyterian minister was found who agreed to marry them, but not in his church. Tearooms were hired – 'they were nice tearooms,' Mum used to tell us – and a makeshift altar and chairs were set out. The Presbyterian minister officiated and everyone was satisfied.

Dad, who had just completed medical school, joined the air force and was posted as medical officer to the Royal New Zealand Air Force Base at Ohakea on the banks of the Rangitikei River. When the war was over they nosed the old Ford through the surrounding peaceful farmlands, looking for a place to settle. They decided on Marton, bought a house and put down their roots in the fertile Rangitikei soil. We five children were not long in coming – first my two sisters, Robin and Janet, then me, and then my brothers, Bruce and Peter.

For us, childhood in Marton was halcyon years of sunshine, unlimited energy and little responsibility. I remember Mum spent a good deal of time coming at me with soapy facecloths and sticking plaster, since I was always falling in drains or crashing my bike or gashing my limbs on fences. 'Next time I'll use a fish hook and string,' Dad would say gruffly, as he stitched me up in the surgery.

We grew up accepting that we would never see as much of our father as other children, for Dad, one of the last of the old-style country doctors, was at the beck and call of patients across a vast countryside, driving many miles each day to outlying farms. Even when he was home we often had to compete for attention with the boats he built in the back shed.

His practice also took in the remote Maori community at Ratana Pa and I sometimes accompanied him there. I became familiar with the old corrugated iron housing and the children in ragged clothes. From an early age I discerned that the smiling Maori on the tourist brochures were light years away from the Maori who lived here. When I asked Dad about it he talked about subjugation, dispossession of land and loss of mana, and seemed quite angry.

'You're young yet, Heather,' he said, as he wrote up his notes in the car, 'but I can tell you that the sickness I see in these houses – and there's too much of it – has something to do with what I've just told you.'

I was intrigued when Dad talked like this, even if I hardly understood, and I began to reach for books on Maori history in our local library. Gradually my interest broadened to include other cultures and the librarian finally rang Mum because she was concerned that some of the books I selected contained specific references to sexual customs.

'You're only eleven,' said Mum crossly. 'Why don't you read the books that normal people read?'

But it was too late; by this time I was well and truly plugged into anthropology. Even the elite private school I was sent to in the hope of refining my personality could not shake my enthusiasm. I was more interested in talking with the Rarotongan cooks in the school kitchen than listening to the governor-general on sports day.

Towards the end of my schooldays I began to think of a career.

'Nursing,' said Mum, who was herself a nurse.

'Physiotherapy,' said my aunts in Dunedin, whose sole aim in life was to help Mum bring us up.

'University,' said a teacher who had often lent me books.

When I finally announced that I wanted to study anthropology the reactions were immediate.

'They don't have toilet paper up the Amazon!' laughed my brothers.

'You could be shoved in a cooking pot and we'd never know what happened to you,' said Mum desperately.

'What's got into her!' exclaimed the aunts to Mum and bombarded me with brochures on teaching.

I went to the back shed where Dad was sanding down the hull of his latest boat.

'You do what you want,' he said gently.

And that is what I did.

Some months after I met Joe I went home for the holidays, determined to tell my family about him. Everyone was home and it was almost impossible to be heard.

'I've met this nice student from Africa,' I began over dinner. 'He's doing a thesis in public administration.'

'I once met this bloke from Nigeria,' said Robin. 'He told me they eat snakes.'

'Pass the gravy.'

And the first hint about Joe to my family went unnoticed.

On the news one night while I was home it mentioned that the Kabaka of Buganda, tired of Obote's repression, had declared Buganda a secessionist state. Obote had responded by sending troops into the palace; the Kabaka and many of his followers were reported to have been killed.

'This is terrible,' I said, worrying about Joe. 'King Freddie was the leader of three million people.'

Peter's head came out of a comic. 'King Freddie? Sounds like a frog.'

'My friend comes from Uganda,' I said icily. 'This news will upset him.'

As soon as I could, I caught the train back to Wellington, dumped my bags at the hostel and rushed along The Terrace to Joe's. As he opened the door I asked him about Uganda. He explained that the Kabaka had not been killed but had escaped to England.

'That's wonderful news!'

'You really care, don't you?' he said quietly and he bent and kissed me on the cheek. There was a wolf whistle from a passing car. Cheeks burning, I rushed back to the hostel to unpack before tea.

Final examinations came and went and, now in my second year, I moved into a flat with Jane and Pam. The work was a good deal harder and I spent a lot of time wading through Levi-Strauss and structuralism.

I began drip-feeding Joe to my parents, dropping his name occasionally into my letters home. When my parents visited me at Easter Joe was there along with a couple of my other friends. Mum and Dad seemed to like him but of course they had no idea of our feelings for each another. I felt guilty for hiding from them the one thing that mattered most in my life.

The second year became the third, and Joe and I were still together. Ours was a unique relationship noted for its stability, loyalty and contentment on a campus that was experiencing sexual liberation, drugs and an increasingly alternative lifestyle.

On Sunday afternoons we sometimes wandered along the beach at Oriental Bay, visited Paul or took a walk to the National Art Gallery. Other times we would listen to Billie Holiday in Joe's flat above the harbour. We often talked about Uganda and Joe shared with me his dream, on his return, to become involved in the development of small local businesses. 'Uganda has so much potential,' he would tell me, describing the opportunities in coffee and cotton production, commercial fishing and local industry.

We never seemed to run out of things to say or ideas to share and I found that being with Joe – living with him in the weekends – became the happiest time of my life.

Final exams rushed towards us and, after weeks of intense swotting, I sat my papers and passed. I now had one more year to go. Joe planned to finish his thesis early the following year. I silently prayed for him to slow up, for under the terms of his scholarship he was to return to Uganda on its completion. The notion of university, of life, without him was too awful to contemplate.

One warm evening after finals as we walked along Oriental Parade, Joe, who had seemed preoccupied, stopped, turned to look at me, and took both my hands in his.

'Heather, I love you. I will never love anyone else besides you. I can't promise you anything more than my devoted love. Is that enough for you?'

'God,' I replied, laughing. 'It's plenty.'

'Then,' he said, 'it's time for me to ask you to marry me. All I can offer you is my undying love, my family, and a life in another country across the other side of the world.'

I was young, excited, desperately in love and I answered without hesitation. 'I don't want anything else but to marry you. I don't care where we live or what we do. I love you so much that nothing else matters.' I waited eagerly for his reaction.

But there was none. He looked into my eyes almost sadly for a moment and whispered, 'Darling Heather, is it fair of me to ask you?'

He turned his head away and I wondered for an instant if I had seen tears.

Janet and Bruce, who had both moved to Wellington earlier in the year, had come to know and like Joe. I rang Janet and asked her to meet me for lunch. Over spaghetti I admitted to her that Joe and I were serious. Her face registered a stricken expression but, after the first rush of feeling had subsided, she said, 'It really shouldn't matter. I liked him when I first met him and I like him now. Why don't you ask him home for Christmas?'

'What . . . what will Mum and Dad say?' I found I was trembling.

'Absolutely nothing. They won't want Joe celebrating Christmas on his own in Wellington. Anyway, it's not as if you're going to marry him.'

I looked up at her, unable to speak.

'Oh my God . . . !' she gasped, and for a minute we sat there staring at each other.

'Tell them after Christmas dinner,' she said after some thought. 'They'll be full of wine and *joie de vivre*.'

'What about the aunts?' I whispered. 'And how will Mum and Dad react?'

Janet began to gather up her things. Her voice became businesslike. 'The aunts aren't coming to us this Christmas. And as for Mum and Dad, we'll remind them why they had to marry in tearooms.'

Joe's head lay close to mine on the pillow. I sighed into the darkness. We had gone over and over how we would break the news to my family. It would be done late on Christmas afternoon when people were full of food, tired and affable.

'Are you prepared for criticism and tears and maybe even estrangement?'

My voice rose in anger. 'Let them! I don't care. They don't know you as I do.'

We were quiet for a few minutes and then I asked about his parents.

'They won't be happy. They expect me to marry a Muganda, preferably Catholic. They'll write and try to stop me.'

It seemed to me much easier to elope.

I thought of Christmas with fearful anticipation. Although I could not envisage my family's complete reaction, I expected something cataclysmic with explosions of hysteria and disbelief and a subsequent diminuendo of pleas to revert to common sense. For the first time in my life I actively dreaded Christmas.

34

Chapter 6

Several days after we arrived at William Street some of the relatives called to finalise plans for my trip to meet Joe's parents. They sat about the living room on boxes and mats. Ted, Joe's older brother, made a flying visit from the game park where he worked as a warden, on his way picking up their younger brother, Henry. I warmed to them immediately. Ted was a large, good-natured man with a happy-go-lucky manner. Henry, on the other hand, was a slim, rather thoughtful young man who played soccer for the famous Express team and who was earmarked for the national team. The two brothers surprised us with the gift of a fridge.

'It's second-hand and a little battered, but it's as good as gold,' said Ted.

'It's a godsend!' I cried. 'A haven from the cockroaches!' They would not listen to our thanks and wandered into the living room to join the others. I was now beginning to understand the language and from the ensuing conversation I gathered that we were to visit Joe's parents the following Saturday. We served chicken and rice, someone produced the inevitable bottles, and the room became lively with stories and laughter.

'I'm worried about Ted driving all the way back to the park tonight,' I said later, as we stacked things in our new fridge. 'He should have stayed with us overnight.'

'Not him! He's spending the night with his girlfriend in Mengo.'

The utter sod!

I thought of his wife and children waiting for him back at the park and slammed the fridge door. By this time I was aware of the problems many of the women had with philandering husbands. It was useless to moralise; I looked at Joe and realised how lucky I was.

Lucky, perhaps, but it did not mean we were without our problems. Joe met up with Musoke and Byron in some bar after work each day and arrived home after dark. This annoyed and hurt me, particularly since he knew I was alone all day. Sometimes, after repeated job rejections, long spells without mail from home, or struggles with the temperamental primus, I quarrelled with him over his lateness. When I asked why I couldn't sometimes join them for a drink, he explained that it was not the way here.

'You're the student of anthropology. You should understand these things.'

It was a lonely existence, and my Indian neighbours did little to gladden the heart. Silent and watchful, they kept to themselves. In the bottom flat was a teacher from Madras, who occasionally greeted me in flowery English to show off to his less educated neighbours. His radio wailed Indian music incessantly. Higher up the fire escape was a shrewish Goan widow who told me she had a retroverted uterus. Then there were two families of Patels. The Spitting Patels, as we called them, cleaned their teeth *en famille* over the fire escape. The courtyard below was blotched with dried toothpaste. Their neighbours, the Spying Patels, suffered from insatiable curiosity. I once caught the grandmother at the clothesline, examining the labels on my underwear. 'But I suppose,' I told myself firmly as I thought of Ted's deceived wife, 'things could be a lot worse.'

The day for our visit to the village arrived. Joe's brothers, the Musokes, Byron, James and several families of relatives congregated at our flat in a noisy throng before setting off. It was a field day for Grandmother Patel, who flew to her entrance like a trapdoor spider every time one of our visitors passed.

36

Sarah Musoke had brought me a traditional basuti to wear to the village. It looked completely wrong on me and I refused to wear it.

'You must! It's protocol,' said Sarah.

But I felt I looked contrived and rather ridiculous and shook my head. Sarah fetched Ted's wife, Mary, a large woman with a baby at her breast. Mary looked at me with pursed lips.

'Leeta Jozefu,' she said, and Joe was brought in.

To Mary's disbelief Joe sided with me.

'The old people won't like it,' protested Sarah, but Joe was firm. I heard Mary cluck with disapproval. In her world husbands did not concede to wives.

In the end I wore an ankle-length Indian cotton skirt and a white peasant blouse. This seemed to satisfy everyone and we all descended to the cars below.

It was a journey of over a hundred miles, well south of Masaka, the country's third largest town. Joe and I travelled at the head of the convoy in the jeep with Ted, Mary and their numerous children. In the car behind us James's pale visage bobbed about in a sea of black faces. Mary reminded me of the customs and taboos in the village, particularly the one pertaining to Joe's father, whom I was not to touch and whose food I could not handle. I already knew most of what she was saying and I nodded off against Joe as her voice droned on.

It was a long, hot drive and we stopped off for drinks at the Tropic Inn near Masaka. Joe pointed out the mayor of Masaka who sat at the next table, sporting a three-piece suit and a flashing smile.

We resumed our journey, Mary's baby, Nakalo, sleeping in my arms. Fifteen miles past Masaka we left the main road and bumped for some distance along a red dirt road. We had to slow down considerably when the road became a rough track, with the bush on each side scraping the jeep. 'We're almost home,' said Joe. A hen with a swarm of chicks pattered out on to the track. The whole convoy had to halt. We continued, bumping slowly between trees and over a grassy verge and finally into a large clearing – the family front lawn.

From all sides rushed members of Joe's family, waving banana palms and cheering. There was a cacophony of tooting from the cars behind. Youngsters jumped up on the moving vehicles, clinging to the sides and laughing. The jeep began to fill up with bananas, pineapples and a variety of vegetables, some of which I had never seen before. We pulled up under some trees and climbed out.

The parents' house stood on a small rise, a simple dwelling of concrete and tiles behind which I could see well-tended coffee groves, pineapple saplings and a vegetable garden that would have made Mum green with envy. A short woman in a blue basuti hurried down the steps towards us, smiling broadly. She was followed at a more sedate pace by a thin man in a white kanzu.

'My parents,' said Joe, taking my hand and leading me through the people to meet them. I felt nervous and remembered how Joe had once told me that they wanted him to marry a Muganda woman.

'Kulika yo! Kulika yo!' cried Joe's mother, as she rushed to embrace us. She was a small bundle of energy, exclaiming over me delightedly, scolding Joe for being late, worrying if I had a comfortable trip and shooing away the curious children. She sat us on chairs in the shade and instantly people came up to us with presents – lengths of cloth, grass mats, woven baskets, fruit and vegetables. I was completely overwhelmed.

Joe's father welcomed me formally in English and then asked me to choose a goat from several that were paraded before me. I selected a dappled nanny, stroking it gently on the nose, and a young boy in a ragged shirt immediately took it away.

'It will be slaughtered and cooked for you,' said Joe.

'Oh dear, I thought it was to be a pet,' and I felt guilty as I watched it trotting unsuspectingly away.

People were now sitting about on mats, catching up with all the news. Aunties bustled about with refreshments and children played at the far end of the clearing. Around us the peaceful shamba shimmered in the morning sun. The aroma of food wafted to us from a thatched cooking hut and from the coffee bushes swelled the rasp of cicadas. Joe's father came to sit with me.

'You have a lovely home here,' I said to him.

'It is true,' he said quietly. 'You are part of our family now. You are welcome here any time.'

Joe brought over a gourd of his mother's home-brew made from bananas and gave me a glassful. With both Joe and his father looking at me expectantly, I nodded my appreciation but found it quite vile. I was relieved when Joe's mother claimed me for a tour of the shamba.

She took me through the coffee to the gardens where she busied herself picking oranges, tomatoes, cabbages and other vegetables, which went into a huge grass basket. At another plot she hacked off matoke, pineapples and pawpaws and ordered the children to stow everything in the jeep for us to take back to Kampala. Then she led me down a track through the bushes to a small mud dwelling with a thatched roof.

'The grandmother lives here,' she said. 'She would like to meet you. She is old and cannot walk.'

I bent to enter the hut and as my eyes became accustomed to the darkness I could make out a wizened little figure lying on a goatskin on the earth floor. For a second I felt I was in a Rider Haggard novel. I knelt down beside her and greeted her in the traditional way. Her smile was toothless and trembling in an old, old face. From the folds of her garments she produced a small grass basket containing six eggs. She gave them to me, wishing me well in a voice that quivered and sighed like reeds in the wind.

I stumbled back into the sunlight, appalled that she should spend her last days in such surroundings. I hurried back to Joe, clutching the precious eggs.

'She's happy and secure,' he said, when he saw how upset I was. 'This shamba has always been her home. If she wants to get around she's pulled along on the goatskin. She'll die here peacefully, surrounded by her family. It's all she wants. She has everything she needs.'

I knew he was right and felt comforted. He added as an afterthought, somewhat contemptuously, 'Here we don't put our old people away in rest homes.'

'Sanctimonious prick!' I said, and he burst out laughing.

In the early afternoon two large tables were set up on the grass and children circulated with jugs of water, soap and towels for handwashing. The aunties bustled back and forth from the cooking hut with dishes of steaming food. There was beef, whole chickens, chunks of my roasted nanny goat and huge parcels of matoke wrapped in banana leaves, with mounds of potatoes and rice and green vegetables.

Joe's father stood on the doorstep and called for silence. Everyone stood as he said grace. Afterwards people heaped their plates and home-brew flowed convivially. I tried some more and this time it seemed almost pleasant; I finished a glassful.

Armed with a plate of food, I went to join my friends under the tree. I sat between Mary and James, trying not to smile as James ate awkwardly with his fingers. There were no forks. He looked cross when he dropped gravy on his shirt and I giggled. I wondered if the home-brew was getting to me.

Around us sat Joe's family. Even the old grandmother had been brought out and was happily imbibing home-brew beside Joe. Fingers flicked food to mouths, black eyes snapped with laughter, breasts like melons suckled babies. I wanted to shout my thanks to them all, for their welcome, for their ready acceptance of me, for the six eggs lovingly placed in a grass basket, but most of all for giving me Joe.

The afternoon drifted on. One of the children settled next to me and dropped off to sleep. I put my arm around him and almost dozed myself. On the doorstep the older aunts gossiped together, tongues loosened by the home-brew.

We began to pack up as the sun dipped behind the hills. I tried to thank Joe's parents for our wonderful day, but in the gracious manner of the Baganda they turned around and thanked us for coming. There was hardly any room in the jeep, loaded as it was with all the food and presents, and Ted's children had to travel back in another car. Relatives crowded round the jeep to farewell us.

'You come back soon!' ordered Joe's mother through the window and patted my face.

'Go in peace,' said Joe's father, moving up beside his wife, 'and do not forget us here in the village.'

It was almost dark as we lurched along the track to the main road.

Chapter 7

I was becoming unbearably miserable.

I had tried to find a job but with no success, so I spent most of my time on my own at home. I hated it. Joe left for work at seven-thirty in the morning and, after stopping off with his friends at a bar in the evening, usually got home after eight. There were arguments over this but the situation remained unchanged. He insisted that it was customary for men to go to a bar after work and relax with their friends.

'But what about me?' I said bitterly. 'I'd like to relax too. You don't seem to think about me. I have feelings and aspirations that you don't even consider.'

'Like what?' His dark eyes gleamed with amusement. 'Do you still want to do the anthropology bit and gallop off into the hills to find some semi-extinct tribe?'

'You won't even take me seriously!' I raged at him.

But no amount of reasoning or pleading or shouting had any effect. Because, at that stage, I relied on him for everything, I could either like his behaviour or lump it, but I couldn't change it.

I tried to arrange ways of filling in the long hours, but with no phone to contact friends or relatives, and no car to take me visiting, I almost always found myself hanging around the flat, bored, angry and miserable. And what a dismal place to have to hang around in! There was not even the diversion of redecorating it because we had no money.

I visited the library constantly and it was not unusual for me to finish a book a day, even though this gave me headaches. When I wasn't reading I would often convince myself that we needed extra provisions, just to have something to go out for. Or I would decide to walk to the post office and clear our box, knowing already that Joe's office boy had probably beaten me to it. There were endless little excuses I invented to give some purpose to my day, but it always ended up in the same way – waiting for Joe.

I determinedly kept looking for work, although, for several reasons, it was not the most auspicious time to do this. Firstly, I had a Baganda surname and under the present government this automatically went against me, even though I was European. Secondly, it was a time of Africanisation, a system I wholeheartedly supported whereby good jobs were offered to suitably qualified Ugandans before expatriates or non-citizen Asians. And thirdly, I suspected some people were hesitant about employing me because of my unusual marital position, assuming, no doubt, that I must be a misfit because I had married a Ugandan.

I trudged from nursery schools to hotel reception desks with no luck. One day I bumped into a German woman I vaguely knew who was also married to a Ugandan. She had landed herself with a good job in the German Embassy in Kampala and suggested I try for a job with my embassy. As there was no New Zealand embassy in Uganda I tried the British High Commission, where my name was politely taken down and I was thanked for my trouble. As I left, I noticed the Israeli Embassy across the road and decided to try there. A muscle-bound Israeli officer who appeared to be on duty at the door asked my business. I told him and he informed me there were no jobs.

'I'd still like to speak with someone inside, please.' The soldier settled in the doorway, blocking my entry. I began to get cross and asked him to move. He smiled apologetically. 'We have all the staff we need here, and in any case we use our own people.'

'Well, I'm one of your people – or at least half of me is.'

But he still refused to budge. I took in the guerrilla beret, the heavy boots and the bulge of his revolver. 'You're absolutely paranoid!' I snapped, and turned on my heel, walking away with all the dignity I could muster. But inside I was weeping tears of humiliation, vowing that this was the last time I begged for a job. My head ached and I felt sick with the heat. I turned into Kampala Road, sat down at a pavement table in front of City Bar and ordered a Coke.

I tried to take stock of the situation. Here I was reduced to walking the streets looking for work. I had hit rock bottom. I needed a job, not only for the sake of my sanity, but also for financial reasons. My family would be shocked if they realised just how bad things were for us. We had no money, no amenities and no furniture. And, although we called it home, we could hardly call it cosy, our cockroach-ridden little flat with its three cups, its two cold water taps and its cheap sheeting curtains. I imagined Mum arriving at the door in her tweed suit and being asked to sit on a box. I wondered how she would cope with stewed primus tea and with being asked to hurry up and drink it so someone else could use her cup.

I sipped my Coke miserably and the throbbing in my head increased. Locating some Disprins in my bag, I washed the first one down with Coke.

'Hello. Aren't you well?'

I looked up. It was the soldier from the Israeli Embassy. I said nothing and swallowed the second Disprin.

'I hope I didn't give you a headache.'

'You did,' I said curtly.

'I'm sorry,' he said. He had dimples, dancing eyes and a riot of dark curls. I had never seen anyone look less sorry.

I suppose he thinks I'm an easy lay!

My head thumped and I wished he would go away. My body felt decidedly peculiar. I could hear the man explaining his conduct at the embassy but it sounded as if he were talking through cotton wool. I felt a heaviness descend on me. I picked up my drink but it was such an effort I could barely bring it to my mouth. Coke slopped on to the table cloth.

'Are you all right?' said the Israeli uncertainly.

A wave of fear swept through me. I was going to die at this

Coke-stained table in this strange country! Dear God, I should never have left those damp, green hills and sparkling rivers and my home in the sunny Rangitikei. My glass crashed to the ground and I began to cry.

I don't recall much after that. I vaguely remember being helped into a taxi by the Israeli and taken home. He used the Madrasi's phone to call Joe at work; then he disappeared.

'Malaria,' said the Muganda doctor to Joe at my bedside. On top of malaria I contracted tonsillitis and, along with malaria shots, had to endure penicillin injections.

'My bum's like a pin cushion,' I moaned to Joe and wished Dad was there to treat me.

My illness, funnily enough, turned out to be a blessing, for it indirectly landed me with a job. Karim, our landlord, came to our door that week, as he did every week, for the rent. When he learned that I had been looking for a job before the onset of the malaria attack he immediately informed me that he had just the job for me, in a nursery school in Nakivubo.

'The woman who owns the nursery is looking for someone to manage it. She's not interested in teaching in it herself.' And he offered to take me there as soon as I was better.

A few days later we drove to Nakivubo. All the way there I tried to visualise myself in the role of nursery teacher. I knew that nursery schools in this country relied heavily on structured methods of learning, since they were expected to equip children with sufficient skills in English, writing and basic mathematics so that, by the age of six, they would stand a good chance of being admitted into Kampala's primary schools. With competition fierce for places, admission was sometimes based on a written and oral test. No lover of regimen, I hoped that if I were lucky enough to get this job I could somehow balance structured learning with equal amounts of creative activity and fun.

We pulled up by the huge Aga Khan mosque, white and majestic, on the left side of the road. 'No, no, that's not it,' said Karim hurriedly, and he pointed to the other side of the road. There was a low-lying swampy expanse stretching back towards the city. Along the bank of the swamp, shoe-shiners, car washers and barbers had set up open-air businesses. They used the swamp as both toilet and rubbish dump.

My eyes, following Karim's pointing finger, came to rest on a squat ugly building crouched halfway down the embankment like a grotesque frog. It looked as though it would, at any moment, leap into the swamp. As it was the only building on that side of the road, I realised, with a sinking heart, that this was it. Paint was peeling off the mouldering walls, and curious vegetation sprouted from the decaying roof.

We left the car and descended the shaky steps that led to the front door. The shoe-shiners and barbers stared at us with unveiled curiosity. This was obviously no place for a Muzungu woman. We opened the door to a crescendo of voices that slowly subsided as fifty pairs of eyes turned to stare at us. Most of the children were Asians and sat at little desks, some squeezed two to a desk, while the overflow sat with two ayahs on mats on the floor. I noticed the impoverished surroundings – the cracked walls, the bare concrete floor, the scarcity of pre-school equipment.

A small, brisk, birdlike woman approached us and Karim began to talk to her in Gujerati. She turned to look at me, gave me a quick smile and turned back to Karim, shaking her head. I knew I had lost.

'I'm sorry,' she said, waving a thin brown arm around, 'but I don't think this is quite your cup of tea. Have you tried Nakasero or Kampala City Nurseries?'

The bird-head was cocked and the bright eyes looked at me enquiringly. I was tempted to offer her a worm. Telling her I had already tried those pre-schools, I turned dejectedly back towards the children who had begun to gossip among themselves. A small boy with bare feet knelt at a table, and with his tongue peeping from his mouth, laboriously wrote on his blackboard. The pixie-faced girl next to him in red ribbons wiped her nose on a dirty cuff and gave me a smile of piercing sweetness. The older black-braided girls whispered importantly to each other behind cupped hands, their eyes sliding from my face whenever I looked their way. I looked around the room – so many children and only one teacher and two ayahs.

The well-equipped nurseries that the bird-woman had mentioned flashed through my mind. I saw the carefully tended playgrounds with swings and slides, the airy classrooms with Beatrix Potter pictures on the walls. I remembered the neat little children in white socks and shoes – Africans, Asians, Europeans – all privileged compared to these little ones at Nakivubo.

I swung round to the woman, my heart beating fast. 'I want this job very much. I don't care about conditions or lack of amenities. You can't possibly know what would suit me. This is where I want to work.'

The woman looked uncertain, but reluctantly agreed to let me wait until lunchtime when the owner, Mrs Rodrigo, came to collect the fees. It was the closest yet that I had come to a job and I nearly whooped for joy.

After Karim left, the woman introduced herself as Miss Alani and informed me she was leaving to get married. With luck, I might be her replacement. She quickly showed me around. A pair of double doors at the back of the room opened on to a broad verandah, about fifteen feet wide, which ran the length of the building. This was the outdoor play area. It was enclosed by a high wire-netting fence, which was just as well because the verandah dropped straight into the swamp.

We returned to the classroom, where the noise level from insufficient stimulation and supervision was almost deafening. I assisted a group of five-year-olds with their writing and then took a group of younger ones out to the verandah for a story.

At lunchtime, after the children had left, Mrs Rodrigo arrived – a large, coastal Swahili woman with a square, forbidding face. She stared at me as though I were something nasty that had crawled in from the swamp. Miss Alani hastily tried to explain who I was. The woman took no notice but advanced on me, hands on hips, head lowered like a bull before it charges. My first impulse was to leap screaming into the swamp.

'What are your qualifications?' she barked.

'Er, I have a degree in anthropology and education.'

'I don't believe in university degrees!'

I looked at Miss Alani helplessly, on the verge of tears.

'S-she seemed to get along v-very well with the children this m-morning,' said Miss Alani.

'Well, I suppose it wouldn't hurt to try you out,' said Mrs

Rodrigo doubtfully. 'Don't expect fancy wages and don't be smart alecky.'

'Oh no, I wouldn't! Never! Thank you, thank you.' I would have kissed her feet if she had asked.

Mrs Rodrigo was a woman of few words. And also a shrewd one – she obviously thought I would add a little prestige to the place, and at very little cost to her. The wages she offered were abysmal but I was too relieved to care.

I arrived at school the next morning at the same time as Miss Alani and the two ayahs, Agnes and Rose. Quite unprepared for the shambles that awaited me when we opened the door, I almost took a step backwards when the stench of cigarette smoke and beer hit me. Miss Alani explained that the premises belonged to an Indian gambling club from whom Mrs Rodrigo rented the building. The gamblers simply walked out on their mess each night, leaving the nursery staff to deal with it in the morning. I looked about me in amazement. Not only were the gamblers' tables and chairs spread out higgledy-piggledy all over the room, but the floor was awash with litter, spilt drinks, cigarette butts, beer bottles, even spittle.

We lugged their furniture back to the committee room that was otherwise off limits to us. It was equipped with a bar and I gasped at the array of beer and spirits. Back in the main room we had to pick up the litter, sluice down the floor and toilets and set out our own tables and chairs. By this time the children were arriving and before too long the school was in full swing.

My first morning was a busy one. By the time we had stored all our furniture away in the storeroom at lunchtime I was exhausted and felt sorely tempted to pinch a nip of whisky from the bar.

Apart from the gambling club's mess, I loved everything about my new job, especially the children, and I must have bored Joe to death with my stories about them. To me they were the loveliest children imaginable. I quickly learned their names and their abilities and soon established some favourites. There was Ali Raza, the cloth merchant's son, who could speak four languages, Abdulkarim the frog collector, and tiny Nita, who had a blood condition and often fell asleep in school. The staff, such as we were, worked well together and, although busy, noisy, over-crowded and understaffed, we were a happy school.

Chapter 8

Two weeks after I started at the school Miss Alani left for marriage and a new life in Kenya. I was on my own with fifty-two children and two ayahs.

The first thing I did was to divide the children into four groups based on ages that ranged from three to six years old. Each group had its own home corner with its own tables and chairs. This left a large space in the middle of the classroom where everyone could come together for stories, singing or some special activity. I rotated among all the groups during the course of the morning, while the two ayahs supervised the others. My main aim was to encourage the development of English in the younger ones and to foster reading, writing and mathematical concepts in the older ones. Although we coped surprisingly well under the circumstances, we desperately needed at least two more English-speaking staff – neither of the ayahs spoke English – and much more equipment.

I took a deep breath and began a nagging campaign with Mrs Rodrigo. I started with a plea for paints and brushes.

'That won't teach them to read and write,' she said scornfully. I pointed out that education was not only reading and writing.

'Typical university hogwash!' and she further complained about the messiness of it.

'I swear to God I'll clean up any mess.'

I wore her down and eventually we got the paints.

We set up a painting table in the middle of the room to which the children came group by group. They were delighted with the paints and I nearly went berserk trying to keep order. I then started pressing for toys and puzzles. Again I was told it was hogwash but I persevered and gradually, but with much grumbling, Mrs Rodrigo allowed me to purchase some of these items. At my own expense I bought flour and food colouring and made dough, and with this, and the toy kitchen utensils I purchased with our electricity bill money, we were able to set up a dough table. Unfortunately in the warm climate the dough went off very quickly and had to be thrown out. I ended up making it once a week or it became too costly.

The main necessity, however, was extra staff. The noise level owing to inadequate supervision nearly drove me insane. Besides this, the children needed extending at every level and one teacher could not possibly provide it all. I asked about the possibility of another teacher.

'Absolutely not!' said Mrs Rodrigo. 'The other teachers never needed help! You must be incompetent.'

Thank you, you bitch.

I humbly suggested that even another ayah, preferably English-speaking, would be an enormous help. In mounting exasperation she told me that the school simply could not afford it. This was an outright lie, for I was the one who collected the school fees and it did not need a genius to calculate that, even after payment of wages, rent and miscellaneous expenses, Mrs Rodrigo was left with a considerable profit. However, worried that she might decide to replace me with someone less bothersome I let the matter drop.

Although I was often preoccupied with the nursery, I could not help noticing the increasing tension about me. Taxation, repression, corruption and nepotism, the hallmarks of the Obote regime, made life for the ordinary person a daily struggle. People lived in constant fear of armed robbery and violence and it was common knowledge that the guns had somehow found their way from the armouries to the common thug or kondo.

I could feel the growing uneasiness in the Asians. Knowing they were plump pickings for kondos, they barricaded themselves in each night, often employing the services of private security guards. And they were nervous about Obote, particularly those of them who had not assumed Ugandan citizenship.

The expatriates, too, were jittery. Life in Uganda meant big houses, a pleasant climate, good wages, servants and social clubs. They began to fear it might all come to an end with Obote's apparent intention of nationalising their companies and replacing many expatriate personnel with Ugandans. The British in particular disliked Obote because he had accused them, with some reason, of tacitly supporting the racist regime in South Africa.

If the Asian and European communities disliked Obote, the Baganda actively hated him. You could feel their hatred simmering. They blamed Obote for the death of the Kabaka and could only watch helplessly as he sought to crush any reference or relic that pertained to the now defunct kingdom. The Baganda, who had become over the centuries one of the most politically sophisticated tribal nations in black Africa, had been brought to their knees by Obote.

The tension and the hatred were inextricably wrapped up in Uganda's history.

The Uganda Protectorate was formed in 1894. Its boundaries, like those elsewhere in Africa, were drawn up by greedy, short-sighted colonialists – in this case the British – who had no regard for the peoples living in the area. The north and south of this new region, areas that could scarcely be more culturally and physically diverse, were lumped together by the new boundaries and expected to move forward together in national harmony.

The south, a lush, fertile, lake-studded region, consisted of four great kingdoms that were highly organised and comparatively prosperous. This was particularly true of the kingdom of Buganda which, with its Kabaka and his three million subjects, was the largest and most powerful.

The harsher, drier northern area of Uganda was home to mainly Nilotic peoples, whose tribal groupings were loosely structured, basic and often nomadic. Unlike their energetic counterparts in the south, these northern people showed little organisational initiative and lived as they had for centuries. The many tribes in this area included the Acholi, Langi, Kakwa, Lugbara and the more recent Nubians who had drifted in from the Sudan.

After the protectorate was formed, development leapt ahead in the south. Buganda in particular prospered, its people showing a remarkable enthusiasm and aptitude for Western learning. As the years passed the north lagged far behind in every way and this resulted in contempt for the north by the south and jealousy of the south by the north.

And so it was that, while the people of the south sought education and developed cash crops on their shambas, the north became a target for army recruitment. By the time Uganda became independent, an army made up almost entirely of northerners emerged. Within its ranks a large, uneducated northerner of Kakwa-Nubian extraction was elbowing his way up to become chief of staff. His name was Idi Amin.

As independence approached, Uganda, known as Britain's 'model' protectorate, emerged as one of the most efficient, productive and well-organised nations in black Africa.

Uganda became independent from Britain in 1962. By a convoluted set of circumstances a northern politician called Milton Obote, a Langi, made a compromise alliance with the Kabaka to beat a third party at the polls. Thus Obote became Prime Minister and the Kabaka became President – a strange and uneasy alliance between a northern socialist and a southern monarch.

Eventually Obote and the Kabaka clashed. Obote sent in the army, filled with his loyal northerners, to ransack the palace and dispose of the Kabaka. The five-hundred-year kingdom was destroyed on that day. The Kabaka escaped to England where he later died, and the troops, incensed at losing their prey, turned their fury on the Baganda. Shocked, leaderless, without arms and with the heart of their tribe cut out, the Baganda were easy to keep down. Hundreds were killed. Obote drew up a new constitution and Uganda became a one-party state with himself as President. His government grew harsh, repressive and discriminatory against the Baganda. He had absolute faith in the army although, unknown to him, Idi Amin was insidiously recruiting Nubians into the ranks. By 1970, when I arrived, Obote had become a confident, ruthless dictator and his country seethed with rumour, discontent and intrigue.

The year progressed slowly and my hopes of earning enough money for extras were, for the most part, unrealised. It seemed we would be stuck in our dismal flat forever.

One morning in early July, Mrs Rodrigo appeared at the nursery in tears. In a rare flash of intimacy she told me that both her parents were ailing in Tanzania and that, as their only daughter, she would have to go and care for them. She had decided to sell up and move with her family to Dar es Salaam. Then she dropped the bombshell.

'I would like to offer you the nursery. I have watched you. You are a good teacher,' and she named a price.

Hell! Where will I find that sort of money?

'Yes!' I said wildly. 'Done!'

We arranged that she would continue to run the school until her departure in December. I would pay her on the last day of school before the Christmas break and then the school was mine.

I rushed home along the swamp to tell Joe.

'How can we raise that sort of money?' he said worriedly.

'I'll get an afternoon job. I'll budget. We've got nearly five months to save.' Joe laughed, took me in his arms and promised to help where he could.

I saved desperately. I haggled vehemently with the vendors at Shauri Yako Market. I bought hard local bars of soap instead of packaged washing powder, and I stuck to the cheap local staples of matoke, beans and sweet potatoes. I farewelled the modern air-conditioned butchery I once frequented and resorted to the cheap market meat that was hacked up on the pavement with pangas, leaving splinters of bone.

I sold Joe's radio to Musa, whom I met in the market one day. I got a good price for it but Joe was furious and wouldn't speak to me for days, even when I told him I'd buy him a better one when the school was mine. Slowly my savings grew and, incredibly, I was able to find a job in a photocopying company three afternoons a week.

One day, as I was browsing in the library, I felt a tap on my arm and looked up into the face of the Israeli soldier. I had been hoping I would bang into him so I could thank him for taking me home when I had come down with malaria. We chatted for a while and he asked if I had found a job. I told him about the nursery school and how I was struggling to buy it.

'I have a proposition for you then,' and the dimples sprang to life in his cheeks. 'Come and have coffee with me at Chez Joseph and I'll tell you about it.'

I hesitated.

'Grant me this wish,' he said, with laughter in his eyes.

'I'm not your fairy godmother.'

'I'm serious.'

'No one can be serious and smile like a Cheshire cat.'

'It's about English tutoring for some kids I know.'

It sounded like money so I accompanied him to the café where we ordered coffee. We introduced ourselves and I learned that his name was David and that he was from the Galilee.

'And you are Heather. That's a flower, isn't it? A beautiful one, I'm sure.'

'The proposition?'

A waiter arrived with our coffee and David told me of an Israeli family who were looking for an English tutor.

'The family's name is Shmuel. They are originally from Iraq. The little boys both need tutoring. The father is contracted to a construction project here. You'll really like them.'

I stirred my coffee thoughtfully.

'Well?' He had an expectant eager look, like a spaniel about to be thrown a ball. I couldn't help smiling and I agreed to do it.

He asked me about the comment I had made when I had been looking for a job about half of me being Jewish. I explained that my father's side of the family were Jewish.

'And what does that make you?' he asked.

'A New Zealander first and foremost, and vaguely mono-theistic.' I sipped my coffee. 'Are you religious?'

54

'Not really. I consider myself an Israeli before a Jew,' said David, going on to tell me about his home, his family and how his parents had coaxed the land into fruitfulness. He mentioned the graves there of a brother and sister, both killed in the struggles. In spite of my initial impressions of him – flirt, ego-centric, bullshitter – I found myself liking him. Beneath a flippant exterior he was intelligent and perceptive.

We talked a bit about New Zealand then, David surprising me by his interest. We finished our coffee and he offered me a lift home. Before he dropped me off he arranged to collect me from the photocopying office the following Monday to take me to the Shmuels.

'I don't like you driving around with this soldier,' said Joe, when I told him.

'Jozefu, you sound jealous,' I teased, but I kept it light. I remem-bered Osman. 'Anyway, while you're drinking with your mates in the bar, I'll be tutoring these kids instead of waiting round for you. It sounds fair to me.'

Fair? One of us earning money, the other whittling it away?

I enjoyed meeting the Shmuels. The father was short and swarthy with the weathered face of an outdoor workman. His wife was plump and motherly, ushering us into an orderly kitchen that smelled of home baking – like the aunts' kitchen, I thought with a pang. The two boys, Avram and Moshe, were both under five, a good age to pick up a new language.

The boys and I started our first session in the living room, later progressing to the garden to have some fun while David and the parents, neither of whom spoke English, sat around the kitchen table chatting. They paid me well and it was arranged that David would bring me twice a week thereafter.

The next few months fell into a pattern around the nursery school, the photocopying office and the Shmuels. I looked for-ward to the drives to the Shmuels and a deep friendship devel-oped between David and me. Joe also liked him and we often invited him to stay for a meal. I took it as a sign of true friendship that he ate the coarse stews cooked on the primus without raising an eyebrow. Sometimes the three of us would sit on boxes in the living room talking politics well into the night and becoming tiddly on wine.

Towards the end of the year Joe confided to me that he was seriously considering the offer of another job. He had been unhappy for some time at the centre. His superiors, Obote-picked and with lesser qualifications than Joe, saw him as a threat, and his initiative and expertise were deliberately ignored. My heart ached for him as I watched his enthusiasm drain away to be replaced with bitterness and resignation.

In mid-December three things happened that were to change our lives forever. Joe accepted a highly paid position with an international company, I bought the nursery school, and we found to our delight that we were going to have a baby. Christmas ushered in the end of my first year in Uganda.

Chapter 9

Christmas was a warm family affair. A few days beforehand we had travelled to the village to spend a day with Joe's parents. Then Ted and his family came from upcountry to stay with us, sleeping on mattresses on the floor.

On Christmas day Byron, Henry, James and the Musokes joined us for lunch. I had borrowed a portable gas cooker for the occasion and Joe and I surprised ourselves by turning out a superb meal.

'Something smells good,' said Musoke, coming into the kitchen where Joe and I were dishing out the food. 'I've been looking forward to Christmas at your place all month.'

I handed him a bottle of his favourite wine with a Christmas bow around the neck. 'How nice, Heather,' and his big face broke into a smile. Sarah came in and we four had a quick drink together. Joe put his arm around me and reminded me of the Christmas at Marton two years before when we had dropped the bombshell of our marriage. We laughed and the Musokes begged us to tell. Ted's wife Mary bustled into the kitchen, her large body stiff with disapproval.

'The kitchen is for women and servants,' she said bluntly to Joe. 'Your wife should push you out.'

I already knew that the more traditional relatives disapproved of the way Joe helped in the kitchen. I had tried to explain that he enjoyed cooking but they didn't believe it and assumed that I coerced him into helping.

'Jozefu shouldn't work like a woman,' said Mary firmly.

Now I've heard everything – a woman encouraging her own denigration!

And yet her attitude was common enough among her sister Ugandans. Their upbringing taught them it was right for the men to loaf while the women cooked and hoed and bore children and carried water. It was the women who saw that the children went to school clean and fed; who worried over straying husbands and empty larders; who sat up alone all night with sick children while their husbands were out carousing.

I tore up lettuce and chopped tomatoes, my mind working furiously as I pondered on a system where males had all the freedom and little of the responsibility. I tossed the salad and dumped the bowl in Mary's hands.

Take that, lady, and lay off Joe!

I looked sideways at Sarah, who was squeezing oranges for the children.

And you – modern and educated – are as trapped as the rest. Much as I like your husband, he's an amiable rogue.

I ran water on the dishcloth and wiped down the bench viciously. Joe, sensing my mood, put his arm around my waist. His face was wide and calm as he looked at me with understanding and dropped a kiss on my brow. Mary's eyes bulged.

Dear Joe, don't ever change.

We gathered up the food and moved into the living room where people were singing Christmas carols. The noise gradually subsided as people helped themselves to food and began to drink. Joe and I sat among them, proud of our spread. During dinner Musoke again asked us to tell about our Christmas at Marton. Joe shook his head, but everyone took up the plea and finally Joe, after looking helplessly at me, laughingly succumbed. The room became silent. Mary put the baby to her breast and settled back against the wall. Joe put down his plate and began.

It began in our large, comfortable living room at Marton. The old piano where as children we had struggled with Brahms and

Schumann was almost completely submerged beneath vasefuls of summer flowers. In the corner, shedding pine-needles and decorated with winking lights, stood an untidy, loose-limbed Christmas tree.

Discarded wrapping paper and strings threatened to trip Dad up as he picked his way around with a tray of drinks. Robin and Janet, in crisp new dresses, sat on the sofa laughing over glasses of wine while Bruce and Peter argued, their mouths full of nuts. My grandmother sat smiling and affable in an armchair with her second sherry.

I looked about me, my heart fluttering in dreadful anticipation of the hour when we would break our news. Joe, who had arrived with me the night before, looked tense and tired and had hardly spoken a word. He picked up a Christmas cracker for us to pull. It exploded and an imitation diamond ring fell out. We stared wordlessly at it as it lay in my palm.

'A ring!' laughed Peter, looking over my shoulder. 'Who are you marrying?'

I was relieved when Dad came with my drink and began to describe the boat he was building. I heard him tell Joe of his plans to sail it to the Marlborough Sounds for fishing.

Stuff the Sounds! I'm dying of nerves. Palpitations. Trembling. Diarrhoea. I'm scared shitless, literally.

'. . . thick with blue cod. You virtually drop your line into a fish's mouth.'

'A bit different from Wellington Harbour,' said Joe and he smiled at me.

Oh God, I love you. Don't let me fall apart.

Mum called us into dinner. Janet in her warm way took Joe by the arm and sat him down by her at the table. We put on bright paper hats and pulled crackers while Dad carved the turkey, then everyone fell on heaped plates with noisy verve. Joe and I picked up our knives and forks in silence.

I cast a despairing eye around – my grandmother opposite in a red paper hat struggling with her turkey and her sliding false teeth; Peter, still a schoolboy, his hand sneaking out for the red wine; Robin next to me, dramatic in dialogue, the silver neck chain I had given her that morning vibrating at her busy throat – and I wished I were a million miles away.

By this evening they will all know.

Peter knocked over the wine. I watched as a dark ragged map of Africa seeped into the white tablecloth. I could take no more.

I felt sanity slip from me as I rose to my feet and said, 'Joe and I love each other and we're going to get married. I shall go with him to Uganda as soon as we're married.'

I clung like a limpet to the table.

If I faint they'll think I'm pregnant.

I looked in misery at the dumbfounded faces staring at me beneath ridiculous paper hats. My grandmother, slightly deaf, ploughed on through her meal unaware. I sank to my seat.

Dad turned to Joe. 'Is this true?'

'Yes.' Joe seemed as shocked as the rest.

'Was this hatched up on the train coming here?'

'No. We planned to marry some time ago,' said Joe, his features taut and strained. 'I have always loved Heather – I only want her happiness.'

'Good Lord!'

'You could have told us before.'

'It's absolutely out of the question' – Mum.

'You're both still studying' – Dad.

'What difference does that make?' My voice shook strangely.

'A lot of difference!' and then, incredulously, 'And living in Uganda!'

'Different cultures! Different countries! You're both dreaming!' Mum looked as if she were too.

'We're not! You're just worried about what the neighbours will say!'

Dad, whose aim in life seemed to be peace at any price, put down his knife and fork. 'Look. We're all getting carried away. Finish your degrees and think about it then. What's a year or two?'

'Joe finishes in a few months, Dad.'

Janet, initial shock over, now faced the table with grim determination. 'What's all the fuss? They only want to marry and live in Uganda.'

'Who, dear?' said my grandmother.

'A wonderful thing, marriage, but you don't want to rush into it. At this stage it's not a very wise idea.' Mum's commonsense voice belonged in the cupboard with her tweed suit.

60

'And why did you have to marry in tearooms?' Janet asked her icily.

'It's not your place to interfere,' said Dad.

'Why not? I'm her sister. I care for her and I like Joe. Why shouldn't they marry?'

'It's not your place to interfere.'

'You forget you were both young once and had to marry in tearooms,' said Janet.

'It's not for you to interfere!'

'What about all those wonderful plans to do anthropology up the Amazon?' Mum, who had once discouraged my notions, was now clutching at straws.

'I'm going to Africa with Joe.'

'You're both too young! Pass the potatoes, Peter!'

'Joe's nearly thirty,' said Janet crossly and snatched the potatoes from Peter. 'You two do what you want, Heather. I have faith in you both. Congratulations. You can count on me.'

I felt the hot tears prick my eyes. Dad, always moved by tears, said, 'This isn't the time to discuss such an important matter. Whoever Heather decides to marry will be accepted by us. Now let's finish our dinner before it gets cold.'

Nobody was particularly interested in food any more and we finished dinner quickly. Mum helped my grandmother into the living room, followed by Dad. In silence the rest of us began taking the dishes to the kitchen. Janet filled the sink and threw in the cutlery.

'We'll work on Mum and Dad later. I'll start the dishes and you others take the coffee to the living room. My God, what an exciting day!'

'I suppose it is,' said Bruce and began to laugh. 'What a pair of silly buggers you are! Why didn't you drop a few hints?'

'Congratulations!' Somebody hugged me.

'Same here!' Peter shook Joe's hand and suddenly the kitchen was filled with noisy voices. Joe's arm came around my waist and the icy knot of fear that had lodged in my stomach began to thaw. We took the tray of coffee things to the living room. Through the half-open door I could see Mum arranging champagne glasses on the coffee table.

'I think,' whispered Robin, 'it's going to be all right.'

The champagne was a sign that Mum and Dad took us seriously but they still tried to dissuade us.

'They bombard me with lectures on cultural conflicts and the miseries of miscegenation,' I grumbled to Joe. When they realised that we were determined, they did the only sensible thing and made an effort to get to know Joe better. In time they became very fond of him and were a lot happier about our marriage.

The aunts wept when they were told, saying that Joe – whom they had never met and never would, thank you very much – was a charlatan and they would not attend the wedding.

Joe's parents were distressed and angry and insisted that he return immediately. But, like my parents, once they got used to the idea they became more accepting, although their letters were cool and distant. I dreaded meeting them.

Mum fussed about with dressmakers and caterers and sent out scores of wedding invitations. As presents began arriving for us in Marton, I was summoned home to help Mum pack china, linen and other gifts into shipping crates.

'Gosh, will you need these electric blankets in Uganda?' she said, on her knees before a crate.

'I don't know.'

'Shall we pack them?'

'If you like.'

'Well, what do you think?'

'I don't know,' I said, surveying the crystal and silver about me. 'I'd be just as happy living with Joe in a tent on the shores of Lake Victoria.'

Mum became exasperated and sent me back to Wellington. Thereafter she disturbed my peace with phonecalls about kitchen tea parties and bridesmaids and, semi-hysterically, about Roman Catholic protocol since, at Joe's request, we were marrying in his church.

'The whole thing's getting bloody out of hand,' I said crossly to Jane. 'I really only wanted a registry office marriage.'

But after the wedding – an occasion of great love and happiness, where Jews laughed with Christians, old danced with young, and Africans charmed locals – I would have had it no other way.

And much later, sated with love and champagne in a luxurious bridal suite, Joe said, 'It's as if my whole life has been a journey leading up to this day. Whatever is in store for us in Uganda, let us always remember this perfect, perfect day.'

We were quiet for a while and, as I often did, I thought of faraway Uganda. 'Tell me again about the lakes and the wildlife and the Mountains of the Moon. Is Uganda really so beautiful?'

'Uganda,' he whispered into the darkness, 'is the Pearl of Africa.'

Chapter 10

Soon after our wedding Joe returned to Uganda to find a job while I finished my studies. A few months later, armed with a brand-new degree and three suitcases, I boarded a plane for Uganda.

Chapter 10

With Christmas over, I had four weeks in which to get my new school ready for the new year. On credit I spent a fortune at Patel Press on Kampala Road where I purchased paper, pencils, crayons, scissors, puzzles, powder paints and sticky paper and had them boxed and delivered to the school. I bought good used toys and books from school fairs and departing expatriates, and an assortment of building blocks from a wood craftsman in Wandegeya. I bought blackboard paint and painted all the little blackboards, which had become scratched and shiny over the years. At a timber yard on Seventh Street I commissioned the Sikh proprietor to make a number of tables and chairs and a bookcase on wheels.

'Are you sure you can afford all this stuff?' said Joe later, his brow wrinkling unhappily. It was to wrinkle a lot over the next few weeks.

The next problem was staff. I wanted a third, English-speaking ayah who would be able to contribute a little more to the school than the basic babysitting skills Agnes and Rose offered. But, more importantly, I wanted another teacher. The ayah job went to Mary, a relative of Agnes, and the teacher's position, after interviewing five candidates, went to Mrs Kherani. She was a youngish Asian woman, estranged for some time from her husband. She had two years of nursery school experience and a quiet steady air about her that appealed to me immediately.

I then had to arrange the rent payments with a certain P. P. Patel, who was president of the gambling club. He turned out to be a fat, repulsive individual who sat in his emporium periodically spitting phlegm through the open window. He ran his eyes over me and with a cackle told me the rent had gone up. When I protested on the grounds of the broken toilets, the filth that the gamblers left for us each morning and the general deterioration of the building, he laughed until he choked. He then cleared the contents of his throat, the thick yellow sputum hitting the windowsill where it sat quivering like blancmange in the morning sun. I declined his offer of tea, agreed to the new rent and hastened away before I contracted some vile disease.

I hurried back to school and sought out John, the young Muganda caretaker who had a room at the end of the verandah. I offered to put him on the school payroll if he did odd jobs for me. He agreed. In my mind's eye I saw Joe's brow begin to wrinkle.

Over the next few weeks John and I scoured the whole building with ammonia. Mould, grime and stench succumbed to our scrubbing brushes. Cockroaches and mice fled in droves from the onslaught. Mrs Rodrigo's mildewed junk was tossed out and my new provisions were proudly stowed in the sterilised storeroom. The Sikh from Seventh Street delivered the tables, chairs and bookcase which John and I painted blue and yellow and put on the verandah to dry.

The week before school started we were still nowhere near ready. While John washed windows I prepared huge wall charts depicting numbers and the alphabet and colours. I fashioned glove puppets from Joe's socks, using buttons and bright scraps of material for faces, and made jigsaws from pictures stuck to thick cardboard. At the nearby dukkas I bought a paraffin cooker, a large sufuria and five dozen plastic cups and staggered back, leaving a trail of cups in my wake.

'Agnes is going to boil up milk for the children each day,' I told John.

'This isn't a hospital, teacher.'

'A lot of the kids don't bring a mid-morning snack. You can't function on an empty stomach, you know.' I had a vision of Joe's brow wrinkling again.

As we were putting away these latest purchases the plumber and two fundis arrived. I took them to the malfunctioning toilets where they dabbled in the cisterns, pulled chains and made diagnoses in Swahili.

'It will be expensive,' they said. 'P. P. Patel has refused to pay.' *The miserable shit!*

I thought of the fifty children who would be using them each day. I thought of cholera and gastroenteritis and worms.

'Fix them,' I heard myself say grimly. 'I'll pay.'

Joe, already exasperated about his vanishing socks, hit the roof about my paying for the toilets, telling me that I was irresponsible and wasteful. I coldly reminded him of the money he wasted at the bar every evening.

On the day before school began, I had to admit to John that we had performed a near miracle. If the place didn't quite sparkle, it looked years younger. I grumbled to him about the gamblers who now had the benefit of my beautiful lilac-scented toilets and well-scrubbed surroundings. They still left their mess for us each morning. John smiled and went to empty the rat traps.

We had bought these some time ago and most days we arrived to find trapped rats in various stages of rigor mortis. Some were as big as small kittens. I shuddered as John threw a couple into the swamp.

I turned to the huge, scratched, old-fashioned blackboard and stand that I had picked up at a school fair and patted it affectionately. We had had one exactly the same when we were children. In good spirits I began to coat it with blackboard paint. There was a knock at the front door. I let John answer it. He hastened back in alarm.

'A soldier,' he whispered. Like most Baganda he was fearful of the army.

'What the hell does he want with us?' I noticed I was clutching my paintbrush tightly. 'What have we done?'

'He asked for you.' He looked at me helplessly. 'But it may not mean kolele. He's a Muzungu.'

'Oh dear God, it's all right then! It's only David.' John sped back to the door and let him in. David, in full jungle combat gear, strode in with a broad smile on his face and an oblong crate in his arms.

'Beware of Greeks bearing gifts.'

'You didn't half give us a fright. We thought you were the army.'

David threw back his head and laughed, the cords on his strong neck standing out. I stood watching him, unamused. John hung his head and walked out to the verandah.

'For God's sake, belt up! You've upset John!' The laughter stopped. I started painting again. 'You'll have to apologise to him, laughing like that. Excuse me, but some of us have to work. We open tomorrow.'

'You look like you've been working for a week.'

I was aware of how I must look, hair flying, face flushed, paint-spattered jeans. David lowered his crate at my feet and settled himself on a box.

'What's in the crate?'

'Something for you.' I put down my brush, pulled off the thin wood tacked across the crate and found myself gazing down at rows of golden oranges.

'They're from home,' said David. 'Much better than the ones here.' The green and fibrous local oranges were used only for drinks. David made me promise to give one to each child the next morning to celebrate our opening.

'What a lovely idea. Thank you.' I tossed him an orange and made him take it out to John and say sorry. When he returned I showed him all our new equipment in the storeroom.

'The bookcase has wheels on it, see? We can roll it out with the books in it each morning. We painted every single desk in here. Come and see the toilets – they are a joy to behold and almost flush in unison.'

'I'll give them a miss.' There was laughter in his voice.

'Thanks so much for the oranges, David.'

'It was my pleasure.' This time there was no banter in his voice. I looked up, surprised. His eyes seemed luminous in the darkness of the store. With the back of his hand he gently touched my cheek, said goodbye and left as suddenly as he came.

I couldn't wait to get to school in the morning. Arriving bright and early, I couldn't help a gasp of pleasure when everything was set up. The sun shone through the open windows on to the scrubbed walls, and everything in the room seemed to be waiting for the children. The blue and yellow tables were arranged at strategic points around the room and on the walls was a colourful mosaic of pictures and charts. By the windows, picked up for next to nothing at a mission fair, stood my most prized possessions – three large old-fashioned rocking horses wearing scarlet saddles and slightly alarmed expressions. The bookcase had been wheeled in to display its exciting new books and in the centre of the room we had set up the activity tables – dough, collage and painting. The box of oranges stood with the cooker and the milk on a table near the front door.

Mrs Kherani, hair swept into a huge bun that seemed too heavy for her small, grave face, busied herself with the admission forms for the new arrivals. The children from the previous year, ecstatic with the changes, ran from table to table in excitement. The big horses rocked back and forth with their shrieking burdens and over at the dough table a bakery was in full swing. Agnes, dumbfounded by the changes, plodded dazedly around looking for brooms, hand-towels and toilet paper.

At break we gave out milk, biscuits and the oranges, which resulted in excited exclamations and heaps of peel, wet smiles and sticky fingers.

'Well, what do you think?' I gasped to Mrs Kherani later as we snatched a cup of coffee at my desk.

'It's busy,' she smiled.

'Oh God, look!' I leapt away to rescue a screaming child down whose mouth a dough cake was being forced by a determined girl in a cook's hat. After I had defused the situation I had the chance to observe the two new members of staff. Mary the ayah had quickly found her feet and was reading a story to a group of five-year-olds. Mrs Kherani had moved to the painting table and was encouraging some of the new children to paint. Patient and gentle, she knew instinctively how to win their confidence. I felt a rising satisfaction with our new staff.

Lunchtime came rapidly and after the children had left I counted up the fees. In spite of the increased rent, the debts I owed and the staff's wages which I had undertaken to raise, I calculated that we were off to a good start. I walked home on air.

As word spread that the nursery school was under new management we were inundated with enquiries for places and we had to start a waiting-list in an exercise book. This grew so rapidly that I toyed with the idea of starting an afternoon session. But my pregnancy, although in its early stages, was becoming irksome and I was perpetually nauseated. Sometimes I had to leave the classroom quickly to throw up in the toilet, returning clammy and weak. Another session began to seem like suicide and I decided against it.

One day towards the end of the first week Mrs Kherani informed me that a man, anxious to have his child start at the nursery, had promised Pepsis and doughnuts for the whole school if the child were admitted. I pointed out that I was not going to subscribe to bribery, particularly when it put others on the waiting-list at a disadvantage.

'Put this Pepsi boy on the waiting-list with the others,' I said.

'I think we should make an exception in this case,' she said. 'It'll be a real treat for everyone.'

I still said no. She had been brought up in the Asian community where bribery was almost a way of life. She looked at me with disappointed eyes that seemed to be saying, 'You won't last long here with your immovable Muzungu ideals.'

'I'm sorry,' I said. 'I must do what seems right to me.'

'Of course,' she said, delicately patting a straying wisp of hair into her bun. She turned from me towards her group of four-year-olds and I sensed disapproval in the straightness of her slim back.

By Friday I was more than ready for the weekend and persuaded Joe to take me to a movie on Saturday night. We walked home after the show, arm in arm. Above us the moon poured a creamy light on to the trees and rooftops. The stars hung low and exceptionally clear in a violet sky and I felt I could reach up and pluck one down. Joe stopped and looked up.

'It's funny, Heather. It's as though tonight is putting on a special show for us.'

Perhaps it was – a grande finale – for that was the last peaceful night Uganda was to know.

Chapter 11

On Sunday we slept late. I felt nauseated and could not eat breakfast. Joe looked at me unsympathetically.

'Morning sickness is all in the mind,' he said, between mouthfuls of egg.

'Oh, rats!' I stomped off to pack my swimming gear. James was coming to take us swimming at Lake Victoria Hotel in Entebbe. On the way we had to stop on the roadside at Najjanakumbi for me to be sick. When we arrived at the hotel Joe tried to forbid me to swim in the pool. 'You'll disgrace us if you vomit in it.'

He ensconced himself in a chair with a beer and a *Newsweek*. Although he was full of quiet pride about the baby, his anxiety showed in his impatience with my symptoms. I tried not to let it bother me.

I followed James up on to the highest diving board. At the other end of the pool I noticed that Joe, the size of an ant, had risen and was signalling frantically for me to stop. Amused at his fear, I waved back happily before sailing downwards into the water. Joe was waiting at the pool edge as I came up. I glided up to him, crocodile-like, hiding a smile beneath the water. James floated towards us.

'Don't do that again,' Joe said testily. 'Think of the baby.'

'Baby?' cried James in alarm. 'I was swimming with her!' Heads on nearby sunbathers swivelled.

'It's not contagious, you oaf,' I said coldly.

He submerged in confusion, drowning his cowlick. He resurfaced slowly, his apology a stuttered telegram. 'Sorry . . . Should've clicked when you spewed at Najjanakumbi . . . Bit thick, I'm afraid . . . Super news . . . Congratulations.'

We sunbathed for a while before going into lunch. After we had eaten we lazed the afternoon away in deckchairs in the sun. I listened to Joe and James discussing Obote's current trip to Singapore for the Commonwealth Conference. Joe felt the British would be blasted by Obote for selling arms to South Africa.

'Those arms are to protect the strategic Cape sea route,' said James indignantly.

'Who from?' I laughed. 'The Commies? Those arms will be used to prop up the government, in other words to suppress the blacks.'

James and Joe began to argue good-humouredly and I dozed off. At four o'clock we packed up and set off back to Kampala. James, anxious to get back to his school, declined to stay to dinner. I cooked up some Nile perch steaks and Joe and I ate out on the fire escape. Joe was going for his driver's licence the next morning so I tested him on questions from the driver's manual. Then, tired from our outing, we went to bed early.

An enormous explosion rent the night air. 'Shee-yit!' Joe sat bolt upright in bed. We became aware of the distant rumbling of heavy vehicles.

'The army's on the move!'

'It must be night manoeuvres.' There was the sound of intermittent gunfire and then another explosion.

We rushed to the windows. The disturbances came from the direction of Mengo and every two or three minutes from our top-storeyed position we could see flashes of fire followed immediately by explosive thunder. In the apartment block opposite us the windows were filled with Asians staring towards Mengo. Below us the Spitting Patels were craning over the sills, the father fiddling with a radio that emitted only static. His lean hand impatiently banged the radio on the sill.

'Hey, Patel, any news?' called Joe.

'I cannot say. Bloody radio won't work. I think it's just army exercises.'

'It could be a coup,' I ventured, 'with Obote away, and all.'

'Not here,' said someone. 'This isn't Ghana.'

'Uganda is civilised.'

'Besides,' put in the Patel with the radio, 'the army is loyal to Obote.'

'What about the Nubians? There are thousands in the army now,' came the educated voice of the oldest Patel daughter, who was at teachers' college.

'So what!' snorted her father. 'They're illiterate. Only good for shining boots.'

Clearly female opinion was unwelcome. I shut my window with a bang and made my way back to bed. Feeling the scrunch of a cockroach beneath my foot, I shrieked.

'Look!' called Joe and pulled me over to his window. Below us, winding up William Street was a lone uncovered jeep. As it passed under our building the glow of a streetlight fell on a spreadeagled heap of inert bodies in the back. A ripple of shock ran through the building. The jeep rattled along the road and disappeared, leaving us gazing down in horror. Frightened whispers sped up and down the apartments and then the faces at the windows began to withdraw. Joe and I went back to bed.

'A truckload of corpses!' I whispered, shivering.

'Several bodies in a jeep,' corrected Joe.

After some discussion we decided that the army was on special manoeuvres, which accounted for the disturbances, and that it was also on a purging exercise to rid the city of criminal elements – hence the bodies. Having whitewashed the whole débâcle, we turned over and slept till dawn.

The egg-beater whirred merrily as I prepared eggs for breakfast. It was a calm, clear morning and the events of the night seemed far away. We were up earlier than usual because it was D-Day – Driving Test Day – and Joe had to report to the Central Police Station at seven o'clock to take his test. We breakfasted at six-thirty and Joe left soon after, clutching his driver's manual. I cleared away the breakfast things and sprayed out the flat with the insecticide on which the cockroaches seemed to thrive. Although it was still far too early to leave I packed my bag and set off for school as there were a few things I wanted to attend to.

I walked along the lonely swamp, engrossed in plans for the day. At this hour the streets were quiet and there was nobody about. A soft breeze rippled across the swamp and from far away a lone frog called mournfully for a mate. The sound made me aware of the greater silence around me. It was too quiet, even for this hour. I became uneasy. No movement disturbed the hushed streets or mute buildings. I felt like the sole survivor of a nuclear accident. I wondered if I should turn back, but as I was nearer to the nursery than to the flat I grimly kept on, fighting off growing panic. I unlocked the school door and ran along the verandah to John's room. He opened at my knocking, his eyes widening with disbelief when he saw me.

'Teacher! Why are you here? Something is up. The radio told us to stay indoors.'

'Oh dear God!'

I wondered absurdly if Musa was safely battened down with our radio. We walked back to the classroom. I sat on a gambling table, wondering whether to stay or go and worried about Joe.

'They've been playing military music for hours,' John was saying. 'I think the radio station has been taken over.'

'Oh dear God! A coup!'

'You will have to stay here for some time, teacher. At least until the military are back in barracks.'

'Oh dear God!' I said for the third time. Nausea engulfed me. I went to the toilets and vomited. Scrambled egg floated forlornly around the toilet bowl. Rinsing out my mouth and splashing water on my face, I glanced in the mirror, realising with a little shock that the pale, frightened-looking creature was me. I squared my shoulders, took a deep breath and went back to the classroom, determined to remain composed.

I nearly blew it when I saw the three children standing there – Nilesh, Abdulkarim and Fatima. John explained that their houseboy had deposited them at the top of the steps and had left before John could warn him.

Holy shit! Five of us trapped here!

I ran to the door but the street was frighteningly empty. 'Can we play in the store?' Abdulkarim and Fatima, brother and sister, stood behind me holding hands. I unlocked the store and the three children scampered in and began fossicking for toys.

'Honestly, as if I hadn't got enough to worry about.' I sat down as another wave of nausea hit me.

'Teacher,' said John, 'oli mulwadde?'

'Sort of.'

'Oli lubito?' Gently.

'Yes.'

'That is nice.' His eyes shone softly.

There was a loud knocking on the door.

'Leave it,' whispered John.

'We should have locked it.' Even as I spoke, the handle turned. A frightened Asian darted in, clutching a briefcase. He had sharp, rat-like features and was nattily dressed in a dark suit and silk tie. It was Nilesh's father. Relieved, I asked him for news. He knew very little except that his office was closed when he arrived at work and that the few people like him who had turned up for work were now rushing home. He had heard that the army was on its way into the city.

'I must take Nilesh and go.'

I asked him to take Abdulkarim and Fatima too since they lived near him.

'Well – er, they're not my responsibility, you know.' His face twitched.

'This is serious, Mr Patel. There'll be roadblocks and soldiers about soon. Their parents may not be able to come for them.'

'I came only for my son. Their father diddled me out of an import licence,' and he left hurriedly with Nilesh. I slammed the door behind them and locked it.

'That . . . that . . . rodent!' I fumed.

'Fear does strange things to people,' said John quietly. Something in his voice convinced me that my anger was futile and inappropriate.

You should be the teacher, John.

Abdulkarim and Fatima sidled up to me, troubled. 'We want to go home.' I swung them up on to the table and sat between them, my arms around their shoulders, explaining that we would have to stay for a while. Taking the book that Fatima was clutching, I suggested we have a story.

There was a rumble in the distance like thunder. The army was coming. I heard several shots. I watched, my heart leaping with fear, as John stacked tables against the door. I turned away from the frail barricade and started the story. 'Once upon a time there was a little girl called Goldilocks . . .'

A heavy vehicle suddenly shattered the quiet of the streets outside, backfiring several times. The children clung to my arms. There was shouting, cheering and gunshots as the truck, obviously carrying celebrating troops, drew abreast of the school. The children began to cry. I held them to me, breathing in their aroma of musk and coconut oil. We heard the truck slow to a halt outside. Doors slammed as its occupants got out and began descending our steps. There was a banging on the door. We froze. A voice in Swahili demanded entry. I held the children tightly.

'What do the buggers want with us?' I whispered to John, terrified.

'They know the Bayindi keep booze here. And cigarettes. They will know there's a school here and . . . and . . .' he stopped.

. . . *and* you, *teacher!*

A jet of pure terror shot through me. There was rough laughter and again they pounded on the door. We watched the furniture jump at each blow. John looked at me. 'The swamp!' he whispered.

We raced outside to the verandah and along to the end where John removed a wire screen that blocked a gap between two posts. He lowered himself down through the gap into the swamp. I saw the mud ooze around his legs. I handed the children down to him and he settled one on each hip. I stuffed my sandals into my shoulder bag and let myself down, replacing the screen securely behind me as I went. I sank into the warm sludge, trying not to think of rats and snakes. I took Fatima from John.

There was a crash from inside as one of the tables fell over. Then another. We headed for the safety of a thick clump of reeds fifty metres away. There was a big crash and a cheer from within the school. 'The bastards are in!'

In a few minutes they were wandering up and down the verandah, drinking a variety of spirits looted from the gamblers' bar. They wore full battledress and were bristling with guns. Their raucous, indiscriminate drinking made them all the more terrifying. From behind the football stadium came an ominous rumble that crescendoed to a roar as a huge tank topped with a revolving gun made its way down the road along the swamp. And, like a nightmare out of control, truckloads of soldiers swung into the far road that bordered the opposite edge of the swamp. I began to imagine they were deliberately encircling us and wondered if we were all to die in the mud.

Yesterday, when I frightened Joe on the diving board, fear was almost funny.

The tank lumbered towards the city like a huge mollusc and the trucks rattled away out of sight. The laughing group on the verandah grew steadily drunker, firing shots into the jackfruit tree that grew at the swamp edge near the road. We could see the huge fruit, each as large as a human head, fall and splatter, all pink and white, over the pavement.

The sun climbed higher, beating down on us in our miserable refuge. The children, tired and hot, laid their tear-streaked faces on our shoulders. Nausea swept over me and I threw up into the swamp, alarming Fatima, who began to cry again. I wondered wretchedly if this day would ever end or whether we would be forever suspended in a time capsule of sludge, fear and droning mosquitoes.

Eventually, around midday, the soldiers on the verandah ran out of liquor. Throwing the last of their bottles into the swamp, they made their noisy way back to their vehicle. We watched as the truck wove drunkenly across the road in a hopeful attempt to return to Mengo. Suddenly the world was still and quiet again.

'Does a coup have a lunchbreak?' I asked John.

'Look, teacher,' said Abdulkarim. A lone figure – a civilian – ran down the road towards the school. Thinking it was Joe coming to rescue us, I sloshed joyfully through the mud towards the road. Fatima bumped about on my hip, whining. It turned out to be the children's father and Fatima almost leapt out of my arms with delight. The man gave a cry, then he was down the bank and into the swamp to meet us, shedding tears as he took his crying children from us, and thanking us profusely. We asked for news and all he could tell us was that the streets were quiet for the time being.

'Go home now, teacher, while you have the chance,' he

advised. He struggled up the bank with the children and we watched them disappear down the road.

I decided to try and make it home. John offered to accompany me, but he had done so much for me already that I felt I had to decline, feeling scared and alone as I did so.

'Where do you live?' he asked. I told him.

'I know the place. Let me take you. I know a shortcut that will keep us off the main roads.' Again I said no and assured him I would be all right.

'I insist on accompanying you.' There was a strange dignity about him as he stood there in his ragged shirt, his young face glistening with sweat and his feet planted firmly in the mud.

'Thank you,' I said humbly.

We set off again through the swamp toward the city, ducking behind vegetation when we heard vehicles. I plodded behind John, wondering again if this day would ever end. He finally stopped at the far bank. I wearily sloshed up to him.

'There's a road above this bank. We'll have to cross it quickly and lose ourselves among the dukkas on the other side.'

Following John up the bank, I paused to put on my sandals. We hurried across the road and into an alley that led upward between the dukkas. Halfway up was a bar whose back door opened into the alley. Voices and laughter came from within. We crept past the door, almost colliding with a tall figure in battle-dress relieving himself against a wall. He was very black, with three straight lines etched each side of his face – the Nubian scarification. It was hard to tell who was the more surprised, him or us. He was very drunk and swayed dangerously. He reached out and touched my hair, blinking in bewilderment.

'Ni malaika wewe?' he said incredulously.

We hastened away, expecting a bullet in the back. We ran upwards, our breath coming in gasps, my bag bouncing all over my back. I turned around once. The drunk was surrounded by laughing soldiers who obviously disbelieved his story that an angel had appeared while he was urinating.

At the top of the alley we found ourselves in a street that connected with the bottom of William Street. I was overwhelmed with relief as we passed the familiar little stores with their whimsical names – Hassan's Fancy Dream Store, Ramji Precious

Goldsmith, Bombay Lucky Emporium. We arrived breathless before the gates of our building. John refused to come in, preferring to look in on relatives nearby.

'I'll never forget what you did for me, John. Thank you for everything.'

'Kale, teacher. Weraba.'

'Weraba.' I watched him hurry along the street and turn the corner. I opened the gates and, muddied, mosquito-bitten and dishevelled, wearily crossed the courtyard, an eyeful for my silent neighbours staring down from the fire escape.

Joe was not home. I wondered if his visit to the police station earlier in the morning could have landed him in trouble. I tried not to worry about him as I made tea. Without doubt there had been a coup led by the army, probably with Chief of Staff Idi Amin at its head. Obote and Amin had been at loggerheads for a while, Obote accusing him, among other things, of gold smuggling and misappropriation of military funds. It had been rumoured that Obote was going to deal harshly with Amin on his return from Singapore. It seemed that Amin had moved against Obote before Obote could move against him.

I refilled my cup and went to the window. I recalled the other rumours over the past year of the secret build-up of Nubian and Kakwa personnel in the army. Loyal to Amin, they could have surprised and overcome Obote's Langi and Acholi friends within the forces. Perhaps it was murdered Langi and Acholi soldiers who were heaped in the truck the night before. I shivered and longed for Joe.

At four o'clock, when I was beside myself with worry, I saw him enter the courtyard. I rushed down the stairs and into his arms. The Patels quietly lined up along the fire escape.

Joe explained that the police station had been surrounded by troops all day and that no one could leave. Joe and the trapped police had played cards all day. Only now were people free to leave the station.

'And what about you, darling? I've been so worried about you. Are you all right?'

'Yes – apart from wading through a sewer and being scared to death by a peeing soldier.' As we climbed up the fire escape arm in arm I told him all about it. We asked for news from our neighbours but no one seemed to know what was going on.

In the flat Joe showed me his new driver's licence.

'You won it at cards, didn't you!' and I burst out laughing. He smiled rather shamefacedly and I kissed him hard. Still laughing, I went to shower away the muck from my flight across the swamp.

Later we sat out on the fire escape with a Patel and the Madrasi teacher who had a radio. The BBC stated in guarded terms that a military coup may have taken place in Uganda. That was all.

'That lack of news is lamentable,' grumbled the Goan with the retroverted uterus, who was sitting in her doorway cleaning rice. The Madrasi turned to the local station where military music had been playing all day.

'If Obote is out, I shall dance all night,' said Joe.

'And I shall get drunk,' said the Madrasi.

'Then do it quietly, for pity's sake,' snapped the Goan, whose interrupted sleep of the night before had left her waspish. Quite suddenly the music stopped. There was an announcement from the army. It was now official. The military had taken over. Obote was out! A cheer went up from the fire escape.

A list of reasons justifying the coup followed. The spokesman finally announced that Major Idi Amin Dada was temporary head of state. Joe and I looked at each other and burst out laughing. Was it possible that a huge, simple, bumbling soldier of doubtful intelligence could assume the reins of government?

'Shh . . .' hissed the Madrasi and flapped a hand for silence.

Amin's thick voice came on air in barely intelligible English. 'I am a man of few words. Everyone has been unhappy under Obote. Now I want everyone to be happy and friendly and then we can have elections and I can go back to the barracks because I am a soldier, not a politician.' He ended up by saying that everyone should return to work as usual the following day and thank God for the army. Martial music followed.

The brusque simplicity of his statement was touching. The fire escape again burst into cheers.

'Obote is out!'

'Amin oyee!'

'Freedom!'

The broadcast triggered simultaneous eruptions of joy all over

Kampala. There was a sudden cacophony of car horns, music and cheering. The jubilant Baganda poured into the city in wild delight, dancing and ululating and waving banana palms and embracing every soldier in sight. Joe grabbed my hand and we ran downstairs to the street below to join the ecstatic crowd. It seemed as if the whole city was dancing.

For several days after the coup people were euphoric and Kampala rang with cheers of 'Amin oyee, Dada oyee!'. Framed photos of Obote, once mandatory in all workplaces, were ripped off walls and hurled outside where they were gleefully smashed by the people on the streets.

P. P. Patel himself limped into school and in front of everyone knocked Obote's picture off the committee room wall with a broom. He gave it to the shoe-shiners on the bank, who fell upon it with hoots of laughter and stamped it into the swamp. Patel stood fatly by, smiling. I could imagine him smiling in the same way among minor Obote officials when the picture was first installed years ago.

'What a turncoat!' I muttered to John, who was sweeping nearby.

'All Bayindi are like that,' he said cheerfully.

I glanced over at Mrs Kherani, who was gently wiping a little girl's nose. 'No, not all,' I said.

Chapter 12

The school flourished amazingly in those early days of 1971, and I was filled with optimism. So, it seemed, was the rest of Uganda. Obote's notorious spy system was disbanded and its members imprisoned. An interim, mostly civilian, cabinet of astute and reputable politicians was established and political prisoners were released from jails where they had languished for years without trial. I watched their joyful parade down Kampala Road to the clapping and cheering of hundreds of onlookers.

Britain, the first country to recognise the Amin regime, was extended a firm, cordial hand of friendship to replace the cool, reticent one of the latter Obote years. 'The British are my best friends,' boomed Amin, 'and I love them very much. In particular I love Queen Elizabeth very much.'

To the British expatriates whose businesses had suffered under Obote's encroaching socialism, this was music to the ear. They welcomed the new President and his promise of a more capitalistic approach and were willing to block out some of his more macabre, sometimes faintly disturbing statements. Sipping evening gins at their elite Kampala Club, they smiled about the black Anglophile who had suddenly landed in their laps.

There was buzzing speculation as to who would replace Amin when he returned to barracks, and it seemed that an election, the first in many years, would soon take place. Everything seemed to be coming right. True, there were disquieting rumours about trouble and bloodshed within the army, but to most Ugandans it seemed remote and insignificant. Local media suppression contributed to the widespread ignorance of what was going on in the barracks and if it had not been for foreign broadcasts, we would not have heard about intra-army dissension.

'What do you make of the latest BBC reports on army atrocities?' I asked Joe as we sat on the fire escape one evening.

'I would say it's sensationalist reporting,' he said. 'I know there's tension between Amin's soldiers and the Langi and Acholi troops, but massacres . . . ?'

'Exaggerations, undoubtedly,' said the teacher from Madras on the next step up.

'Agreed,' said a Spitting Patel, his mouth full of sim-sim seeds. 'We're all happy now. Why look for kolele?'

'Hear, hear!' shrilled the Goan woman through her window. 'We should all be glad that rotten dictator is gone!'

I often wondered afterwards why we were all so ready to make excuses for Amin, so eager to protect him. Even in my letters home to New Zealand I found I was unconsciously defending him. I tried not to think about the bodies in the jeep on the night of the coup because it raised disturbing questions in my mind. Like everyone else, I was happy to believe that Amin's soldiers had rescued us from a tyrant. This was relatively easy to do, for day and night – on TV, on the radio and in the newspapers – Obote's crimes were denounced. Although a lot of what was said was true, some was also fabricated.

Most Ugandans laughed at the bizarre accusations about the former regime that imaginative army officers dreamed up. At one stage Amin went on the air to condemn prostitutes. It was they, he claimed, who had infected all the former cabinet ministers with venereal diseases. 'No wonder the cabinet couldn't sit still and do their jobs,' he said. There was always some new story for the media. One thing that remained constant, however, was the repeated vilification of President Nyerere, who was harbouring the deposed Obote in Tanzania.

During the day, the army was visible everywhere. Jubilant bystanders threw flowers and plantains into the jeeps and trucks as they drove through the streets. Army vehicles were hailed with cries of 'Amin oyee!' and cheering children ran alongside the big green trucks as they passed through the city. Amin became a common sight around Kampala driving himself about in an open jeep, sleeves rolled up and enormous ham-fists clutching the steering wheel. He had a big moon-face and smiled all the time.

'He's an overgrown child,' said an American Peace Corps worker next to me as we watched Amin career down Kampala Road in an Israeli jeep.

And so, with good-humoured indulgence, we sat through the military government's circus and waited for the elections.

As the days of the new regime turned into weeks, an uneasiness seemed to settle on us at times. There were rumours and incidents, all difficult to ignore, which were always hastily explained away on Radio Uganda. Stories filtered down to us of the early murders of several prominent people just after the coup, among them ex-Army Chief of Staff Brigadier Hussein, who was supposed to have been beaten to death by Amin's soldiers. According to a wild rumour that swept round Kampala, Amin had demanded his head and kept it in his refrigerator where he could take it out at will and scold it. Then, it was said, a certain Dr Ebine was dragged from the operating table in Mulago Hospital by Amin's soldiers and murdered for suspected Obote sympathies. Other victims' fates were whispered, often in tones vacillating between shock and disbelief.

One night when Musoke, Joe and I sat up discussing the situation until dawn, we came to the conclusion that the alleged murders were mostly a result of rumour-mongering and an attempt to discredit the new regime by pro-Obote factions.

'Not even Amin would be stupid enough to put a head in the fridge,' said Musoke with his infectious grin. 'It would curdle the milk.'

We talked, too, about the impending elections, an event that was on everyone's mind.

'I can only hope that there's large Baganda representation in the next government,' said Joe quietly. 'We must regain our former position. How we Baganda have suffered!'

'Amin appears to want to please us. He's going to fly the Kabaka's body back from England,' said Musoke. It was a promise that had instantly endeared Amin to all Baganda.

We were shocked a few days later, however, when, on 22 February, Amin went on air, without the knowledge of his civilian cabinet, and declared that the military government, with him as its head, would be in power for the next five years.

It was a bitter blow to the country, but since there was nothing anyone could do against the military machine and since Amin had promised a large degree of political freedom and lack of government interference, the people put disappointment behind them and prepared to go along with Amin's plans in a spirit of goodwill and optimism. Incredible though it seemed, Amin had inspired a universal feeling of commitment towards Uganda.

Amin proved to us, however, that he had neither the concentration nor the desire to work at his presidential desk for very long. When he got bored, he would take off by helicopter or fast entourage for distant parts of the country where he would delight in the huge rallies awaiting him. As Big Daddy, he would earnestly listen to the people's grievances and make the naive promises that the people loved. He would turn to his accompanying Minister of Health (or Education or Works) and say, 'The people here want a new hospital (or school or road) – build one.' When informed once that there was not enough money for one of his schemes, he angrily ordered the Minister of Finance to print more money.

At this stage, such behaviour endeared Amin to us. We weren't too worried about his ignorance because it was generally assumed that he would remain a colourful, blustering figurehead while the country itself would be run by the astute and competent cabinet behind him.

A curfew had been imposed for some weeks following the coup. I never complained about this because it meant that Joe could not meet up with his friends in the bar after work and drink all evening. Instead we would sit on the fire escape in the cool dusk and plan for the baby, talk about New Zealand, or indulge in idle gossip. Sometimes we were joined by our neighbours but this did not happen often. It was a sad fact that, even after a year, there was no real friendship between any of us.

Soon the curfew was lifted and life in Kampala returned to what could almost be described as normal. Our fire-escape chats, which I had grown to love, stopped, and once again Joe sought out his friends in the bar each evening. Determined not to let my hurt and loneliness take over my life, I threw myself into preparations for the baby and for the school. Joe and I ended up doing most of our talking in bed at night, always with the faint but persistent background of gunfire from the Mengo Barracks. Some nights we could also hear military movements on the outskirts of the city, on others the sirens of the military police, or the harsh staccato of automatic weapons. Everyone heard the disturbances. No one wanted to question them. And each morning dawned calm and peaceful.

Now that we were both on better incomes we could make definite plans. The first priority was to move out of our slummy little flat into a decent place with modern conveniences. I had never got used to living out of suitcases, sleeping on the floor or doing the laundry in cold water with hard soap bars that chafed my hands. I used to daydream about switching on a light at night and not seeing cockroaches flee in all directions, or lying in a soapy bath and turning on a tap with my toe when I wanted to add more hot water. I threw myself into flat-hunting with enthusiasm.

We finally decided on the nearly completed apartments being built by the Israelis in Bugolobi, the ones I had seen from the back of Osman's motor bike. We arranged to move in June, a month before the baby was due, and even that was not soon enough for me.

The new flats were light, airy and sparkling clean. Each had a tiled bathroom with hot and cold running water. There were three bedrooms, cork-tiled floors throughout and loads of cupboard space. After eighteen months of living out of crates and cases the sight of those empty cupboards filled me with something close to desperation. The living room had glass sliding doors opening on to a balcony that overlooked the green surroundings. To the right, rimmed by low hills, lay the shores of Lake Victoria. To the left in the distance was Mbuya Army

Barracks and ahead, almost lost in the bush, were the quaint thatched buildings of Silver Springs Hotel.

'It's divine – absolutely gorgeous!' I said to Joe after our first tour of inspection. 'And it's even got two toilets!'

'One is for the servant.'

'A servant!' Things were really looking up.

'And I'm going to buy a car.'

'A baby! A servant! A car! Oh, brave new world!'

'I'm serious,' said Joe. 'I've ordered a Mercedes Benz.'

'O-o-hh, I see,' I hooted in disbelief, 'and now if you'll excuse me, I'm off to lay the archbishop.'

The Mercedes Benz was delivered several weeks before we moved to Bugolobi. It looked very wrong in the shabby tenement courtyard with screaming children playing ball around it. We had become 'Wabenzi' – members of the Mercedes Benz tribe – overnight and every tenant in the building hung over the fire escape to watch our first drive when, with Joe at the wheel, the car leapt backwards and mangled the Madrasi's bicycle.

Having transport opened up an entirely new way of life for me. I was able to explore Kampala, call on friends and relatives, and drive to my ante-natal clinics. I no longer struggled with shopping – into the cavernous boot went groceries, school equipment and market produce, with still room for more. I must have been a common sight in those days, tearing round Kampala in the big car with the windows down, radio blaring and hair streaming. For the first time since I had come to Uganda I felt in control of my life. No longer was I trapped and miserable within the grimy walls of our flat; no more those long, lonely afternoons that I had endured for eighteen months. Things were looking up.

At the end of June we said goodbye to our Indian neighbours and moved to our new flat. What luxury it was to pack drawers full of underclothes and closets full of sheets and towels. How enthusiastically we hung our clothes in wardrobes and stocked the gleaming pantry with foodstuffs.

'And not a fucking cockroach in sight!' I crowed.

I spent several happy days looking at lounge suites before choosing a sumptuous one in a beautiful Sanderson print. 'I don't care,' I explained to a doubtful Joe as it was delivered one

Saturday morning. 'We sat on boxes for eighteen months. We deserve only the best.'

'What's this?' said Joe, as the furniture was followed in first by a king-size bed with mahogany headboard and side tables, and then by a short barefooted man struggling under a pink and cream mass that was our curtains and bedspread. This fabric was a big gamble. It could prove to be a brilliant choice – or a discordant disaster, reminiscent of strawberry ice cream chunder. I held my breath as the yards of cloth were unravelled at the window. It looked absolutely beautiful and I smiled with relief.

'We can't pay for all this!' gasped Joe.

'We can and we will,' I said firmly.

And we did.

A few days later our crates from New Zealand finally arrived. I felt like crying as I unpacked our belongings, most of them wedding presents from my family. There were linen sheets and silverware, crystal and china, electrical appliances and kitchenware, blankets and towels. Each item came with its memory of home and the easy intimacy that I so missed. Out came the china coffee set from the aunts, who disapproved of my marriage but still cared enough to give something, and I wept. Tears dropped silently among the parcels and paper and, overwhelmed with longing for home, I crawled through the debris into Joe's arms.

'You're the only person I've got. Promise you'll always love me?'

'I promise, darling.'

He stroked my hair and rocked me gently against his chest until the crying stopped. We sat quietly together on the littered floor as evening descended around us. A cool breeze drifted through the wide open balcony doors and we could hear the distant croaking of amorous frogs and the soft rasping of nocturnal tree insects. I shivered at the sudden burst of artillery fire from Mbuya Barracks.

Chapter *13*

The first six months of Amin's reign saw our fortunes change rapidly, not as a result of the new government but in spite of it. My school and Joe's new job took off like twin rockets and we were now able to plan for our future with some certainty.

A fortunate beginning for us – a terrible one for Uganda. The real story of those first months under Amin will probably never be known in full because most witnesses to the horrific events were slaughtered by an Amin who became increasingly paranoid as time went on. From the day he took control, the murders and wholesale slaughter began. Hushed-up killings in the army were on a massive scale and so capricious in nature that an accurate estimate of deaths is impossible. The most incredible, and probably the most chilling, aspect of the whole grisly business was its almost total concealment from the civilian population. While people on the streets were hailing Amin as a saviour, mass murder was being committed in the barracks.

From day one of the coup, Amin's prime targets were the Acholi and Langi troops who made up a large proportion of the forces. These groups were systematically murdered and truckloads of their bodies left the barracks in the dead of night for unknown graves.

His other victims, officers who held the rank of lieutenant colonel or above at the time of the coup, were quietly murdered because Amin saw them as a threat. Their places were filled by sadistic, inexperienced Nubians, by Amin's Kakwa people or by privates whom Amin had befriended and whom he would promote several ranks in as many days. By the middle of the year – about the time we were ferrying our belongings from William Street to our new flat in Bugolobi – the number of murdered soldiers, particularly Langi and Acholi, had climbed into the tens of thousands.

Makindye Military Prison, on the outskirts of Kampala, became a black Auschwitz and featured prominently in the massacre of army personnel. The notorious Singapore cell in this prison was periodically awash with blood and body tissue and the screams of the dying could be heard beyond the prison confines.

By early July, despite the secrecy surrounding the army, stories were leaking out. The brief love affair between the people and the army had begun to fade after Amin's announcement of the military government, and had vanished completely as Amin assumed more power and disturbing rumours were given more credence.

About this time, prominent civilians began to disappear. Former politicians were picked up off the streets and never seen again. High-ranking police officials failed to turn up for work; their bodies were washed up in the Nile. Fishermen told of half-eaten bodies in the lake and villagers of graves in Namanve Forest.

'Can this really be happening?' I asked Joe, shocked, and the despair in his eyes gave me the answer.

Shortly after the arrival of my crates from New Zealand, there were two great massacres, one each at the Jinja and Mbarara Barracks. The slaughter was so enormous that it could not be contained and news of it overflowed into the civilian sector. Horrified rumours flew in all directions. Two Americans named Stroh and Seidle – one a freelance journalist, the other a university lecturer – travelled from Kampala to Mbarara Barracks to investigate the reports of the great massacre. They were never seen again.*

---

*The Americans had been murdered. Much later, in a court of inquiry forced on Amin by the American government, two army officers were found guilty of the Americans' murder. The verdict so enraged Amin that the presiding British judge had to flee for his life. The two army officers were subsequently promoted.

The disappearance of Seidle and Stroh signalled the end of any illusions we still had about Amin and the army. Up until now the killings, disappearances, corpses and kidnappings had been hardly more than rumours, and they were on the whole concerned with army personnel, but the disappearance of the Americans meant that no one was safe, no one was exempt from the madness which had insidiously crept up around us. It had taken the disappearance of the two foreigners to wake us all up.

At the time of the great massacres Amin, in need of cash and arms, was winging his way north to Israel and London to visit his 'good friends Golda Meir and the Queen'.

The cash was urgently needed, for Amin had squandered money recklessly. From the start, unable to understand basic economics, he had used the Bank of Uganda as his personal money box. He allowed no limitations to be set on the amount of money he could withdraw and, as his power grew, murdered any bank official he felt disapproved of him. The Governor of the Bank of Uganda was one of his victims.

He ordered rash building programmes – hotels, an airforce base, conference centres – most of which were completely unbudgeted.

On top of this, public funds supported his personal lifestyle. He ran several family homes where his three – later four – wives and at least thirty children were housed. He also supported Kakwa relatives and friends and numerous girlfriends, who had to be fed, accommodated and entertained with trips abroad.

And then there was his pride and joy – the army, for whom his crackpot schemes were always costly and bizarre. He spent enormous sums on the importation of luxury goods for the troops, including woollen Scottish kilts to be worn on parade. And he insisted that land-locked Uganda would set up its own navy of warships and submarines to float around on Lake Victoria. 'Guess who will be admiral of the fleet,' said Henry with a grin. Besides this, the army had to have better pay, better uniforms, better equipment, more promotions, more luxury goods and more training.

Amin's attempt to procure funds from Britain was unsuccessful but he proved popular with the press, who followed him wherever he went. After dining with royalty at Buckingham Palace –

'How will he cope with a knife and fork?' asked Mrs Kherani cattily – Amin was taken to see the latest military hardware, which was demonstrated for his benefit. He ordered two dozen of the latest British vertical take-off Harrier jet fighters, commenting to an astounded British entourage that he needed them to bomb Tanzania – a fellow member of the British Commonwealth – so that he could grab a strategic corridor to the sea through northern Tanzania. Needless to say, he did not get his jets. Nor was he treated any more generously when he flew on to visit Golda Meir. Disillusioned, he returned to Uganda to be met with the unwelcome news of the two missing Americans.

I continued teaching at the nursery school until the baby arrived, but after the Stroh-Seidle affair there was a subtle difference in the atmosphere. Fear was never far away, and its ripples filtered into the classroom. If we heard the high-pitched wail of a military police siren, the whole classroom suddenly became silent, the children turning to me anxiously. If there were soldiers in the area, I kept the children indoors, all morning if necessary, to avoid drawing any unwanted attention to the school. The children often asked me if the army could get them and I always replied no, although it was not the truth. Several African children left the school at this time. Their parents explained that they felt their children would be better off with the grandparents in the obscurity of the villages.

In spite of the tensions, Mrs Kherani and I were making great strides with the children. The three- and four-year-olds were beginning to communicate in English, while the older children were developing skills in writing and maths.

'These kids,' I said firmly to Mrs Kherani one day as I looked at the diligent little heads bent over their papers, 'are going to fly through the entrance tests and be admitted to the best primary schools in Kampala.'

I gathered up a group of five-year-olds for reading and we went to my desk with a story book. Immaculate Kaggwa, shy and breathless, started the first page. Mrs Kherani appeared at my side, whispering that there were some parents at the door wishing to enrol their children. I looked up at her with some surprise, since she knew the procedure for dealing with this situation.

'Just put them on the waiting-list as we always do,' I said.

'Well, this is different. They don't want to go on the waiting-list because . . .'

'They'll go on the waiting-list like everyone else,' I retorted, wondering why Mrs Kherani and I always bickered over this subject.

I turned back to Immaculate, who was staring at the door with wide eyes and dropped jaw. I followed her gaze to find myself looking at two terrifying Kakwa soldiers in combat battledress. Each man had a gun at his belt, a knife strapped to his leg and the biggest pair of black boots I'd ever seen. Clinging to their hands like scruffy appendages were four small children. The soldiers stood immobile at the door, staring at me from blank silent faces. On their temples were the three vertical marks denoting a tribesman of Amin.

Mesmerised, I stared at them across the hushed classroom for a few seconds. Then I pushed back my chair and hurried over to greet them, smiling warmly and extending my hand. They shook my hand briefly and the taller of the two men, who had the small, round eyes of a pig and an upturned snout to match, began to bark at me in Swahili. Mrs Kherani was summoned to translate. Pig Face repeated his diatribe to her, and then swung round to face me, his little eyes glaring fiercely.

Mrs Kherani hurried to explain. 'He says they have moved to this area and that the children will join this school. Tomorrow.' She stopped and looked at me, the corners of her mouth twitching. 'Er . . . shall I tell him about the waiting-list?'

Fear of the army permeated every walk of life. People went out of their way to avoid soldiers on the streets or in buses. The troops were always served first in shops, banks and doctors' clinics and if they deemed a price too high it was lowered immediately.

Amin's three security organisations, which emerged at about this time, were to become even more feared than the army. The first was the military police, stationed at Makindye, whose development into a vicious terror unit was the work of its new head, Major Hussein Marella, a Nubian whose name became synonymous with death. His victims came from both the armed forces and the civilian population; once thrown into a military police vehicle, they were rarely seen again. The military police could call on homes at any hour of the day or night. A dreaded late-night knock on the door became a death knell for many people.

The Public Safety Unit – 'What a misnomer!' exclaimed David – was set up ostensibly to protect the public from armed robbery. Under Ali Towelli, another Nubian, this organisation became notorious for its thuggery and its execution tactics. The unit and Towelli were a law unto themselves. They were given orders by Amin to shoot on sight anyone they suspected of being a thief and this gave them free reign to terrorise the population at large.

The third and most awful of the security organisations was the State Research Bureau. This terrifying annihilation machine, an amalgam of the Ton-ton Macoutes, the Gestapo and Mickey Mouse, was run by Nubian thugs who were, for the most part, illiterate, sadistic and completely amoral. Nattily dressed in bell-bottomed trousers, floral shirts, platform shoes and dark sunglasses, these bullies walked freely among the population, bringing with them death and destruction. They arrested, robbed and killed without fear of reprimand. Their victims – mainly wealthy, professional, Christian and from the south – were dragged from streets, shops, bars and offices in broad daylight and bundled into the boots of State Research vehicles. Horrified onlookers were powerless to intervene and any enquiries were suicidal.

Seven months into the new regime, we watched helplessly as Uganda plunged into an abyss of destruction. There was no secret now about the corpses that were dumped regularly into the Nile for the crocodiles to consume. As the number of bodies climbed into the thousands, the crocodiles, fat and replete, could not dispose of them and the corpses were swept to the banks or carried to the power station near Owen Falls Dam. Musoke, who frequently drove to the dam on business, told us of the divers he had seen disentangling bodies from the hydro-electric machinery.

Bodies were found in the sugar fields at Lugazi, in the forests at Namanve and on the shores of Lake Victoria. Businessmen were threatened with death and then forced to pay bribes for their safety. Men were imprisoned or killed if army officers desired their wives. People fled Uganda in droves. Those who remained became close-mouthed and reluctant to confide in anyone who was not family. Fear and suspicion stalked the country.

Into this chaos our lovely baby daughter was born.

Chapter 14

The birth of Tanya turned our lives upside down. I had always envisaged motherhood as that happy state where a sweet young mother rocked and hummed to a perpetually sleeping baby in a golden glow of contentment. But I was sadly deluded. There was no sweet mother and sleeping baby in our house, only two cross and wakeful combatants who seemed determined to upset each other. Orderliness and routine flew out the window. Everything revolved around the small bundle with the waving hands. Nights were spent rocking or feeding her, meals were missed to attend her, personal indulgences such as reading or trying out new eye make-up became forgotten luxuries. Her crying summoned us, on the run, from any part of the flat.

At night Joe and I would fall exhausted into bed, only to be woken almost immediately by Tanya, whose outraged face and bare gums filled me with something close to panic. I could always recall Dad saying to someone many years before, 'Never disregard crying in a baby. It always means something – maybe a wet nappy, maybe meningitis', and I would feel a clutch of fear as I picked up my screaming daughter.

There was another memory, too, so far away and misty that it may have been a dream, of a Maori family who drove twenty miles to our house one night with a dying baby. Their urgent knocking brought my father to the door where he was handed the blanketed baby. It died in his arms, and the wailing began immediately, horrifying us children in our beds.

Besides caring for our baby, we also had to go to work each day. We had a new housegirl called Florence whose job was to care for Tanya while I was at school each morning and then to do the household chores in the afternoon. I never had much confidence in Florence and could hardly contain myself until lunchtime when I was reunited with the baby. For the rest of the day I was Tanya's eager slave, although my enthusiasm waned as the afternoon slowly wore on. She never slept in the afternoon – if I tried to put her down she screamed and I would hastily pick her up again – so I carried her about in my arms, cuddling and crooning and rocking, reinforcing her determination to stay awake. Sometimes I was so tired that I actually nodded off to sleep while I was walking.

'How on earth do mothers in New Zealand cope?' I asked Joe incredulously. 'When do they get time to cook and iron and do housework and laundry and everything? We're so lucky to have a housegirl to do all that for us.'

But several days later Florence, with a pile of our sheets under her arm and my high heels on her feet, ran away with next door's houseboy, never to be seen again.

Tired and furious, the only thing we could do the next morning was to get up extra early and bath, feed and dress Tanya and take her and her assorted paraphernalia with us. She was all sweetness and smiles that morning, blissfully unaware of the complications.

'How intrigued my parents will be when they learn that their grandchild started school at two months,' said Joe with a laugh. I wondered if he would have been so cheerful if the baby had to go to *his* work.

The children at school were captivated by Tanya and clamoured to see her. For the first time I became aware of the running noses and hacking coughs that were a normal state of affairs in the classroom. I looked down at the eager children, seeing only a mass of germ-ridden facial orifices and upreaching fingernails rimmed with colonies of bacteria.

'I must have been mad to bring her here!' I gasped to Mrs Kherani and for the millionth time since Tanya's birth I wished that my mother or a Plunket nurse or *someone* was here to guide me.

'We're all the same, we mothers – over-protective.' Mrs Kherani clucked and cooed as she took the baby from me.

She never talked much about her past, but I knew that she had married into an influential Ismaili family and had, as was customary, lived in that household. They had had three children, after which there had been an argument over her husband's womanising, and he, supported by his entire family, had thrown her out. Having no family of her own in Uganda, she had moved into the boarding house of an Asian widow, and had returned to teaching in order to support herself.

'Did you worry about your babies as much as I do?' I asked her.

'I suppose not. I lived with my husband's family, remember. They all had lots of children and lots of advice and I felt reasonably confident.'

'If only you knew how much I'd welcome a visit from my mother. Every decision I make about babycare is a stab in the dark.'

For a minute I felt close to tears and turned away. I looked at Pig Face's two scruffy boys who, defying all the laws of genetics, showed promise of intelligence; I watched fragile Nita building a castle with blocks, and the twins Kato and Wasswa helping Rose heat milk for morning tea – and wondered if any of them had turned their mothers into neurotic messes.

Turning back to Mrs Kherani, I took the baby from her. 'I'd love to meet your children, Mrs Kherani. Why don't you bring them to school some time?'

She picked up a box of crayons and began distributing them among the children. Mary followed her with papers. 'I'm afraid I don't see them much. I'm not permitted to.' She turned away, the silken edge of her sari falling across her face, but not before I saw an indescribable sadness in the dark features. I handed the baby over to Agnes, reminding myself firmly that there were many, many people worse off than myself.

Although we tried several housegirls after Florence, none proved suitable and Tanya ended up coming to school with me each morning.

Around us, the country still seethed with uneasiness and fear. Every few days the awful murder of some prominent person would occur and rumours about who would be next would sweep round the city. In Kawempe a well-known doctor was dragged from his clinic and murdered because Amin was interested in his wife. Several lawyers, who expressed concern at the Public Safety Unit's intention to shoot on sight 'anyone suspected of being a thief', were taken from their offices in broad daylight and never seen again.

Next there was a spate of disappearances among insurance personnel after one insurance company gently hinted to Amin that they could not keep paying out on vehicles stolen or lives lost because of the army. John Kasasa, a very dear friend who had a child at my school, lost his life at this time because he was an insurance salesman.

'How long will this go on! Why doesn't someone assassinate him!' cried Joe in his grief. And when I saw Kasasa's son at school a few days later, I had to leave the room and weep.

Each evening Joe and I discussed the day's news. We often spoke of leaving Uganda but, like everyone else, we felt it could get no worse and that at some stage the British or the Americans would rescue us from Amin. Henry, coming in from soccer one day, dispelled that notion.

'Why should they intervene? Their nationals aren't the ones being murdered.'

'But they won't want a ghoul like him around, any more than they wanted Hitler,' I argued.

'Foreign companies are getting a good deal here at the moment,' said Henry, his young face tightening. 'So long as that happens there'll be no international involvement in any plots.'

I looked at Tanya asleep in my arms. The soft downy head seemed so vulnerable that I was swamped with emotion. 'I could kill the bastard myself!'

Shortly after Tanya was born we had taken her to the village and, as was the custom, she had been given her Kiganda names by the proud grandparents. When she was nearly four months old we decided on another trip to the village. This time we invited the Musokes to come with us.

Sarah was aghast at the quantity of baby things I was packing for the trip. I looked at the assortment in the suitcase – baby oil, bibs, gripe-water, milk mixture, Vaseline, towels, nappies – and snapped at her. Musoke sided with his wife, saying that we were wearing ourselves out unnecessarily over the baby. It was on the tip of my tongue to tell him to mind his own business, but when I looked at the big, kindly face I softened. I closed the suitcase wearily, knowing he was right.

At about this time I had begun having two recurring nightmares. The first one showed my father, late at night, silhouetted against the dimly lit doorway. Beyond him on the doorstep was a shadowy knot of people who handed him a blanketed bundle. I watched as Dad opened the blankets to reveal a lifeless baby very much like Tanya. In the dream I cried and screamed so much that I could not catch my breath and woke up gasping.

The other dream concerned a desperate attempt to leave Uganda. It was my job to pack our belongings, but I seemed to have difficulty in choosing what to take. Most of the dream consisted of frenzied and desperate packing, unpacking and repacking. I never finished the job and was in a constant state of anxiety. I invariably woke up from this dream with a headache.

My restless, thrashing nights were obvious to Sarah. 'Circles under the eyes,' she said sternly, marching me to the mirror. I saw she was right. My face was thin and washed out and my hair hung pale and limp to my waist as if it, too, were exhausted.

Get me a wig! A face-lift! A blood transfusion!

I trailed dejectedly after the others to the car.

The relatives were overjoyed to see us all. We had brought salt, sugar, flour and tea for them from Kampala, things that were becoming difficult to procure in the village. They told us of the hardships they were experiencing. According to a toothless uncle, an army lorry had recently stopped nearby and the soldiers had raided the shambas. Girls were raped, bicycles and foodstuffs stolen and several people beaten up. Two days ago a body had been found on a relative's shamba. The people were too scared to go to the police so the body was buried. To the

gentle villagers, these incidents were shocking and unprece-
dented; the violence affected them deeply.

There was little laughing and merriment that day. The villagers
were still upset by the latest events and I was depressed about my
face. I sat glumly between Musoke and Sarah under a pawpaw
tree while Joe lugged the suitcase from the car. Curious relatives
looked on as I took out Vaseline and nappy liners. Irritated and
slightly envious of their bare-bummed babies, I went through the
procedure of changing Tanya's nappies.

Joe's mother joined us. Slowly the quiet magic of the village
prevailed and I began to relax. Musoke got up to bring us lunch
from the cooking hut where two aunties in long basutis were
busily engaged. As we watched his departing figure, I told Sarah
how fond we were of him. She intimated that she had problems
with him.

'He's rarely in before midnight – every night.'

'What does he do?'

'I don't question. Drinking, socialising or worse.'

Worse? Musoke and women? Surely not!

'Doesn't it bother you?'

'I have a husband, a job, a home, lovely children and security.'
Sarah was echoing the sentiments of many Baganda women.
'What else do I need?'

'But what about *you*?' I longed to say, but her face was young
and sweet in the shade of the pawpaw tree and I kept quiet.

Musoke came back with two plates of food and we were joined
by some of the relatives. Joe's mother took Tanya on her knee,
Joe joined his father on the verandah where they became
engrossed in conversation and I leaned back against the tree
trunk, listening to the quiet voices around me and feeling
pleasantly tired. We chatted lazily on until the shadows lengthened and the children came in from play. As we prepared to
leave, Joe's mother rushed about collecting pineapples, matoke
and cabbages for us to take back.

Dusk descended as we got into the car. I hated to leave the
quiet, predictable village. By comparison Kampala seemed a
tense, fearful place, riddled with rumour and corruption. Joe
broke into my thoughts as the car lurched along track.

'My father and I have been talking about the times. Things are bad now and we have a child to consider. Tomorrow you and I are going to my lawyer. We'll have to make a will.'

A will! If ever a word presupposed death that was surely it. I clutched the baby to me and longed for New Zealand.

Chapter 15

The state of the country, our sleepless nights and taking Tanya to work each day did not make this an easy time for either of us but nothing could detract from the feelings of love and admiration we experienced as we watched our baby grow. She became plump and responsive, kept wonderfully healthy and she had an irresistible smile that resembled Joe's. She was our pride and joy, but she still ruled our lives tyrannically.

The earlier rising in order to get the three of us bathed, breakfasted and out the door by eight o'clock was telling on us. Joe and I snapped at each other, Tanya was often cantankerous in the afternoons, and I was always exhausted. I never had time to finish the washing – all of which had to be done by hand – or to keep up with the daily chores. I felt I was carrying everything on my own shoulders. Joe usually returned after dark, mellowed from a few hours in the bar, and this did little to restore my humour.

There were numerous arguments in those days, yet if I had not been so tired or so overcome with relief at seeing him safely home, there would have been many more.

His indifference to my feelings hurt me more than anything else. I could not understand how he could profess to love me and yet leave me alone night after night.

'I couldn't hurt *you* like that,' I said bitterly.

'It's not a matter of who hurts who. It's a matter of a lifestyle that you refuse to come to terms with.'

'But I married you, not a stupid lifestyle! I'm scared and lonely here on my own. What if the State Research boys come round?'

He took me in his arms and tried to soothe my feelings. 'I love you and Tanya more than anything in this world. But I need time out for myself. It's not too much to ask.'

I knew it would never be any better than that.

One afternoon near Christmas, David came around. I hadn't seen him for ages and I felt embarrassed at the shambles around me – piles of ironing, dishes, Tanya's mess. As I went to the kitchen to make coffee, a growing resentment filled me.

'It's bloody well not on,' I burst out finally as I dumped his coffee down. 'I work at school all morning – with Tanya, of course. Then I have all this pig-sty to contend with in the afternoon as well as one squalling baby, not to mention mashing vegetables and sterilising bottles. And do you know what?'

'Nope.' The dark eyes looked amused.

'The bastard walks in at nine o'clock expecting a meal. I'm so tired I'm walking round in circles and we start fighting.'

'Perhaps you should give up the school. You're trying to do too much.'

'Never!' I saw my classroom and its mass of chattering, squirming, bright-eyed children. 'That place is part of me.'

David, sipping his coffee thoughtfully, told me I was taking motherhood too seriously. 'You need to get out more. Meet up with other mixed couples like you and Joe. You'd have lots to talk about and you'd find your frustration a lot easier to bear.'

I knew what he said made sense. I had in fact struck up an acquaintance with a dumpy Swiss woman called Eva who lived in another apartment block with her Muganda husband and their two-year-old daughter. And then there was Clarice, a handsome copper-coloured woman from the Caribbean who lived in a downstairs flat with her Ugandan husband and four children. I was drawn to Clarice from the first time we met. She was a laughing, self-assured woman whose orderly flat with its soft lace curtains and polished furniture was an inspiration to me. But with so much to do I did not have much time to establish real friendships with either of them.

David reached over and grabbed my arm. 'Let's go and visit the Shmuels and then buy some beer and samosas and picnic at Lutembe Beach.'

'No. How can I with all this mess?' I almost said but my mind raced ahead. I had stopped tutoring the Shmuel children when Tanya was born and I missed them. And Lutembe Beach and samosas were memories from a lost world – a world before Tanya, when life was free of constraints, when spontaneity was allowed.

'Let's!' I cried, surprising myself. I looked round at the shambles, picked up the baby's bottle and some clean nappies and stood up. 'Come on, before I change my mind.'

We sped down Port Bell Road in David's car, stopping at Silver Springs Hotel to pick up beer. As I nuzzled the baby's curls I wondered if Joe would be annoyed with me. Then I thought of all the long lonely evenings waiting for him and I didn't care. The sun was shining, David was singing and it felt good to be out.

Mrs Shmuel and the children were delighted to see us and we had afternoon tea in the garden. After tea Mrs Shmuel claimed Tanya, and the children took me to see their new pet monkey which they kept in a cage behind the garage. They called it General. 'But not after General Amin,' the boys assured us. We all laughed and the monkey shrieked and grimaced.

Leaving the Shmuels, we stopped near Katwe to pick up samosas. Tanya and I stayed in the car, watching the people swarm about their business – large basuti-clad women selling vegetables, ragged Luo charcoal-burners, Moslem butchers waving flies from their meat. David returned and we continued along Entebbe Road into the countryside. Here, extending for as far as the eye could see, were the strong colours of Africa – the rich russet of the soil, the intermingling greens of the bush, the shimmering tawny hue of the distant hills. Everywhere were the distinctive banana plants, pale green and waxy, their broad, fringed leaves arching protectively over clusters of fruit. I wondered what this land would be like in ten years from now, or even five. Would it be gobbled up by the sprawling suburbs already creeping out from Kampala? Or would its silent beauty be ravaged by civil war?

We turned off Entebbe Road and after ten bumpy minutes arrived at Lutembe on the shores of Lake Victoria. We wandered along, listening to the birds scolding in the bush and watching the fishermen haul in their catch. Finding a peaceful spot, we settled ourselves in the sand. It was warm and we opened the beer. I watched David throw back his head and drink deeply. The sun made the beer bubbles glint and sparkle as they rushed up the bottle.

'"Beaded bubbles winking at the brim." Keats.' I scrabbled in the bag for a samosa. 'You're a damn good friend, David.'

He put down his beer. 'Thanks,' he said, a little surprised.

'You've taught me a few things today. I've been like a prisoner – a self-imprisoned prisoner. I'm going to stop worrying about babies and housework. I'll find a decent housegirl. I'm going to read books again. I'm going to buy a car-seat for Tanya and get out and about again in the Mercedes.'

'Baby will like that, won't you, baby?' He held out a finger to Tanya. We laughed as her plump fingers clamped on to it like a leech and she pulled it to her mouth.

We finished the samosas and sat with our beer, watching the fishermen set out again in their boats. Tanya clucked and cooed beside us, investigating sticks, stones and shells with damp, inquisitive fingers. I surprised myself by my lack of reaction. Somehow fussing over hygiene seemed inappropriate. I rolled over on my stomach, buried my face in her soft tummy and made a gobbling noise. She shrieked with laughter, patting against my head with soft hands.

I felt a firmer hand on my head, gently stroking my hair. I froze. 'I love you, you know.'

I jerked my head up and looked at him. He was serious. His eyes were beautiful, a changing mixture of brown and green in the sunlight. I quashed something inside me that threatened to panic.

Dear God, he's so attractive!

I slowly removed his hand from my hair and said somewhat primly, 'You don't know what love is. Love is different from wanting. I shall forget you ever said what you did.' I made the mistake of looking at him again. Beneath the dark tangle of curls his face looked strangely forlorn.

'Oh David,' I whispered and turned away, my heart aching for him.

'I'm sorry. I shouldn't have said that.'

Struggling with my feelings, I could think of nothing to say but, 'I love Joe and I love my baby and that's that.'

'I understand. Let me remain your damn good friend. Please?' He put on his spaniel look and I had to laugh. The tension dropped and we had another beer.

Later, as we got back into the car, I remembered somewhat guiltily that I hadn't changed Tanya's nappy all afternoon. David said I was improving.

After Lutembe, I made a real effort to get more enjoyment out of life. I became more friendly with Eva, Clarice and my other neighbours. Joe, at my instigation, arranged with a colleague to pick him up in a company car after lunch each day, leaving the Mercedes for me. I bought a car-seat for Tanya and took to the roads again. I called on relatives I had not seen for months and on several occasions took Eva and her daughter Andrea swimming with us at Silver Springs. With new determination I did a round of the chemists and came away with cosmetics, hair rinses and vitamin tablets. I discovered an excellent local dressmaker and commissioned her to start on several new garments. Then, skipping into a boutique owned by a fabulously wealthy Asian couple, I bought myself designer jeans from Italy and three blouses from Paris.

'All for the resurrection of Mummy,' I told Tanya as I plonked the parcels into the car beside her. 'I was beginning to look like something off Skid Row.' Tanya gurgled and I kissed her soft cheek.

My new attitude worked wonders for my morale. I felt better than I had in ages and my nightmares faded away.

David remained my damn good friend and we went on outings from time to time when he was off duty. Sometimes we took Tanya swimming at Silver Springs or visited the Shmuels or he accompanied me on my expeditions to purchase equipment for the school. Once we went swimming at Lake Victoria Hotel and as I watched David dive from the top board I remembered how upset Joe had been when I had dived off it the day before the coup. It seemed so long ago, but not even a year had passed.

Although I was much happier, as a family we still had our little problems. We didn't rise every morning like normal people – we erupted with the alarm clock. From then on it was a race against the clock to get us out of the house by eight when we would hurtle downstairs, leaving an indescribable shambles behind us.

We would return at lunchtime to face congealing breakfast things on the table, clothes all over the floor, dishes in the sink, cold water in the baby's bath and heaps of washing and ironing. I bad-temperedly attempted to clean up when Joe went back to work after lunch, but I never seemed to finish. I longed for a washing machine, since it was the washing that took up most of my time, and I would swear long and loud over the slightest mishap. Then I would give up and escape in the car with Tanya.

'What I need,' I thought grimly as we drove away, 'is some sort of miracle.' It came in the form of Abby.

When Agnes informed me one morning that she had found a domestic ayah for me I groaned inwardly. Agnes had provided me with several possibilities and all were hopeless.

Abby stood before my desk – short, stocky and seemingly stupid with downcast eyes, and bare feet firmly planted on the floor. Agnes stood back, beaming proudly. I greeted Abby in Luganda, adding that I was no longer looking for an ayah and thanked her for coming.

To my immense surprise she replied softly in good English, 'I thank you too, Madam. I was prepared to work hard.'

I sat up and looked a little closer. She had a solemn face and her fingers twisted nervously on the cane basket she was holding. Her basuti, although old, was carefully patched and her hair, neatly plaited in Congolese style, was healthy and shining. There was an air of competence about her that the others had lacked.

I wavered, undecided. Rose came up with Tanya to hand me some school fees and Abby, catching sight of the baby, smiled at her with a sweetness that transformed her whole face. Tanya replied with an instant smile and Abby, delighted, put down her basket and took the baby. Her hands, dark against the pink jump suit, looked strong and capable. I smiled and extended my hand to her. 'Okay Abby, you're on.'

She started the next morning and as Joe and I drove to work without Tanya I was full of misgivings. I stared unseeing at the early morning crowds. A rickety bus, bursting with passengers and laden with chickens, crates and bunches of matoke, lurched past us, spraying us with dust and fumes.

'Shit,' said Joe.

'What if she steals everything and runs off, leaving Tanya alone?'

'I thought we agreed to forget about housegirls.'

'She might let her slip when she's bathing her . . .'

'It was your idea to employ her, not mine!'

'But I needed the break. It is impossible taking her to work each day.'

'Only Bazungu need to have relief from their kids.'

'What bullshit! Your people have on-tap relief in the form of extended families.'

We drove to school in angry silence. I was still cross when he picked me up at lunchtime.

It was like entering a strange new apartment when we walked in on our return. The place was spotless, almost empty-looking without its usual mess. The beds were made, the washing was on the line, the floors were washed and the kitchen gleamed as it had not gleamed for ages. The novel smell of lunch simmering on the stove was almost too good to be true and, best of all, Tanya sat propped up in her playpen, washed, fed and happy.

Joe and I looked at each other with smiling faces. 'Whoopee!' and we were in each other's arms.

With Abby's arrival, the last vestiges of domestic disorder disappeared. It was hard to believe that one short, stocky little person was responsible for this revolution. I was delighted with the way she cared for Tanya and a strong bond developed between them. If Tanya was a problem, she was simply tied on Abby's back, Kiganda style, and carried about the house while Abby worked.

I began receiving Christmas cards from family and friends back home. Mum wrote me a long letter giving all the current family gossip. Janet, who had married earlier in the year, was expecting a baby and everyone was very excited for her. Bruce and Peter had bought some beautiful bush-clad land in the Marlborough Sounds and Robin was off to Australia to start a new job. Everyone was holidaying at Whangamata at Christmas – wouldn't it be nice, Mum said, if we could come too. It was two years since I had seen my family. So much was happening to all of us I wondered if we would all ever really catch up.

'I've blown it this Christmas,' I said disappointedly to Clarice over coffee, 'but next Christmas for sure, we'll go home. It just seems such a long time away.'

'Don't you go wishing for time to hurry by, girl. At my age time goes by too damn fast.'

'Something will happen,' I grumbled. 'Amin will ground all flights or Joe will become bankrupt or Tanya will become ill and we won't be able to go. I don't know why we stay here anyway.'

Clarice laughed. 'This is Africa, girl. Anything can happen. That's why we stay.'

Amin began bullying the Asians. The country needed a diversion from the fear and misery Amin had inflicted, and he went on air to castigate them. Asians were rich, he claimed, because they cheated ordinary Ugandans. They refused to socialise with Africans, fraternising instead in their own cliques, attending their own schools and places of worship, patronising only their own businesses.

'The Europeans mix far more freely with the Africans,' said Amin, 'and that is why I love them all.'

He went on to accuse the Asians of smuggling, tax evasion, currency racketeering, undercutting African businessmen and supporting only their own charities. Worst of all, in Amin's eyes, was their refusal to allow their daughters to marry Africans. While some of these accusations may have been warranted, the hatred that ensued was not. The army made a point of humiliating Asians in the streets and in their workplaces. Asian parents told me of girls being molested, cars being taken at gunpoint, merchants being intimidated into giving away their goods to army personnel.

Bhavna and Minesh Patel's parents argued on the school

doorstep about the wisdom of leaving Uganda. Mrs Patel had family in Nairobi and desperately wanted to move there, but her husband felt it was overreacting.

'Yesterday he hated Tanzanians, today he hates Asians, tomorrow he will hate the British,' he argued. 'It won't last. You'll see.'

Mrs Patel didn't want to wait and see. Her husband became impatient. 'Here we have a good business and a comfortable home. I was born here. I belong here. We'll stay here.'

Mrs Patel gathered her two children up and left abruptly, her face a mask of despair and anger. Patel shrugged his shoulders and said to me, 'This is Africa, no? You go up and you go down. Why can't she accept that?'

'Because she's more sensible than us,' I said and turned away, worried.

Chapter 16

In January we went for a short holiday to Fort Portal near the
Zairean border. It was not a successful break. We discovered, on
arriving at our hotel, that the manager had been murdered by
the army two days before. Tanya developed diarrhoea and there
were cockroaches in the bedrooms. Several loud Nubians,
flashing money and diamond rings, moved in with their girlfriends on our second night and stared curiously at us over
breakfast. One of them, after eyeing me thoughtfully, asked Joe
what white women were like in bed. We packed up straight after
breakfast and left.

We returned to Kampala via Mbarara so that I could see the
beautiful highlands of Kigezi in the south-west. It was a mistake
because we were subject to countless roadblocks owing to a
sudden transportation of prisoners from Kampala to Mutukula
on the Tanzanian border. It was a relief to reach home.

Nineteen seventy-two got off to a bad start. To start with, there
was another spate of disappearances, among them a classmate of
Joe's. Then I arrived at school one morning to find an almost
decapitated body lying across the school doorway. An hysterical
Agnes ran for the police who came to remove it, but not before
several children had arrived and had had to step over it to get
inside. And then came the horrifying news of a massacre at
Mutukula. The very prisoners that we had passed on our return

from Fort Portal had been transported to the remote prison at Mutukula and annihilated. Of these six hundred prisoners, none of them criminals, about twenty managed to escape to Tanzania where their story was picked up by a journalist. As usual, we learned of the incident only through foreign broadcasts.

Again the country cowered in terror. The cabinet could do nothing, the police could do nothing, the people could do nothing. In vain we waited for international outrage, but none came. Instead the world laughed at Amin because he said he was interested in Princess Anne.

In February Amin prepared his Israeli jet for another trip to the West to look for arms and cash. Uganda was heavily in debt and Amin was still fired with the idea of invading Tanzania and seizing the northern part of its territory, across to the port of Tanga in the east, thus giving him an outlet to the sea.

Again his trip was unsuccessful and on his way back he decided to visit Colonel Gaddafi, Libya's volatile head of state. The fact that he was flying into Libya on an Israeli jet and could be blasted out of the sky at any moment did not occur to Amin. He met with Gaddafi and a strong bond was established. Amin led Gaddafi to believe that Uganda was a Moslem state and Gaddafi promised Amin arms and cash in return for Uganda breaking off ties with Israel. On his return, Amin went on radio and television expressing support for the Arab cause in its struggle to drive the Zionists into the sea.

The nation was shocked. Israelis had been in Uganda for over ten years as part of their country's aid programme in military training and construction. Ugandan-Israeli friendships had developed on construction sites, in the armed forces, in school playgrounds and on the cocktail circuit. Amin himself had always spoken highly of Israelis – indeed he had on numerous occasions declared them his best friends and publicly stated they had the best army in the world. He had visited Israel several times, obtained his executive jet from there and had himself undergone paramilitary training there. A stunned nation wondered initially if this were not a sick joke.

Amin's broadcasts prompted swift complaints from the Israeli ambassador in Kampala, with whom Amin had previously been very friendly. Amin refused to see him. A Libyan delegation arrived in Kampala shortly after with further promises of aid for Uganda. Amin, sure of his friends now, told the nation that the Israelis, in league with the Tanzanians, were responsible for the subversive activities and bloodshed of the past year.

I asked the gentle Shmuels how they felt about being accused of mass murder. 'Don't worry about us. One grows used to such talk after two thousand years,' said little Mr Shmuel.

The situation became tense, and personal friendships between Ugandans and Israelis were now viewed in a sinister light. Although I continued to see David during these troubled times, I often wondered if it were wise. One day at Silver Springs I was sure we were being watched. We decided there and then that we would stop meeting until the trouble died down. Looking about him quickly, David stood up.

'I'll crawl out of the woodwork when it's all calm again.' He angled his beret rakishly over one eye, saluted Tanya and, with a little Charlie Chaplin kick, walked briskly away.

Late one March afternoon when Abby was off duty, I put some lamb chops under the grill and started to prepare a salad. Tanya, trapped in her playpen, was grizzling and I turned on the radio to block her out. Amin's voice came over the air, accusing the Israelis of exploiting Uganda.

'They milk the country of three million shillings a day in their construction projects,' he was saying. 'Our Libyan friends could provide us with far better and far more honest aid. Israel should be wiped off the face of the earth.'

I could hardly believe my ears. It was like a declaration of war. I rushed downstairs to Clarice, who was on annual leave from work at the time, and told her to tune in. Amin was ranting about Jews this time, not Israelis. Clarice turned it off quickly.

'I don't want to hear it,' she said. 'That sort of talk makes me sick. Let's have tea.'

I declined her offer and went back upstairs to Tanya, only to find that the wind had blown the door shut. I was locked out. In dismay I ran back to Clarice, who returned with me to try her keys in the lock. None of them fitted. I heard Tanya crying inside and I felt myself becoming hysterical.

'We've got to get in! Have you got an axe?'

'Hang on, girl. If Tanya's in the playpen she'll come to no

harm.' She tried forcing a key in the lock. Tanya, hearing the noise, cried harder.

'Shit, Clarice! Do something!'

Clarice straightened slowly. She insisted we ring Joe and see if he had a spare set of keys.

Joe was furious. 'My key is on the ring with the car keys. I left the car keys with you. Where are they?'

'Inside,' and I burst into tears.

'I'll call the fire brigade,' he said in an icy voice.

Joe and the fire brigade arrived in due course, sirens wailing. People poured out of the block to see what was going on. A ladder was extended to reach our balcony four storeys up. Two firemen climbed the ladder and disappeared over the balcony. Joe stood with me and watched.

'Some mother you are!' he said tightly. Clarice pulled Joe away and made him go upstairs to take the baby when the door opened. He returned a few minutes later with a red-eyed, shuddering Tanya. The crowd cheered. I rushed to her but Joe refused to let me have her. Tanya, though, stretched out forgiving arms to me and Joe had to relinquish her.

'You've put a lot of people to a lot of inconvenience.'

'Jozefu, it's all over,' I pleaded. 'Let's put it behind us.'

'It's not all over. The firemen are still up there!'

'What on earth for?'

'They found the kitchen on fire.'

'Oh God! The lamb chops!'

We spent a wretched evening. It was a minor fire but our dinner was in cinders, the kitchen curtains – what was left of them – were in black, dripping tatters, and the whole flat smelled of burning. I couldn't put Tanya down, so shocked was I that she could have gone up in flames. I longed for Joe to comfort me, put his arms around me and absolve me from all blame, but he refused to talk to me at all.

I crept into bed much later and lay there huddled, shivering and miserable. I heard Joe get in heavily beside me. I moved up beside him, feeling cold and in need of love, and put my arms around him.

'Joe . . . ?' He pushed me off and turned away.

Bitterly humiliated, I stared at his unyielding, angry back and wished to die.

I dreamed I was a child again and had crept to the front door at the dead of night. Dad stood with a group of people in the shadows beyond the light. I tried to stop the dream, for I knew what must happen, but in greater detail than ever before I saw my father reach out for a bundle and part the blankets. And there was the baby! A lovely baby with black curls and golden skin and a soft little mouth . . . A cold baby . . . A still baby . . . My baby . . . I thrashed myself into wakefulness and lay there, exhausted and drenched in sweat.

I attempted to talk with Joe in the morning but it ended up in a shouting match. Abby, with a blank face, took Tanya to the other end of the flat. The shouting had purged my guilt, leaving me only very angry. We regressed to sullen silence as we drove to school. I became more and more angry over his unrelenting attitude and his determination to keep me suffering for what had happened the day before. By the time I reached school I could scarcely contain myself. I jumped out of the car and slammed the door.

'You,' I said, putting my head back through the window, 'are a fucking bastard. Twice over!'

His mouth opened in angry shock and I left hurriedly. School dragged that morning. My head ached, I felt sick and weary over everything that had happened and I bitterly regretted my parting words to Joe that morning. John found me on the verandah staring into the swamp.

'Are you all right, teacher?'

'Oh yes. Just thinking. I have fond memories of this swamp, don't you?'

'It was an awful day, teacher.'

We stood together and looked out over the sodden expanse. I thought of Joe and Tanya, and the fire and the fighting and wondered if things would ever be right again. I went back into the classroom with a heavy heart.

Mary approached anxiously with a sick child on each hand. One of them suddenly vomited and they both burst into tears. We cleaned up the mess, sponged them down and sent them home with Mary. No sooner were they on their way than a boisterous child shot over the head of a rocking horse and landed face down on the floor. My heart missed several beats as I rushed to pick him up. He sat on my lap for twenty minutes, roaring, refusing to be comforted. While he was still on my knee, a rat ran out of the storeroom and zigzagged among some children at the painting table. There were screams and a jar of paint splashed across the table, ruining a picture belonging to Saidi, one of the Pig Face boys. He burst into noisy tears. I wondered if his father would shoot us.

At ten-thirty we took the children out on to the verandah for their morning tea. As I had administrative work to do, I left them all and went inside. I sat down at my desk in the empty classroom and took out the accounts book. Fees for March were already due and I hoped there would be no need for embarrassing reminders. I turned to the back of the book where we kept the names of the 'welfare children'. These were the poorer children who paid partial fees or no fees at all. I began to tabulate the fees we would get, those we wouldn't get and those we'd have to nag for. There was a knock at the door. David walked in, his stride urgent. There was no greeting.

'Amin's kicked us out! We've been given three days to leave.'

I stared, unable to gather my wits.

David approached the desk. 'Yesterday,' he went on, 'Amin said Israel should be wiped off the face of the earth.'

'I heard that.'

'Well, today he's ordered us all to leave. I came to say goodbye. I won't try to see you again.'

He stood there in a way that was inherently his, head tilted slightly to one side and a hint of cockiness about him that neither Amin nor anyone else could take away. The implications of what he said were beginning to sink in. A sick, heavy feeling grew in my stomach.

'It's terrible,' I whispered and wanted to weep.

'What's happening to Uganda is one of the saddest things I've seen. I've come to love this country,' his voice dropped, 'and some of the people in it.'

I toyed uncomfortably with a pencil.

'I worry for you, Heather. You're half Jewish and he said some terrible things about Jews last night.'

116

'Nobody here knows except Joe. Don't worry about me. I'll be all right.'

I tried to imagine life without David. There would be that much less laughter, that much less fun, that much less camaraderie. The pain that filled me was unbearable.

'I can't even write to you or it will put you in trouble,' he said. He was silent for a while and then he spoke quietly. 'I wish you'd come back with me to Israel.'

I remembered Joe and his hard, unforgiving back and the tears overflowed, splashing down on the accounts book.

'You're not altogether happy, Heather, are you.' It was a statement, not a question.

I stared blindly into my book where the ink was forming baby Rorschach blots on the paper. I could say nothing. He bent over the desk and kissed me lightly on the forehead.

'Goodbye, dear Heather,' and he walked quickly away. I never saw him again.

Chapter 17

David was gone. Joe was incommunicado. Life was grey, empty, mechanical. I wondered if I would ever smile again. My heart weighed like a stone inside me. I dragged myself about, carrying out my usual activities automatically, aware only of the ache that drained me of all energy.

Our estrangement lasted for weeks but early one morning Joe and I broke out of our mute prisons as the sun breaks through a cloud. 'We must never quarrel like that again,' said Joe. It was Sunday morning and we were lying in bed. 'These last few weeks have been hell.'

I told him how inadequate, despised and wretched I had felt and how he had acted as though I had deliberately locked Tanya inside. He pulled my head on to his shoulder and looked down at me, his eyes growing soft with love.

'Of course it wasn't deliberate. I'm sorry. I overreacted. Perhaps it's because you're so much younger than me that I cry "irresponsible" whenever you do things I don't like. I know it's unfair and I know I overreact but it's because you and Tanya are my life and I can't bear to have anything happen to you.'

The sun, diffused through the closed curtains, poured an amber glow over us, softening the striking contrast of our skins. His profile was thrown into relief, the strong contours of his face highlighted like polished bronze. Not for the first time

Student days. Joe and me at Paraparaumu Beach, 1967.

Our wedding, taken in the garden at Marton, July 1969.

Joe, Tanya and me at Joe's parents' village.

Under the trees at Luzira – Abby with Joseph aged three months.

Waiting for afternoon tea – Joe, Tanya and Joseph in the garden at Luzira.

The Christening day, outside the guesthouse, July 1973.

Some of the children at my school. That's Mum in the background.

Another view of the school, taken from the swamp.

Mum and Dad with Joe's parents in the village.

The Lubowa house.

Tanya and Joseph in the garden at Lubowa, December 1974.

Eva took this picture of the children and me.

Joe and Bella – dog obedience class on the front lawn at Lubowa.

Joe, Joseph, Tanya, Moira (on my knee) and me, December 1975.
Our last picture together.

Celebrating the fifth anniversary of the coup: storm-troopers in armoured vehicles parade along Kampala Road.

The smile of a ladykiller – Amin and his third wife, Kay, whose dismembered body was later found in a sack in the boot of a car near Kampala.

A brooding Idi Amin, his chest heavy with self-awarded medals, stands with his fourth wife, Medina, at an agricultural show in Jinja.

The bodies of slaughtered Ugandan 'rebels' are loaded onto a truck
at Mbarara army barracks for mass burial: hundreds of thousands
of Ugandans died during Amin's reign of terror.

I wondered if the intensity of my love for him was not self-destructive. Would I forgive and compromise and be hurt forever if it meant retaining his love?

'I suppose I would,' I thought. 'There's simply no life for me without him.' Then, 'Gosh!' I said aloud, 'I'm getting as bad as Sarah Musoke.'

For a while, David was never far from my thoughts. I only had to pass the library or drive by the Shmuels' former home to be reminded of him. Whenever I smelled samosas, I thought of him. Whenever I heard a shout of laughter, I remembered him.

'You've got to understand,' I said to Clarice when she grew impatient with me, 'that for as long as I've been in Kampala there has always been David.'

Although I missed him I refused to mope and I made an effort to deploy my energies in other directions. I developed an interest in the local cuisine. Abby and I would drive to the market where we would buy ensenene (grasshoppers), dried fish and ground-nuts and Abby would give me lessons in Ugandan cooking. Tanya began to acquire a taste for a range of European and Kiganda food, which worried the conservative Eva, who watched with growing concern as we consumed grasshoppers, goat tripe and long, stringy mushrooms.

I was also interested in the local weaving and watched Abby as she wove grass mats and baskets. She tried to teach me but I never quite grasped the art, noting with frustration how her quick, strong fingers looped and plaited the fibres with ease while mine bungled and spoiled everything they touched.

The Israelis were sadly missed. Over a decade they had done much for Uganda and their contribution in the areas of agriculture, the armed forces, education, health, building construction and defence was incalculable. The Knesset stated that Israel had lost almost twenty million dollars as a result of the expulsion.

Amin warmed to his role of persecutor of the Zionists. Calling a press conference, he claimed that the Israelis had tried to poison the Nile at its source in Uganda so as to kill the Arabs in Sudan and Egypt through which the river flowed. He sent a telegram to Prime Minister Golda Meir in which he advised her to pull up her knickers and run to the United States if she wanted to stay alive. He jetted in, uninvited, to an Arab Presidential Council meeting in the Middle East and advised the astonished heads of state of his willingness to lead Ugandan troops in the next war with Israel. He then took off in his jet to Rabat, the venue of the Organisation of African Unity Conference. It was a large, important gathering attended by all African heads of state except South Africa's. While Amin was demonstrating to horrified delegates how he had strangled Mau-Maus with a handkerchief, word came through of trouble in Uganda. It appeared that Christian Lugbara tribesmen in the army had staged a revolt. Amin pocketed his handkerchief and flew back to Entebbe. He put down the revolt viciously, imprisoned and killed scores of Lugbaras and, with the blood barely dried on his hands, flew back to the conference in Rabat.

We watched in fear as his troops, incited by the bloodbath, rampaged up and down the country plundering and killing.

'Surely, now, *someone* will intervene and save the country,' I said to Joe. 'They can't allow it to go on.'

We waited for Britain or the United States – anyone – to condemn Amin. But the world stood by and watched in silence. Then Britain sent in a military training team.

'How *could* they!' cried Musoke in disbelief. 'How *could* they support Amin!'

'It's inexcusable,' snapped Joe, 'utterly inexcusable! The only country in this whole world with any guts is Tanzania.'

As if to add fuel to the fire, Amin, on his return, handed over the empty residence of the Israeli ambassador to the Palestine Liberation Organisation. This caused a wave of silent outrage throughout the country, but nothing could be done. Amin had the guns.

Joe received two threatening phone calls at work. We had almost expected this. Joe was educated, successful and well known. He was also a Wabenzi. In other words, he was an ideal target for a blackmailer; the caller wanted money to ensure that Joe stayed alive.

Callers of this type were springing up everywhere. They could be army personnel who informed prospective victims on Amin's death list of their intended fate. For a large financial consideration they offered the victim protection, by means of a safe escape or removal of his or her name from the death list. Lives were often saved this way.

Then there were the bogus callers who, purporting to be army officers, falsely informed their victims that they were in immediate danger and convinced them to hand over protection money. In this way thousands of shillings were needlessly handed over. And then there were the malicious callers prompted by fitina – jealousy – who got their kicks by frightening those against whom they held a grudge. The dilemma for the recipients of these calls was to decide whether they presented a real threat or were simply a hoax.

Joe was taking no chances and made arrangements to pay. But it must have been a fitina call, for the caller neither collected the money nor made another approach. Nevertheless we were badly frightened by the incident and decided to leave the country. Joe arranged for his brother Ted to have the car, and for his parents and his younger brother Henry to take the contents of the house after we had left. My school was to be run by Mrs Kherani and managed by Musoke until our eventual return. We told no one else of our plans.

Joe then went to arrange our air tickets. He found that the procedure for buying tickets involved an initial application stating the reason for travel, which then had to be approved by the government. This meant that the government knew everyone who wished to leave the country – and those people ran the risk of being watched, or worse. Those who did fly out risked reprisals against their families remaining in Uganda. This ensured that no one who left the country talked.

'Don't apply unless you have a bona fide reason for travelling,' warned the Muganda airline clerk, and Joe came away without the tickets.

'We're trapped,' I said to Joe and my heart fluttered in panic.

'*You're* not,' said Joe. 'As an expatriate you can come and go as you please. It's only Tanya and me who can't.'

'I'd never go without you!'

I tried to think of other ways we could leave. We could drive

121

to Busia near the Kenya border and walk into Kenya. We could even take the train to Nairobi, although they checked the passengers thoroughly when they embarked at Kampala. There was also a way of getting out through Rwanda. A family we knew who had been on the death list had fled to the Rwanda border and, disguised as peasants, had followed the mountain trails into Rwanda.

Some weeks later, to Joe's delight, his company manager told him he had been selected to go to England on company business later in the year. 'Company business' was always approved on air ticket applications, so now two of us were free to leave. Joe was confident that Tanya could leave with us for 'medical reasons'; his cousin Sylvester, who was a doctor, could arrange the documentation. We discussed plans late into the night. I felt relieved and excited to be going but Joe cautioned me.

'Heather, *no one* is to know we are leaving, and we mustn't arouse any suspicions. Don't make any arrangements or do any packing. Continue to behave as if we are going to spend the rest of our lives here.'

Joan, a hairdresser from the United States, moved into our block. She had married a Ugandan student from Busoga whom she had met in Pittsburgh. I introduced her to some of the families since she knew no one at all in Uganda. By this time I was friendly with many of our African neighbours and found them to be warm, generous people. We who were foreigners – me, Clarice, Eva and Joan – were never made to feel like outsiders and we discussed children with our neighbours, swapped recipes and accepted invitations to tea. I often found myself comparing them with the cold Asians back on William Street.

After I had introduced Joan to the neighbours, we went on a tour of Kampala. A few days later I took her, with Eva, Andrea and Tanya, to Silver Springs for a swim. I felt sad as we drew up at the hotel, for it brought back memories of David. Joan enjoyed her swim, applying lipstick and powder after every dip and buying drinks all round for everyone.

With her baby-blue eyes and trusting nature, Joan was both vulnerable and appealing, although Eva didn't think so. 'That sugary innocence is put on. I don't think she's at all well brought up,' said Eva disapprovingly when a besotted Sikh merchant presented Joan with a silk scarf one day. 'And she's thoughtless,' she continued, when Joan spilled popcorn through Eva's car while playing peek-a-boo with the children. Her attitude made it difficult for me because I liked them both.

But it was Clarice whose company I valued most. Since she worked all day, we met in the evenings, in either her kitchen or mine. Over beans or baking fish we would catch up on the events of the day. She was familiar with my unhappiness over Joe's lateness every night. Eva, whose husband and household ran like Swiss clockwork, would have told me it was all self-inflicted because I was too unassertive. Joan, who happily read movie magazines and watched television until her husband came in, would not have recognised that there was a problem. Only Clarice understood.

'Baganda men are like babies,' she declared. 'They eat when they want to eat, they drink when they want to drink and they sleep when they want to sleep.' She threw groundnuts into a saucepan of boiling water. 'They come home when they want to come home and they love when they want to love.'

'It's so unfair. What would happen if I stayed out boozing?'

'You wouldn't. Nor would most women. Men trade on it. They're utterly selfish.'

I remained silent. I didn't like to hear other people call Joe selfish. Clarice shook salt into the thickening groundnut sauce.

'Your Joe isn't as bad as the others,' she continued, 'but that won't make you any happier.'

'He was so different in New Zealand.'

Clarice went on as though she hadn't heard me. 'In some ways the women here are their own worst enemies. From birth men are coddled and pampered by mothers who reinforce the attitude of male importance. It makes my hair stand on end!'

Clarice was saying nothing new. I had observed it over and over again and it sickened me.

'On the other hand,' she went on, 'you've got to admire these women. They sit up all night with a sick child while their husbands are out boozing or womanising. They till the soil and feed the family and stoke up their husbands' egos day after day after day. And what do they get for it? A pregnancy every year, a husband who spends the school fees on a mistress, an arthritic spine from carrying heavy loads!'

She whipped the sauce vigorously. 'Beautiful women! Anyone who can put up with so much shit and still smile at her children in the morning is beautiful!' Onions disintegrated rapidly under her knife. 'Don't let Joe's lateness get you down, girl. You and me are so much better off than many others – we've got financial independence. In my home the kids and I do as we want – my husband does what he wants. It suits me perfectly. Shit, I'd rather die than live in subjugation to him!' She tossed her head in contempt, her earrings flashing.

'But that wouldn't suit me. I want my marriage to be the way it should be. The way I was taught it would be. The way it is at home.'

'How many marriages did you know at home? I mean *really* know?' She glared at me.

'Lots. They were all happy.'

'They *said* they were happy.'

'Oh hell, Clarice. They *were* happy.' I picked at a piece of raw cabbage wondering if they really were.

'People like you should be taught that love just isn't enough. Marriages *aren't* made in heaven. They don't live happily ever after.' She yanked open a drawer. 'Where the hell's that friggin' spoon?'

Bold, beautiful Clarice.

As Amin became increasingly pro-Arab, his behaviour became more bizarre. His determination to create a Moslem state in Uganda, where Moslems formed less than ten percent of the population, was foremost in his mind. He introduced a bribery system to encourage Christians to convert to Islam. Daily reports and television spectacles described mass conversions and Amin praised the converted for their wisdom and far-sightedness. It was obvious to all of us that only the financially needy and those who wanted favours from Amin became Moslems. In a concession to the Islamic world, Arabic and French, of absolutely no use to most Ugandans, joined English and Swahili in the news broadcasts, resulting in an unbelievable waste of television and radio time.

If Amin sought to polarise the Moslems and Christians he hardly succeeded. They had lived side by side for nearly a hundred years. Every tribe, every clan, almost every family had both Moslem and Christian members and their dual presence was an accepted fact of life. Troubles were far more likely to be along tribal than religious lines. Most Moslems, apart from Amin's Nubians, would have been glad to see the dictator fall. Amin, who considered himself a saviour of modern Islam, would never have believed this.

Within the army, Amin's recruitment programme sped ahead. At night empty trucks rumbled across the southern Sudan border to pick up waiting Sudanese and Nubian recruits who had eagerly signed up, knowing from their predecessors that a powerful, profitable employment awaited them. Owing no allegiance to Uganda, they raped and plundered the country mercilessly in the following years.

It was frightening to see the influx of Nubians and Sudanese on Kampala streets. They were tall, thin, very black people whose jerky gait and sudden gesticulations reminded one of string puppets. Like the Kakwa, to whom they are related, they often bore the three-lined tattoo on their temples, hence the local nickname for them – the 'one-elevens'. The women had narrow, ebony faces and wore gold in their noses and ears. They dressed in flowing robes of yellow and red and talked in harsh, alien voices. These unwelcome strangers stood out markedly from the local Bantu population.

With the Sudanese came the Libyans and Egyptians. The latter did not fill us with apprehension and fear as did the Sudanese. Rather, they were regarded as a bit of a joke. They came in as 'experts' and 'advisers' but their well-qualified Baganda and Asian counterparts were usually far superior to them. It appeared that Gaddafi and Sadat considered Amin worthy of only third-rate personnel.

Amin's rhetoric became increasingly unpredictable. He was in turn bombastic, conciliatory, threatening and jovial, peppering his speeches with newly acquired words such as 'imperialism', 'neocolonialism' and 'Zionism'. Any person he disliked could be a racist, a CIA agent, a communist, a Zionist, a Boer, or all of them at once. Nor did he confine himself to the ears of Ugandans. He sent telegrams of advice and condemnation to leaders all over the world. John Vorster, Edward Heath, Kurt Waldheim and Chairman Mao were among the initial recipients. To his arch-enemy Julius Nyerere, who was harbouring the deposed Obote, he sent a particularly vicious telegram, accusing him of being a whore and spreading verbal gonorrhoea all over Africa. It became common for the Western television sit-coms screening on Uganda television to be interrupted with an 'important announcement' as a government spokesman laboriously read out the latest telegram in the mandatory four languages.

For the local population these telegrams were no cause for humour, as they were in the rest of the world. We knew that they were the product of a crazed megalomaniac mind that knew no moral or legal bounds. To us the situation was deadly serious.

But life had to go on. The cabinet, although impotent, still met regularly. Amin rarely consulted them and they usually learned their directives from the radio, as they did the news about which of them had been transferred, promoted, disgraced or sacked. Life for them had now became fraught with anxiety, harassment and humiliation. It was an ordeal for them to watch as able colleagues were reprimanded, abused, arrested or murdered. Amin usually replaced those he banished or killed with inexperienced, semi-literate Moslems.

We lived from day to unpredictable day through times that were never free for long of fear, grief and death. Sometimes peaceful weeks would pass by and we would be lulled into a false sense of security. And then there would be a flurry of 'disappearances', a mass arrest of 'confusing agents' or an execution of people who were 'resisting arrest'. We were afraid when friends were late for appointments. We were reluctant to answer unexpected knocks on the door.

We made the most of good times – there were still family celebrations and parties and Henry's renowned soccer team to cheer – and because life was suddenly more precious we derived growing pleasure from friendships and family, a deeper satisfaction from our work and a greater awareness of the beauty of the country around us.

Lapsed churchgoers began to attend services and lawyers had a boom in the business of wills. All over the country, people clung assiduously to daily routines as if a semblance of normality would somehow create the reality. The villagers worked their shambas and the land continued to produce food. The taxi drivers still rattled their battered Peugeots between far-flung towns and the Indians still opened their shops at the same time each morning. The tourist industry continued to draw visitors by the thousands and foreign investments remained secure. Ugandan sugar, tea and cotton were eagerly sought by world markets and high-quality beans ensured the country's continuing status as the prime coffee producer in the British Common-wealth. Blessed as it was with a perfect climate, natural beauty and abundant wildlife, Uganda was to maintain its image, for a little longer, as the pearl of Africa.

Chapter 18

Mrs Ssali joined our staff at the nursery. She was a Muganda woman, a former primary school teacher with a passion for wigs and for mini-skirts which were definitely unsuited to her thick legs. With this welcome addition to the school, we now had a permanent staff of six, plus John.

'You'll have to raise the fees,' said Joe, whose brow still furrowed when he thought about my financial handling of the school. 'You can't afford to engage new staff without adjusting the incoming fees.'

I pointed out that we were managing well. It was amazing, but we were. Although some families could only afford partial fees and several virtually nothing, I was able to pay good wages and we always managed to chalk up a small profit at the end of each month.

'Other schools charge twice as much,' he said disgustedly. His attitude disappointed me. He had lost a lot of the idealism that he had brought back to Uganda. His efforts, once directed to encouraging small, local business development, were now turned upon his own little side business that dealt in the importing of spare parts for German cars such as Mercedes, Volkswagen, BMW and Audi. He planned to run the business from England.

It was already July and our proposed escape in October to coincide with Joe's business trip was never far from my mind. When

I saw the sinister BMWs and Mercedes with their Nubian occupants cruising around on their missions of death, I wondered if we would last until October.

The political situation deteriorated. Two of Joe's colleagues were picked up by State Research Bureau goons in a bar. Joe watched helplessly as the Nubians dragged their victims outside and bundled them into the boot of a military vehicle. They were never seen again. Shocked, grieved, angry at his powerlessness, Joe lay awake in anguish all that night.

A few mornings later a little African boy named Nsubuga rushed into school, screaming and sobbing hysterically. It was ten minutes before we could get the story from him. Apparently Nsubuga's father, a policeman, had set out for work that morning with his son, whom he intended to drop off at the nursery on the way. As they approached the school a car that had been tailing them stopped and three bell-bottomed thugs leapt out. They set upon the father, beating him unconscious and then throwing his body into the boot of their car. They drove away, leaving four-year-old Nsubuga distraught on the footpath.

Horrified, I dispatched Rose to inform his family while I gathered up the shuddering little boy and walked out on to the verandah. I cradled the child against me, angry tears in my eyes, wondering how much more the people in Uganda could endure.

We had entered another cycle of terror. It went on for weeks. Lawyers were dragged from their offices, public officials and cabinet ministers were snatched off footpaths, doctors were hauled from their clinics in full view of their patients. No one knew why. No one dared ask.

Expatriates were, on the whole, left alone by Amin and were to a great extent unaware of the constant fear in which the Ugandans lived. We foreigners who were married to Ugandans were entitled to protection from our embassies, but with our support and loyalties lying so strongly with the local people, and our family connections running deep into the heart of Ugandan society, we doubted whether we were really safe. We celebrated with our families at weddings and wept with them when close friends disappeared. We never lost hope that Amin would be assassinated.

One of the barbers near school had written down on a scrap of paper the car registration of Nsubuga's father's abductors.

'You take it, teacher,' he said handing the number to me. 'The police will listen to you.'

Leaving Mrs Kherani in charge I went to the Central Police Station with the car number. The officer who interviewed me was courteous and sympathetic but was unable to take the case any further for fear of army reprisals. He knew Nsubuga's father, who was a well-trained, thorough, highly moral police officer.

'But it doesn't pay to be thorough or moral in this business,' he said sadly. He informed me that the abducted police officer's body had been found, minus its arms, in a shallow grave in Namanve Forest. There was nothing the police could do. They were as much at the mercy of the army as anyone else. Sickened, I turned to go.

'I trained for years as a detective in England,' said the officer, 'and I sit around doing nothing.'

'So do the British,' I said sourly and walked out.

In this new wave of terror, threats, bribes, abductions and flight were daily occurrences. Eva and I, shopping one afternoon in Kampala, were amazed and uneasy at the increased presence of State Research goons on the street. Suddenly it seemed that wherever we turned we saw men in sunglasses, bell-bottoms and platform shoes.

'Shit, they're spooky,' I whispered and we made our purchases quickly and hurried back to the car. Eva settled Andrea on her lap and speculated on an eggless chocolate cake recipe she had heard about. I hardly heard her, for as we pulled out of our parking place I looked in my rear vision mirror and saw two men glide out from behind a vehicle, watching our departure with interest. They were wearing sunglasses, bell-bottoms and platform shoes.

In the middle of this fearful time, Tanya had her first birthday. I threw a party for her, inviting some of the toddlers and their mothers from the surrounding flats and, of course, Eva, Joan and Clarice, who had thrown a sickie for the occasion. Eva had made the eggless chocolate birthday cake and iced it in pink. There was

130

ice cream and jelly, pikelets with raspberry jam and Abby cooked a pile of samosas.

Tanya, a picture in a smocked white lawn dress and new shoes, glowed with excitement. As I was pouring tea for the adults and wondering whose miserable child was blubbering cream and cake into my curtains, there was a loud knock and Byron walked in. His bifocals panned around the room and finally settled on me. He hurried over.

'I'm afraid it's bad news.'

They've picked up Joe!

The cup I was holding crashed to the floor. For a second there was complete silence in the room. Abby took the teapot from my hand. Eva went for a broom. The startled baby in the curtains held its breath for an instant and then resumed its blubbering, dribbling strings of cream and saliva.

'It's not Joe. It's his brother, Henry.'

'Oh dear God! What happened?'

'They're bringing him up here. He's badly hurt.' It turned out that Henry's soccer team, Express, had been invited to play the army. Express had of course won and the army, in their fury, had turned on the team and beaten them up. Henry, as the most prominent player, had been held down while half a dozen army players jumped on him.

Byron went on to explain that a taxi had taken Henry to Joe's office. 'We can't get him to a hospital yet. The army are swarming all over town looking for Express supporters.'

I looked about me dazedly. The party was rapidly turning into a nightmare of cream and babies and raspberry jam. Joan stood transfixed at my side. 'You'll have to finish the party,' I said to her.

'I'm not really sure how to . . .' The blue eyes fluttered unhappily.

'Run at them and say shoo!' snapped Eva, picking up broken china.

'Come on, girl,' and Clarice and Joan circulated the mothers who quickly began packing up. Someone unwound the regurgitating baby from the curtains and Abby rushed round with a broom. The room was rapidly put to order and a procession of babies began to leave the flat. There was no reluctance, no embarrassment, no questions asked. Everyone understood. This was Uganda.

Ten minutes later Joe and his doctor cousin Sylvester arrived with a badly beaten Henry. His face was swollen beyond recognition and he groaned as they lowered him onto the couch. I sponged down his face in silent horror while Sylvester checked him over quickly, feeling the jaw, the neck, the collarbones and ribs. Henry groaned at every touch.

'A rib or two, I'm afraid,' said Sylvester. Joe and I exchanged despairing glances. 'I want to look at that right ankle. That's what's going to prove the biggest worry.'

The ankle was so damaged that the boot and sock had to be cut away. We gasped as the ankle appeared, huge and shiny like a ripe aubergine. We could not risk getting it x-rayed and set until late the following day when the army had returned to barracks. The ankle was severely damaged and broken in two places. There were other fractures to the ribs, nose and fingers.

Over the weeks Henry's face and body slowly healed, but not his ankle. He was in plaster for months, on crutches for a year, and had two operations to try to stop the seepage of fluid into the tissues around his ankle. Both operations were unsuccessful and his ankle was to remain permanently swollen. He would always limp and he would never play soccer again.

Chapter 19

Six days after Tanya's birthday, Amin appeared at Tororo Military Barracks and announced that God had appeared to him in a dream, instructing him to expel all the Asians from Uganda within three months – all eighty thousand of them. Those who did not leave would be herded into detention camps. 'They milked the cow but failed to feed her,' he told the press, referring to the Asians' supposed treatment of Uganda.

The country was rocked to its very foundations. Although the Asians were never popular, this mad decree shocked even their strongest critics. It was an indisputable fact that, injustice aside, the economy would simply cave in if the Asians left, but the local people did not dare to raise a voice in their defence. They waited instead for international outrage. 'Someone's got to bump the bugger off now,' I said to Clarice.

Britain, the country most affected by the decree since many Asians held British passports, at first attempted to treat the whole thing as mere bravado on Amin's part. After all, they said, the man was unstable, a bit of an ape, prone to changes of mind. They were forced to take him seriously, however, when Amin began a daily countdown on the radio of the days remaining till the deadline – 8 November 1972. They believed him when he warned that any Asians remaining after this would be dealt with severely and that any holding meetings would be shot. The

Asians rapidly prepared to leave. Troops, offering 'assistance', gathered about them like vultures as they packed, helping themselves to Asian goods and taking over their houses as they left.

Mrs Kherani, like many others, was deemed stateless. She told me she was born in Tanzania, where her parents, British passport-holders, had been killed in an accident when she was a small child. She had been passed from relative to relative before ending up with an old aunt in Uganda, long since dead. Family documents had been lost over the years with all the moves and she had nothing at all that could shed light on her nationality status. Her husband's status did not cover her, since they were now estranged.

'My children are all I have in this world. I suppose they will go to Britain with my husband's family and we will be separated forever. God alone knows where I will end up. In a detention camp here, probably.' She put her head in her hands and wept.

With the soldiers engaged in 'assisting' the Asians, the pall of terror lifted somewhat from the African population. Carloads of Asians heading for the borders or for the airport were flagged down, robbed and beaten. One family fleeing to Kenya were stopped and forced at gunpoint to consume a bag of chillis they were carrying with them. I was told that the two younger children later died of asphyxiation when their burnt throats swelled up. It soon became a common sight to see soldiers driving about in commandeered Asian vehicles.

Then a rumour circulated that Amin had succumbed to international pressure and would now allow Asians with Ugandan citizenship to stay. Mrs Kherani and other stateless individuals succumbed to the overtures of an infamous little group of Asians bent on making money out of everybody's misfortune. These opportunists had, through bribery, access to blank Ugandan passports and for an exorbitant sum sold them to their desperate fellow Asians. I warned Mrs Kherani not to fall for it but she did, withdrawing her entire savings to buy a passport. She came to school one day with her new Ugandan passport, her shaky smile reflecting her relief, and I conceded that perhaps she had done the right thing.

Shortly before lunch John came in with his radio to tell us there was to be a special announcement by the President. We sat around the desk and listened to Amin proclaim that all Asians, including those who held Ugandan passports, were subject to the expulsion order. Mrs Kherani's expensive new passport lay immobile in her long, slim fingers. I could hardly bear to meet her eyes. Mrs Ssali caught her breath in sympathy, her eyes filming over with tears.

Asians began to descend on Kampala from all corners of Uganda to line up in front of foreign embassies, ready to emigrate to any country in the world that would take them. Delegations from sympathetic countries – the United States, Canada, Europe – flew in to deal with the Asians who could not be repatriated to Britain, India or Pakistan.

International condemnation at last began to appear in foreign newspapers and Amin blasted all resident reporters, threatening to kick them out with the Asians. A British reporter, who was illegally detained at Makindye and destined for almost certain death, was released only on the orders of the Chief Justice, Benedicto Kiwanuka. By openly defying the President, Kiwanuka became an overnight hero, but Amin never forgave him and later exacted his terrible revenge.

I decided to intervene on Mrs Kherani's behalf. She had become apathetic, almost defeated, and seemed incapable of making any plans. I went first to the British High Commission. As I rounded the corner off Kampala Road I stopped in utter amazement.

A mass of sweltering Asians, their saris splashing every colour under the sun into the mayhem, streamed from the double doors of the building, spilling out on to the footpath and sweeping on to turn the corner and flow along Kampala Road like a huge multi-coloured serpent. There were opulent lawyers in Savile Row suits and tubercular pimps playing cards in the gutter. There were fat merchants with oil-sleeked hair clutching parcels of documents and tired wives who snapped at clamorous children. The aristocracy, heads high, their women resplendent in silk and gold, stood with ragged half-castes.

I pushed my way to the head of the queue, pretending to be high commission staff. Once inside I was taken upstairs to the office of a balding gentleman with a pink and white complexion.

I told him about Mrs Kherani and her statelessness. I told him she had to get to Britain. I told him I would guarantee her, sponsor her, do whatever was necessary for her and explained what a fine teacher she was and how she would never be a burden on the British taxpayer by bringing over her parents and siblings and cousins because she didn't have any.

'We're only concerned here with those who have British passports,' said the pink and white man.

'Her parents were British passport-holders.'

'We'll need to see the passports.'

I explained how she had no documentation for herself or her parents owing to the unfortunate circumstances of her childhood. He seemed to be in no hurry to help.

'I'd like you to give me the passport application papers for my friend. And I'm formally requesting you to provide confirmation of her parents' British nationality status from your records.'

'I'm afraid your friend will need to make representation herself.' I thought of the interminable queue. 'We have certain procedures for the Asian situation. I'm sorry I can't be of more help. Now, if it were for you it would be different.'

'Then you're a racist and you stand for a racist system. I don't think I want my friend to go to your country.'

The pink and white man became a red and blotchy man and I found myself on the crowded pavement again.

I turned my steps towards the German Embassy where I was seen by a smiling young man who listened politely to me. He asked if Mrs Kherani was a scientist, if she spoke German, if she had friends or family in Germany. I answered no to each question. His smile thinned. Was she a communist? Had she criminal convictions? Did she suffer from epilepsy? I replied in triple negative. He saw me to the door, assuring me they would give the matter some thought. The arctic little smile told me otherwise.

I decided to try the Canadian High Commission. There was a long queue of Asians and, using my staff impersonation strategy, I pushed my way through and found myself in an office with a purse-lipped typist. I told her that I had a passport problem and she informed me that I would have to wait a little while. She typed rapidly, her keys clattering away like the guns at Mbuya Barracks. After some time I enquired how much longer I had to wait.

'He's out front doing the Asian applications. You can see him when he's through.'

'That'll be November 8!'

'He does have coffee breaks,' she said reprovingly and turned back to her machine.

A few minutes later I was directed to his office. Suddenly nervous, I took a deep breath as I entered. A middle-aged man sat behind a desk, drinking coffee. His tie was loosened and I noticed lines of weariness on his face. One of the lenses in his spectacles was whited out. I decided it was a bad omen. People with eye-patches smacked of trouble – pirates, highwaymen, Moshe Dayan. The man smiled as I approached his desk and he asked me to sit down. His smile was tired but sincere, the first real smile I had received all afternoon. I took it as a good omen.

I told him I had a problem, an Asian problem. The fingers on the coffee cup gripped convulsively. Definitely a bad omen. With a sinking heart I relayed for the third time the predicament of Mrs Kherani. 'She's stateless, familyless and frightened,' I said.

'There are hundreds, thousands, out there in the same boat,' he gestured in the direction of the queue outside, 'and more every day.'

I pleaded for Mrs Kherani as I had never pleaded before. The white lens regarded me blankly, but behind the transparent lens a kindly eye twinkled.

'My dear lady, I certainly don't intend to leave your friend in the clutches of Amin. I'll give you passport application forms to take to her. She must complete them and return them as soon as possible. And yes, a character reference, particularly with regard to her work in your school, will be a decided advantage for her in Canada.'

I felt a prickle of tears and had to blink rapidly. The man handed me a sheaf of papers.

'Get these filled in and returned immediately. The sooner we get them back, the sooner we can process her documents. And tell her when it's time to leave she and the others will be escorted to Entebbe in a guarded convoy. And, of course, my government will pay the air fares.'

'I – I can hardly believe it.' I carefully folded the papers and put them in my bag and got up to go. 'Thank you for everything.'

I stopped at the door and turned back to him, my heart beating fast.

'Is there something else?' he asked.

'She . . . she . . . has three children.'

'You'd better take some more forms then,' he said, and as the light caught his opaque lens it seemed to wink.

Mrs Kherani was ecstatic about her sudden news. We went to the library, looked at maps of Canada and read up about the country. Once she had completed and returned the forms she was issued with Canadian travel documents for herself and the children. The remaining concern was her husband's refusal to allow the children to go to Canada with her. As she was an orphan with no family to support her, her husband bullied her into submission.

But as the weeks passed and the husband's documents did not arrive from the British High Commission and as atrocities against the Asians increased, the husband and his family decided that the children must get out at the earliest opportunity. If the British documents did not arrive before Mrs Kherani was to leave, the children would go with their mother to Canada. The husband, to whom money was no problem, would come for them when he and his family were settled in Britain.

'That's what he thinks, the swine!' and I rushed back to the Canadian High Commission to see the man with the whited-out lens.

'It's all arranged,' I told Mrs Kherani when I returned. 'They're putting you and the kids on the first airlift out. Even if your husband turns up at the airport waving his British visas he can't take the kids back. They're under your protection by Canadian law. Once you're in Canada a good lawyer will protect your rights as a mother, and you're bound to win legal custody.'

Her smile transformed her whole face.

I felt sad as I watched her moving about the children at school in those last few weeks. She had been with me since the day I took over the school and we had been through a lot together. I gathered my maths group around me and started them on problem-solving exercises. I was lost in thought as I handed out pencils and papers and counters and the old abacus.

I now had to arrange for someone other than Mrs Kherani to

run the school while we were in England. I surmised that Mrs Ssali and two other teachers would be able to handle the day-to-day grind while Musoke took care of the business side of things. When Amin was finally overthrown I would come back and take over.

I thought of Mrs Kherani forced to accept a new life on the other side of the world; of our own escape to England in a few weeks; of Nsubuga who had watched his father killed on the foot-path – all because of one man. There was a shriek and a clatter of wooden balls as Ali Raza dismantled our ancient abacus. Life had to go on.

Chapter 20

As the city apartments began to empty of Asians, Nubian soldiers moved in with their large extended families bringing with them their belongings from the north – enormous clay pots for fermenting millet, livestock, agricultural implements. Goats and chickens were driven upstairs. Cooking fires were lit on concrete floors. Garbage accumulated in courtyards. One by one the Asian stores and dukkas closed and commodities became scarce.

The friendship between Britain and Uganda that had been so eagerly cemented after Amin seized power now began to crumble as the Asian situation came to a head. Amin's orders from God meant that at least thirty thousand Ugandan Asians would be foisted on Britain. When Amin claimed that Britain was also responsible for the twenty thousand Asians with Ugandan citizenship – a blatantly racist decision – the British stopped all aid to Uganda. An enraged Amin expelled the British military team.

'It was impossible,' said a departing British officer in charge of intelligence training. 'One expects a modicum of raw material to start with in intelligence training.'

'Good riddance,' said Joe of the British. 'They had no business training Amin's army in the first place.'

Amin then expelled the British High Commissioner, Richard Slater, claiming that Slater and the expelled British military team had tried several times to assassinate him but that God had warned him in time.

Amin went on to accuse the Asians of blackening their faces with boot polish to pass themselves off as Africans so they could stay in Uganda. He announced a new law whereby anyone who used boot polish on the face would be shot. He then sent a telegram to Kurt Waldheim, the then United Nations Secretary General, praising the Palestinian commandos for their recent slaughtering of the Israeli athletes at the Munich Olympic Games. He decreed that a statue of Adolf Hitler was to be erected in Kampala and he sent off more telegrams around the world expressing his admiration for the gassing of six million Jews.

As the world recoiled in horror, Amin's anti-semitic fervour increased. Signs and billboards were erected around Kampala expressing solidarity with the Palestinians, support for Moslem brotherhood, commitment to anti-Zionism. I shivered in the knowledge of my Jewish ancestry. The United States withdrew its financial aid and several embassies threatened to pull out. James, as part of Britain's aid programme, was forced to leave. As we waved goodbye from the airport roof I felt I had lost an old, old friend.

Meanwhile the tension in Kampala heightened. The Asian queues at embassies grew longer. Warnings continued about boot-polished Asians. The army, clad in Scottish kilts, roamed the city looking for currency which they claimed Asians were hiding in drainpipes, biscuit tins and Sikh turbans. Every day the radio warned the Asians of the fate that awaited those who remained after the deadline. Then Amin went on air to proclaim: 'Though the British hate me, I love them and respect the Queen.'

It was into this scene, rapidly assuming the proportions of a mad opera, that Obote launched his ill-fated invasion from Tanzania. It was badly planned from the start and the Obote forces were massacred. Amin flew above the battles in a helicopter, exhorting his troops by radio and enjoying the carnage below. As the battles dwindled he sought to create further excitement by sending fictitious reports to Kampala, hundreds of miles away, that the capital was surrounded and about to be overrun.

I was making purchases for the school when a radio announcement in a shop claimed that Kampala was about to be invaded.

I left my parcels on the counter, picked up Tanya and ran for the car. People poured out of shops and offices by the hundreds and began a stampede out of the city. Caught up in a traffic jam, in a panic I switched on the radio. The newsreader stated that Indian, Zionist, Tanzanian, British and Boer troops were poised around the capital. I realised then that it was a hoax. Around me, Kampala headed for the hills.

At every barracks around the country that night there were wild victory celebrations. The troops went on the rampage, killing Acholis, Langis and anyone even remotely connected with Obote's defunct party. Joe and I lay in bed that night listening to the troops at the nearby Mbuya Hill Barracks, hooting, dancing and drinking till dawn.

Ted's house at the game park was visited by troops who claimed that the wardens were implicating (and quite rightly) the army in recent poaching and ivory-smuggling activities. Ted, fortunately, was in the arms of his girlfriend in Mengo and the soldiers told Mary they would be back for him. The other wardens, not so lucky, were taken away. Ted fled with his family to a remote village south of where his parents lived.

Joe and I began to make regular trips to Masaka with scarce commodities for his parents and for Ted's family – commodities such as flour, oil, soap and milk for which people now had to queue up. Henry, who was still with us after the soccer beating, always accompanied us to the village and there we would sit with the relatives quietly discussing the deteriorating situation. Often the old grandmother joined us and once she drew Henry down onto her goatskin, running her old, gnarled hands over his slowly mending face. 'Why did this happen to you who are so young?' she said sadly.

Henry could still not use his right leg and relied on crutches to get around. He was also prone to spells of dizziness and headaches and was forced to spend most of the day inside with Abby and Tanya. In all the weeks he had been with us I had never once heard him complain. As we sat together on those warm afternoons I wondered how they would all fare when we went to England – Henry, Joe's parents, Ted's family with Mary expecting another baby. I wondered uncomfortably if we were not deserting them.

My nightmares returned. Dead babies, unpackable suitcases, prickly fear. Sometimes, in need of solace, I would stand on the balcony at dawn with a shawl over my shoulders, watching the sun rise beyond soft flushing mists and silent bush. I learned the awakening calls of the robins, shrikes and hornbills. It was so peaceful, so beautiful, so utterly perfect at this hour that it seemed in all the universe there was only Uganda and me.

Soon we'll be in England where policemen help old ladies cross the road. Things will be all right again over there. Joe and I will relax and laugh and go for walks in the park with Tanya in a pushchair. Our marriage will grow strong again. Joe will leave for work with an umbrella each day and eat sandwiches for lunch instead of goat. Tanya will attend a kindergarten with carpets and hearty chilblained teachers and I shall have to get involved with fund-raising and cake stalls, and my school on the swamp, with its sunny verandah and the jackfruit tree, will be a thing of the past.

One morning as I watched a group of shrill lake birds fly through the fiery, dawn-streaked sky, it came to me with terrible clarity that I did not want to leave Uganda.

I could not tell Joe. Disillusioned and heartsick about Uganda, he now seemed anxious to be gone. His little importing business of car spare parts was growing and he planned to diversify it from England, with Musoke and Byron managing the Kampala end. He had obtained medical documents, along with a passport and an exit visa for Tanya. His trip on oil company business was approved and air tickets were purchased for the three of us. He was ready to go.

With a heavy heart I made arrangements with Mrs Ssali for the running of the school while I was away. I had to swear her to secrecy. The incredulous eyes blinking beneath the Afro wig assured me she would have great difficulty in keeping the news to herself. Mrs Kherani was still at the nursery, accompanied now by her prospective replacement, Miss Mubiru. Mrs Ssali was to engage a third teacher, already interviewed, after Mrs Kherani and I had left. There was nothing further to do but wait.

At the end of September, the Chief Justice, Benedicto Kiwanuka, was killed for his defiance of Amin in the case of the imprisoned journalist. In full view of the other judges, Kiwanuka was dragged from his chambers in the High Court and taken to Makindye Military Prison where he was slowly dismembered. The horror of his abduction swept the length and breadth of the country. If the Chief Justice, the supreme symbol of law and order, could be summarily disposed of, what hope was there now for Uganda? The enormous implications of what Amin had done demoralised the people more than any other single incident.

Kiwanuka's death was followed some days later by the equally grisly death of Mayor Walugembe of Masaka, the suave, good-looking man I had seen at the Tropic Inn on my first trip to the village. Troops had assembled the staff at gunpoint on the hotel lawn and publicly castrated the mayor, who was kept alive, in dreadful agony, for further torment before the soldiers finally killed him.

The people went about their business subdued, stunned, filled with utter hopelessness. At school, as I sang songs, wiped noses and mixed paints, I was consumed with sorrow for this vulnerable generation of children. If Amin were to survive for another five years, what permanent damage would be done to their developing minds?

I tried to shake myself out of the prevailing gloom, to become enthusiastic over the freedom and happiness that awaited us in England. When I had almost succeeded I would suddenly picture stolid Abby sitting under a tree doing her basketwork or Joe's mother, her head tied in a tattered scarf, hacking off pineapples for me to take back to Kampala, and I would long to remain. Or else I would find myself in Clarice's comfortable kitchen with Clarice at the stove stirring soup and laughing at men, and I would know that nothing in England could replace this camaraderie. I tried to tell myself that it was best for Tanya to be out of Uganda but I would see her trudging on damp, woollen-stockinged legs along a wet English street, her nose red with cold, her fingers encased in grubby mittens.

Joe became increasingly withdrawn after Kiwanuka's death. His shoulders, indeed his whole body, seemed to sag. His face appeared closed over, as if brooding on a dark secret. He would gather up Tanya in his arms and stand on the balcony, staring silently over the bush. Sometimes I would catch him looking at me and when I asked what was the matter he would sigh and shake his head. He talked for hours into the night at Henry's bedside, recalling their youth and their aspirations in happier times. On one occasion as he left Henry his face was drawn with despair and there were tears in his eyes.

'What is it, darling?' I begged as I put my arms around him.

'I feel I'm dying of pain,' he whispered and would say no more.

'I can understand.' I imagined how I would feel if people ravaged my country, mutilated my family, forced me into exile. Our carefree student days in New Zealand when we listened to Billie Holiday and discussed Vietnam in his room above the harbour seemed a million miles away.

'When we're in England it will be different,' I said one night as we lay in bed.

'Oh, Heather, I'm miserable beyond belief,' he said and his worries poured out at last. 'I'm tormented with indecision. Whatever I do, I'll be hurting people. If we go to England, I'll be abandoning my family here. If we stay here, we'll continue to suffer under Amin. I'm pulled in two directions and I can't reconcile myself to any course of action.'

I thought of the early morning mists and the hornbills in the bush.

'Joe, you know I love Uganda.'

'I know that. You are almost one of us now.' There was a hint of a smile in the darkness.

'I'm trying to tell you something,' I said gently. His arm about me tightened apprehensively. 'Joe, let's stay here.'

It took him a few seconds to digest it. 'God, this is Uganda! Are you quite, quite sure?'

'Absolutely,' and I was. Joe pulled me to him wordlessly and I became aware of a shuddering deep within his chest.

'Are you crying, Joe?'

'No.'

But his face was wet as I cradled him in my arms.

We undid all the arrangements for our exile. Mrs Ssali stood stock-still in disbelief when I told her that our plans were scrapped. Then she smiled, said she was glad and laughed heartily. Today's wig, an unstable affair that looked like a coconut husk, seemed in danger of falling to the floor. Feeling happier than I had in weeks, I joined in the laughter.

One still dawn as I leaned over the balcony observing the slowly awakening world, I felt a wave of dizziness pass over me. I straightened, clutching the balcony, and waited for the twinge of nausea I felt certain would follow. It came gently at first, then in lapping waves. I tiptoed back to the sleeping Joe, shook him excitedly – 'Wake up! We're having a baby!' – and rushed to the toilet to be sick.

We had a farewell party at school for Mrs Kherani and her three children, splashing out with cakes, Pepsis and potato chips. The ayahs, Miss Mubiru, Mrs Ssali and I were damp-eyed as the nursery children presented the Kheranis with a gift and said their goodbyes. For the last time we had coffee together at my desk – we could not face the food – and our tears flowed into our cups. The following day Mrs Kherani boarded a plane and, like David and James before her, flew out of my life forever.

By mid-October most of the Asians had gone. No one really knew where – they just seemed to vanish. I often wondered about them. Was Osman now burning through Gujerat on his motor bike or had he made it to Hollywood? What country had opened its doors to a shrewish Goan with a retroverted uterus? And what of Musa and the Madrasi and fat old P. P. Patel?

No more the colourful wedding crowds at mosques and temples; no more the bright saris and pungent cooking smells in Asian kitchens; no more those bright-eyed children with oiled braids chattering on their way to school in the morning. A vital, flourishing sub-culture was lost forever. It was the end of an era in East African history.

Chapter 21

We eventually went to England on the business trip, leaving Henry in the care of Abby. England was cool, peaceful, utterly predictable. We stayed at a private hotel in Paddington and, while Joe was out all day, Tanya and I shopped and explored. I bought a pushchair and we went for long walks.

One day in a park I met up with some young New Zealanders who were wandering the world on the smell of an oily rag. They were the first New Zealanders I had seen in three years, and I eagerly struck up conversation with them. They gave me no news of home but dwelt on their travels in India, Nepal and Morocco, where they had lived off the charity of the local people.

'I actually got scurvy,' enthused a young man who looked like Jesus. The father of one of the girls was a judge in New Zealand. She thrust out her arm to show me a set of silver bracelets she had duped a retarded Indian girl into selling for a few rupees.

The group turned to me. They wanted to do Africa. Jesus thought it would be a gas to do Uganda, especially with Amin there. I thought of Nsubuga, who had watched his father die on the footpath. I sadly gathered up Tanya and left them.

Joe and I learned to laugh again in England. The first weekend we rode on the underground and promptly lost our bearings. We emerged at a funny little suburb – all bricks and chimneys and shedding trees – and wandered about eating fish and chips from a paper bag. Later a fine drizzle came down, so we were wet and cold when we got back to the hotel. Stripping off hastily, the three of us jumped shrieking into a hot shower.

We rang up James, who lived near Oxford. He listened avidly to our news of Uganda and thought we were mad to go back. We also met up with some of Joe's exiled Ugandan friends, who were saddened by the news from home.

Just before we left we rang my parents. It was three in the morning in New Zealand and we were amused by their sleep-slurred voices. To my joy, they told us they were planning a European tour the following year and would visit us in Uganda on their way home. There were happy exclamations when I told them I was having another baby. 'But we're worried about you all in Uganda. We hear such awful stories,' said Mum. We told her they were exaggerated.

In all we spent about three weeks in London and enjoyed every minute of it, but as we boarded our KLM flight for Uganda, our suitcases stuffed with goods, I felt glad to be going back. We arrived at Entebbe in the early evening. There had been some sort of security scare and the airport was surrounded by troops.

'We're home,' said Joe, as he peered out at the green and black military uniforms, and the laughter lines of the past three weeks slipped back into their former grooves of sadness.

There were presents for the relatives and for Abby and, at the bottom of my suitcase, the cosmetics ordered by my friends. While Eva, Joan and Clarice pounced on the face creams and perfume, I got busy with my new hair rinses.

'You shouldn't titivate your hair,' said Eva. 'It's already far too conspicuous for Uganda.'

'Rats!' and I convinced them that they all needed streaks. We sat on my balcony in perforated shower caps, sprouting strands of lightening hair. The neighbours thought we were mad.

Mrs Ssali and Miss Mubiru had run the school competently in my absence. By the time I returned all the Asian children had gone and the school was made up of Africans, a good number of them newcomers from the north. Speaking only Nubian, these children had different customs from the locals and it took patience and understanding to gain their confidence and help them settle in. It was a busy time for the school, not made any easier by continual morning sickness that was to last right up until the birth of my son.

As the end of the year approached, the older children prepared for their primary school interviews. Several of them, I knew, would do well. Saidi, the son of Pig Face the Kakwa soldier, was one. Pig Face seldom came to the nursery but once when he did I told him how well Saidi was doing. He gave an awkward grunt of laughter and cuffed Saidi's ear, but he looked pleased. Applications were sent off to the local primary schools and all my children were given places.

The mosque across the road, like all public buildings left by the Asians, was now under the umbrella of the newly formed Moslem Supreme Council. So was the school building. I was ordered to meet with a council official to explain my tenancy. It was the most fruitful meeting of my life. With all the beautiful mosques and temples and commercial buildings to grab, no one seemed to care what happened to a ramshackle old building on the swamp and the entire building was given over to me at no extra rent.

We cleared out the committee room – the remaining alcohol and cigarettes were distributed among the car-washers and barbers – and turned it into another classroom. A carpenter was commissioned to make tables and chairs for the new room and the children's art livened up the walls. Now that the main room was no longer used at night by the gamblers, we could leave our furniture out permanently. This freed the storeroom to become a third classroom. Mrs Ssali, Miss Mubiru and I now had a room each. It was marvellous. The overcrowding was immediately alleviated, the noise level dropped dramatically and the teachers could give more individual attention to the children.

'It's an absolute dream,' I raved to Joe. He felt the improvements warranted raising the fees. I indignantly pointed out that the fees were more than sufficient and that he still appeared to have limitless funds with which to drink in the bar each night.

The departure of the Asians saw almost every store on Kampala Road close. A committee had been set up to allocate these businesses to the local people but it was a charade and most of the shops went to Amin's soldiers, mistresses, relatives and friends. A fully stocked pharmacy shop went to an illiterate Nubian who knew nothing about pharmaceuticals; I saw him cheerfully selling off poisons, antibiotics and narcotics as if they were peppermints.

Soon Africans – Black Patels, the locals called them – were sitting behind the Asian counters, many of them semi-literate, with no idea about stocktaking, reordering or budgeting. Some sold off all the goods in the shop and restocked the shelves with bananas; others simply uplifted all the stock, locked up their shops and headed north, never to return. Months later the empty shops had to be forced open and reallocated. Being given a business on Kampala Road was not without its drawbacks – Amin could change his mind at any time about an allocation and have the new owner murdered and replaced with someone else, usually a new mistress.

There was a state of relative calm after the Asian exodus while troops were busy feathering their nests, but this was short-lived and all too soon there was another wave of slaughter. As usual, it seemed to be without rhyme or reason. Village chiefs and government officials simply disappeared. Mayors, town clerks and prominent office holders in local marketing boards were picked up and never seen again. Even villagers were arrested, their lowly assets grabbed and their bodies thrown into swamps. The killings went on and on, with horrified gasps of recognition at the deaths of well-known people. By this time hundreds of thousands of people had died but the country still recoiled as if each death were the first.

And now details of the way in which these innocent people met their deaths began to leak out. Some had their heads bashed in with hammers; others were castrated and then disembowelled; some had parts of their bodies amputated piece by piece and were thrown back, still alive, among other prisoners to frighten them. In some cells there was enforced cannibalism, where soldiers would cut strips of flesh off live prisoners and force others to eat it. There were eye-witness accounts of deep, dark holes in Makindye Prison, which were filled with ice-cold water; the prisoners, fed once a day, remained in the holes until they died.

There was the chain of hammers method at the Public Safety

Unit at Naguru, where victims were lined up and the person at the beginning of the line given a hammer. This person had to smash in the head of the second man. When the second man died the hammer went to the third man to kill the first and so it went on down the line until the last man remained. He was then clubbed to death or shot by an officer. Women, too, met violent deaths by gang rape, bayoneting, and torching.

'Why don't the CIA or the Poms bump him off?' I would say. 'Haven't they learned from Hitler?'

'As long as only black people suffer, they'll do nothing,' Joe replied.

At this dreadful time, news came to Joe that Ted, still in hiding, was not safe. One Saturday when Clarice, Henry and I were chatting in my living room, Joe came in with Musoke and announced that they were going to Jinja. I could tell something was amiss and asked why. Joe told me a friend was in trouble and they were putting him on the Kenya train at Jinja.

'Let someone else do it!' I said, dreadfully afraid.

'It's Ted, isn't it?' Henry's voice was sharp with concern. 'It was only a matter of time. We all knew that.'

They'll catch you! What about me and Tanya and the new baby?

'You can't go!' I heard my voice rising in fear.

'We'll be back before dark. Besides,' said Musoke, his big face breaking into a grin, 'I smell pork for dinner. There's no way I'll miss that.'

As they moved to the door, I grabbed Joe's shirt, weeping and pleading with him to stay.

'Heather,' whispered Henry, leaning across and wrenching the shirt from my hands. 'Ted must be given a chance.'

I turned to him angrily, observing the disfigured features, the battered cheekline. I looked down at the pathetically crooked fingers that gripped my arms and I knew I had lost. They had done this to Henry. Ted must be given a chance.

'Go then!' I cried, my throat clogged with tears, and ran to the bathroom. I sat on the toilet seat, weeping into a towel. This brought on nausea and I vomited into the bowl. Clarice came in, sponged my face and led me back to my chair.

'Come on girl, they'll be back, God knows, and before too long you'll be grumbling about Joe again. You should take something for that nausea, you know.'

If they're caught they'll be thrown to the crocodiles in the Nile.

Clarice played Happy Families with the children, Henry and I joining in half-heartedly. The afternoon seemed to drag. When Clarice and her children left at six, I bathed Tanya and put her to bed. By eight o'clock they still hadn't returned. In the kitchen the roast pork sputtered and I turned it off. I sat with Henry in the hushed living room, trying to stay calm. At ten o'clock a car stopped outside and I rushed to the balcony. 'It's them!'

They clambered up the steps and swept noisily into the room. Ted had got away and all was well. We all talked at once, even the normally quiet Abby. When Joe put his arm around me and kissed me, I smelled the alcohol on his breath. Musoke was telling us that the train had departed at five.

Then they should have been home hours ago!

We brought out the pork and a bottle of wine and drank to Ted's safe arrival in Kenya. We were all hungry, talkative and relieved for Ted, and the meal was happy and noisy, but once I caught Joe's eye and had to turn away.

You were drinking while I spent an entire afternoon in anguish.

Chapter 22

Towards the end of the year Amin married his fourth wife, Medina, a nubile young Muganda dancer whom Amin claimed had been given to him by the grateful Baganda. This was, of course, both untrue and a dreadful insult to the Baganda, whose people had been systematically disappearing since Amin came to power. Medina was brought home to Amin's command post in Kololo to join his three other wives, Kay, Nora and Malyamu. The young bride was coolly received by the senior wives, Amin making no secret of his preference for her. Cracks appeared on the domestic front at the command post.

The year finished as it had begun, in a spate of murders. A Greek was machine-gunned down in the main road on Christmas Eve. Two prominent lawyers were abducted from their offices on 28 December and never seen again. Former cabinet ministers, next on the hit list, were rounded up and arrested or murdered. Over one hundred and thirty chiefs around the country were killed and replaced by army officers. The chairmen and secretaries of state companies were swooped upon in their offices, to vanish, along with thousands of other Ugandans, into the black void.

Amin did not stop at Ugandan personnel. Kenyans and Tanzanians were dragged from the East African Community offices and slaughtered along with the rest. Seven young Tanzanian students reporting for job interviews with the East African Community in Kampala were arrested and killed. When Kenya and Tanzania protested strenuously, Amin promised an enquiry which, of course, came to nothing. The shocking death of Father Clement Kiggundu, editor of a national Catholic newspaper, heralded Amin's persecution of key Christian personnel.

And then a new phenomenon took place. Amin's civilian ministers began to desert him, knowing full well that if they were caught in flight they would be killed. Dan Nabudere, Chairman of East African Railways, Edward Rugumayo, Minister of Education, and Professor Banage, Minister of Animal Industry, Game and Fisheries, were among the first to flee. They were followed by others – Barigye, Amin's ambassador to Bonn, Kibedi, the young Minister of Foreign Affairs, and at least ten more soon after. It heartened the whole country to witness Amin's humiliation and to know that these people had, by deserting the President, publicly denounced his murderous regime.

'It'll soon be over,' everyone said. 'The military government without the experienced ministers will bring itself down.'

'It won't be soon enough,' said Henry, looking sorrowfully at Abby. Over in the corner she was packing her bag to attend her uncle's funeral. Tears slid quietly down her face. Her uncle, a taxi-driver, had been shot on the road. His taxi was now being driven by his murderer, an army captain. No one could do a thing.

Worse was to come. Public executions, the first in seventy-five years, took place in various venues around the country. The victims – some of them only schoolboys – had to wear white aprons so that the television cameras would get good views of the spurting blood. Crowds were forced at gunpoint to attend the executions. When several heads of state objected to this performance they were bombarded with Amin's wrathful telegrams. President Kaunda's accused him of whining like a sobbing, frigid woman unable to please her man.

'Kino kitalo,' said Abby, shaking her head.

It was obvious to everyone that the economy was faltering. The government had neither the expertise nor the inclination to prevent it. Amin nationalised thirty-five British companies and refused to renew trading licences for ninety others. Expatriates were forced to leave, taking with them much technical and financial expertise. The enormous Asian-owned sugar empires of the Madhvanis and Mehtas ground to a halt and, unbelievably, Uganda was forced to import supplies. Factories all over the country began to close as machinery broke down and could be neither repaired nor replaced. Weeds grew up through workshop floors. Car maintenance became almost impossible owing to the lack of trained mechanics and spare parts. Fridges, washing machines, stoves and a vast array of appliances that could no longer be repaired without Asian or European technicians were simply thrown away.

And so Uganda – once Britain's 'model' protectorate, a land-locked little nation of mountains and lakes – plummeted into an abyss of despair.

In late March, Henry left us to take up with a young woman called Violet who lived in an outer suburb. We were pleased for him, as his life with us must have been very boring. His girlfriend was a quietly spoken receptionist whom he had met at an out-patients' clinic when he was receiving treatment. Henry, mobile now with the aid of crutches, had found a job in a government department and was eager to gather up the threads of his life again.

I was well over eight months pregnant – 'It was April Fool's Day, for God's sake,' I said later to Joe – when Joe received a phone call at work from a Major Hussein at Makindye Military Prison. The major asked him questions about his personal life and then ordered him to report to Makindye at two o'clock that afternoon. Joe knew immediately that he was on the death list.

'We must go to the British High Commission,' I said, terrified, when Joe picked me up at lunchtime, but he pointed out that, as a Ugandan, he would be afforded no protection. I suggested driving home, picking up Tanya and continuing straight on to Kenya.

'I think that's what they want us to do. They would follow us and shoot us for resisting arrest. Or fabricate a motor accident. A car accident is convenient and plausible, particularly in your case where foreign enquiries are to be expected.'

We should have stayed in England!

Immediately after the phone call Joe had discussed the situation with his managing director, an expatriate, who had offered to help in whatever way he could. With this in mind, I convinced Joe that we should both report to Makindye. With me, a foreigner, accompanying him, the army would be much more cautious in its treatment of Joe. If we were not out within the hour, the managing director should ring the British High Commission. When they intervened, as they would on my behalf, there was a chance that Joe might be rescued as well. We decided not to inform the high commission of our plans in advance as they would try to convince me to stay out. We also decided to take Tanya with us. A child in Makindye would prompt an even greater effort on the part of our rescuers and put a lot of pressure on Amin. There was no other way. If Joe went in without us, he would never get out alive.

'It's wrong to involve you and Tanya,' worried Joe.

'If we're to die, we die together,' I insisted.

We picked up Tanya and drove to Joe's work. By this time it was one-thirty. The managing director, when we would not be dissuaded from our course of action, agreed to alert the British High Commission if we were not back by three and suggested we use his car and driver. He felt that an international company car and its uniformed driver seen waiting for us at the gates of Makindye might prove to be a deterrent for Major Hussein. We agreed.

Mohammed, the driver, seemed as nervous as we were and his fingers drummed irritatingly on the steering wheel. We drew up outside the high walls of Makindye Prison. 'I will pray for you,' whispered Mohammed as we got out.

We stood holding hands before Makindye – Joe, Tanya and I. The baby within me lurched, as if recoiling from the place. It settled, pressing uncomfortably into my groin. Joe picked up Tanya and we walked over to the gates.

'Major Hussein, hah!' said one of the soldiers when Joe had explained. The gates were opened and two soldiers escorted us through, across a courtyard and along a path beside a row of barracks. The place swarmed with military police who stared at us. Some laughed. We came to a long, low building with barred windows. The cells.

156

'This is the wrong place,' said Joe uneasily to our escorts. 'We should be going to administration.'

Ignoring him, the soldiers took us inside to a small empty room. They left us there, locking the door behind them. I stared out through bars, unable to formulate any thought. The window looked out onto a grassy square beyond which was a squat building where groups of military personnel came and went continually. There was a sudden scream from a neighbouring room followed by thumping and crashing. Someone began weeping. Joe took me in his arms, Tanya crushed between us. We stood like that until the screaming and thumping stopped. In the distance a door slammed and we heard angry Nubian voices approaching. A key turned in the lock and a balding, very black man wearing the red and khaki of the military police, strode in. He was flanked by two orderlies.

'Why did you come here? What do you want?' barked the balding man, whom I assumed was Major Hussein – he never bothered to introduce himself. I could smell the whisky fumes from where I stood. Joe explained about his phone call. Hussein denied phoning anyone, particularly a stuck-up Baganda with a Muzungu wife. With much relief I realised the whole thing was a hoax. Now we could go. Hussein looked at me.

'You're a reporter! An American! You've come to spy!'

'You're wrong, major,' said Joe calmly. 'She has identity with her. We'll show you.'

'Hapana! Not here! You'll come with me to the Singapore Block.' He glared at me. 'I'll come back for the Muzungu spy later.'

The orderlies grabbed Joe and pushed him out of the room. Hussein followed and locked the door. I was left with Tanya clinging to my legs. Terrified, I knelt beside her and drew her to me.

Oh God in heaven, look after us all. Protect this little girl who has hardly started her life.

I looked at my watch. Barely quarter past two! The managing director would not call the high commission until three. There was more thumping, crashing and crying from the nearby room. Tanya began to cry. I picked her up and carried her to the window, pleading with God not to let the cries be Joe's. In the squat building opposite us a group of officers emerged and walked across the lawn towards us. As they approached the window I stared in disbelief. One of them was Pig Face, Saidi's father. It was now or never. In a minute he would be gone.

'Wewe!' I shrieked into the courtyard. 'Baba Saidi! Ni mimi! Mwalimu!' The group of soldiers stopped and looked up. Pig Face recognised me and started. He said something to his companions, who shrugged and walked on. Wandering up to the window, he looked up at me, his little eyes squinting against the sun. I tried desperately to tell him what had happened. He was not very bright and my Swahili was not very good, so it took a while before he understood. He told me that his uncle was one of the bosses here – he would see what he could do. He gave a sudden smile, looking momentarily like Saidi. Then he turned and strolled away. I watched him go, the sun gleaming on the fat oily coils of his neck.

Hurry then, you pig!

I leaned against the wall, Tanya still in my arms. I wondered what would happen if I went into labour and delivered a baby on this hard, cold floor. I tried to pray but my mind seemed unable to conjure up words. The crying and crashing continued in the nearby room. It seemed an eternity before I heard footsteps approaching my door. The key turned and Hussein and Pig Face entered.

'You're just a teacher, I understand. That is good. That is very good. You can go.' Hussein's whisky breath blasted me as he spoke.

'But my husband?'

'You go. He will join you later.'

I did not believe him. 'I would rather wait here.'

'You go!' barked Hussein. 'This is Makindye! I shoot if my orders are not obeyed. Fuluma mangu!'

Pig Face escorted us back across the compound.

'Please, please make sure they release Joe,' I begged him.

'We watch people like him. He's rich, he drives a Benz.' He told me that even though we were there as the result of a bogus call they already had a file on us.

'Oh God!' I shivered. 'Tell me honestly, will they release my husband?'

'Yes, because of me. He was on the list. Now no more.'

'I'm very grateful. Thank you.'

'I'm a powerful man, teacher. I have killed many people.' He pulled out his revolver and aimed it at Tanya's head. 'Bang, bang! Ha ha! You are frightened, teacher! I'm only joking.'

Shaking, Tanya and I passed through the gates to freedom. We sat shivering in the car with Mohammed. At ten to three Joe was released.

'Allah is great,' said Mohammed with relief. He released the handbrake quickly and we were away. For some minutes we drove in silence. Joe felt for my hand.

'They have a file on us inches thick,' he said in a monotone. 'Hussein would have killed me if your fat friend had not intervened.'

'Are we still in danger?'

'I don't think so. A friend in Makindye is an insurance policy. My name is off the list. God, they know everything about us. They even have photographs. Me in a bar with friends. Driving the car. Some of you too. Mostly from a distance. You stand out because of your hair.'

We tried to think who had engineered the hoax that could have sent us to our deaths. Joe felt it could be someone after his job who hoped we would flee to Kenya. But we could think of no one who would do such a thing. We drew up at Joe's work. Still in shock, I begged him to take the afternoon off and come home with me. But he had things to do.

Like celebrating with your friends in the bar after work!

'You're bloody unfeeling,' I shouted after him and began to cry as the car drew away.

And I went into Makindye to save you.

That evening Joan cut my hair. I watched the long blonde tresses hit the floor in pale disarray. Then she applied the dye.

'Are you sure you had to be this drastic?' she said. I thought of the photographs, of the goons cruising about Kampala watching behind dark, blank sunglasses.

'Yes,' I said, but when she had finished and I saw my short, mouse-brown hair, I burst into tears.

Chapter 23

A week after our Makindye experience the radio announced that the flats on our estate were to be vacated by the end of the week so that the army and their families could move in. Anyone who remained would be severely dealt with. Nobody wanted to stay around to see what that meant, so over a hundred families scrambled to find other accommodation.

I was heavy and tired, due to have my baby at any moment, and Joe seemed to have priorities other than packing, so we employed a houseboy called Ernest for a week to help us move. Even before we had moved out, hooting trucks full of soldiers arrived with their belongings, haranguing the packing tenants and taking over the flats before they were vacated. Departing families panicked, throwing everything unbreakable out of windows and over balconies to accelerate their departure.

Joe had found us a house to rent at Luzira near the shores of Lake Victoria. Our new home was in an isolated area surrounded by beautiful wild bush that came down to the water. From our windows we had breathtaking views of the lake and sometimes we could see fishermen on the rickety Port Bell jetty. The immense shamba contained a guesthouse, a swimming pool and servants' quarters, all set out with doll's house-like precision on manicured lawns. The long shaded driveway was lined with scarlet canna lilies and flowering shrubs.

'Far too grand for us,' I said delightedly, as I followed Tanya's excited legs to a swing that hung from a huge tree in the middle of the lawn. The truck with all our belongings rumbled along the drive behind us, with Joe in the rear in the Mercedes with the last of our belongings. Ernest and Abby were already starting to unpack when Joe looked at his watch, observed it was midday and said it was time to go. I asked him to be in early that night, not only because we needed his help to move in but because the baby was due.

'Okay, I'll try, Brownie,' and he ruffled my hair with a laugh and strode back to the car.

'What do I see in such a cocksure shit!' I said aloud as he drove away.

For the rest of the day Ernest, Abby and I worked against the clock to get the house ready by nightfall. After we had unloaded the truck we made beds, unpacked clothes, and put away all our belongings. Daylight was fading by the time we finished. We were exhausted. After dinner I sent Ernest and Abby off to the servants' quarters to start their own unpacking. I bathed Tanya, drew the curtains and locked the doors. Tanya refused to settle in her strange bed, so we wrapped ourselves in a rug on the sofa and read stories.

I felt lonely in the new house and longed for Joe to come home. I missed having Eva, Joan and Clarice nearby. I heard sirens wailing in the distance. Tanya nodded off to sleep against me. I sighed resignedly and cuddled down with her beneath the blanket. I heard the sirens again. It was nine-thirty. High time for any man to be home with his nine months' pregnant wife in a lonely house in an isolated area in a barbaric country, the aunts would have said.

'I agree,' I murmured aloud. The baby was born the following morning.

Joseph was a placid baby endowed with crisp, black curls and dark, soulful eyes. He was brought home from the hospital with far more confidence than was Tanya and, as a result, was remarkably easy on the household.

In the afternoons I would sit out on the verandah overlooking the peaceful garden with the baby feeding at my breast and Tanya curled up at my side. It was a far cry from the mayhem of Tanya's infancy with its clutter of baby bottles, endless laundry and frenetic sleepless nights. I would smile down on Tanya's head wondering how I had let one little girl cause such havoc.

How alike you are with your curly heads and baby-bright eyes. How innocent, how utterly dependent . . . and my heart would almost break with love for them.

The household marvelled over the baby's steadily increasing weight and sweet disposition. The pet names were not long in coming.

'Jo-jo,' said Tanya.

'Bwana kidogo,' said Abby and Ernest.

'Nnabe,' smiled Joe as he drew the little body into his huge embrace.

I was still able to work at school each morning, thanks to Abby and the baby's bottle, but by the time I arrived home for lunch milk was beginning to seep through my blouse and Joseph was more than ready for a feed. Ernest, who was meant to be temporary, somehow never left us. Quick and efficient in the kitchen, he became the houseboy-cook, which meant that Abby was able to devote her time solely to the children.

Like many private homes we employed two night guards, or askaris, armed with clubs and bows and arrows which, although useless against machine guns, nonetheless provided some semblance of security. We also bought two guard dogs from a departing European – Bella, a slim Alsatian beauty with friendly manners, and Mengo, a black Dobermann-Alsatian cross.

Our household was further increased by a gardener or shamba boy called Kerasese, who did all the outside jobs. He was a sour-tempered old man who grumbled as he worked, cursing the dogs, quarrelling with Ernest and muttering about me. The only person he treated with any consideration was Tanya, allowing her to water the flowerbeds, giving her rides in the wheelbarrow and showing her where the birds' nests were. In spite of his surliness, he had a way with the garden, which bloomed beneath his knobbly old fingers.

In the afternoons, after Joseph was fed and sleeping, Tanya and

I sometimes walked down to the jetty where we watched the fishermen bring in tilapia, perch and lung-fish. The men grew used to us and often greeted Tanya in Luganda or Swahili. It fascinated me to hear her answering in the appropriate language. Sometimes I bought fish from them which we would carry home on reed strings and Ernest would make fish curry for dinner.

We filled the pool and I began to teach Tanya to swim. She had always enjoyed the water and was now able to float unaided. Sometimes my friends came over for the afternoon but it was a long trek to get to Luzira and I didn't see them often. After the army had kicked us off the estate Eva had moved to Tank Hill and was often without a car. Joan had moved across town near the university and relied on Eva to bring her. Clarice, who lived further away than either of them, worked in the afternoons. I missed terribly the companionship we had shared at Bugolobi. My neighbours here were a few staid expatriates whose lives mainly consisted of comparing housegirls over gins at the Kampala Club. Luzira never really felt like home and I would gladly have given up my beautiful house to be back in Bugolobi with my friends.

Every few weeks Joe drove to Masaka to check on his family and deliver provisions. Although it was possible to survive solely on the land – fruit, vegetables and nuts grew everywhere and the lakes were full of fish – the villagers craved salt, sugar, flour, items such as soap, matches and medicines, and a variety of other manufactured goods that for many years had been available to them through the ubiquitous Indian dukkas. I did not always accompany Joe on these trips, because it was a tiresome journey for the two children and therefore for me, but I waited eagerly for his return. On one of his trips he brought back the news that Ted was living with friends in Nairobi and working with a firm of accountants. It was the first real news we had had of him since his escape from Jinja.

About the same time I received a lengthy letter from Mum, scrutinised, as all mail now was, by the censors in the President's office. The letter was posted in Switzerland, the first leg of their European trip, and it gave me details of their proposed visit to

Uganda in July, a month away. I could hardly wait. We immediately began preparations for their stay. Abby and I spring-cleaned the guesthouse from top to bottom, polishing the wooden floors and cleaning the lounge windows and washing the curtains. Tanya helped us to dust and polish the furniture and to air the blankets and mattresses in the sun.

'Nana and Pop are coming,' she told a smiling Abby as they hung clean towels in the bathroom.

'Nana and Pop are coming,' she told the surly Kerasese when she borrowed his twig broom to sweep the guesthouse porch.

'This Nana and Pop means more work for all of us,' grumbled Kerasese when I sent him up on to the guesthouse roof to clean the spouting.

I asked Joe to arrange for a fence to be erected around the pool before Mum and Dad arrived, knowing how they would worry about the children's safety. He agreed to do it, but he was so pre-occupied with his work, his own business and Musoke and Byron that the job was never done. I found an odd-job man in Luzira who agreed to build the fence. He needed a cash advance to buy the materials which I duly gave him and he never returned. 'You're far too trusting,' said Joe crossly. 'Leave it to me.'

Tanya was to have her second birthday during my parents' stay. Since she had not yet been baptised – we had agreed that the children would be raised as Catholics – we decided that, on her birthday, she and Joseph would be christened in Kampala with a reception at home afterwards where friends and family could meet my parents (or farewell them, as it turned out, for, unknown to us, my parents had already booked a flight out of Uganda that night).

Joe arranged for local caterers to cook the traditional food for the party. 'And Mum and Ernest and I can make the European fare,' I said.

Our guest list came to nearly a hundred people. 'Thank God for the garden! We'll set up tables under the trees.'

Eva agreed to make the christening cake. It took contacts, a healthy wallet and time, but eventually I was able to supply her with the ingredients via the black market and I deposited a carton of dried fruit and a sack each of flour and sugar on her doorstep.

'I'll need a concrete mixer for all this! How many people are coming?'

'Over a hundred. We'll need a big cake.'

'Oh,' she said faintly. 'How awful.'

We had invitations printed and for fun sent some out to friends overseas. Jane's, sent to her last known address in Australia, was returned. Paul telephoned us from New Zealand to decline his. He told us about our friends, with whom we were slowly losing touch. Jane was in Britain somewhere, Pam was married and lost in the South Island. Others were travelling to India to find themselves.

'It's time I made a move somewhere,' said Paul.

'Come over here,' I begged.

'What for? A free lobotomy from your lunatic President?' I hoped the wiretappers were out for lunch.

Joe went to the village to set a date with his parents for Mum and Dad to visit them; I knew the relatives would begin preparations days ahead of the visit. Mum rang from London a few days before they were due to arrive.

'I know there must be shortages there,' she said. 'What can I bring?' I thought of the books and pencils and paper we needed for the school. And soap and milk powder and cheese and bacon. Flour, sugar, butter, jam. Clothes, film for the cameras, toiletries, towels.

'I wouldn't know where to start, Mum. Thanks anyway.' She made me promise to cable their London hotel if I changed my mind.

The day before their arrival I brought up the subject of fencing the pool. Joe was apologetic. 'If I can get someone to start on it today we could get most of it up before they arrive,' he said. 'I'll sort something out.'

He forgot. He came in that night at nine-thirty with Byron and Musoke, expecting me to wait on them at the table.

'When Tanya drowns you'll realise you killed her,' I said as I thumped down the vegetables. Byron and Musoke looked shocked.

'That's enough,' said Joe quietly. I could tell by the tightening of his jaw that he was angry.

I stalked out of the room, slamming the door, and headed for my room. I heard the door open and slam again as Joe strode angrily after me. Pushing me into the bedroom, he shoved me up against the wall where he began to shake me. My head hit the wall again and again.

'Rude in front of my friends! Rude in front of my family! When will you learn some manners?'

'When you assume some of the responsibilities that go with being a father. That pool's dangerous! I'm tired of being the one that does everything around here.'

My voice rose with each thump of my head. 'It's me who feeds the kids, arranges their inoculations, buys their clothes, rushes around looking for scarce commodities and sees to all the shit like fused wires, broken windows, burnt fingers and leaking gas cylinders. You're just never around. I may as well be an unmarried mother!'

He thumped my head hard one more time and pushed his face into mine.

'I'm sick of your Muzungu ways! I'm not a lump of clay to be moulded as you will. That bloody pool has killed no one yet, nor will it ever!'

He pushed me from him and I collapsed on the bed. He walked out, slamming the door. I stood up too quickly so that my head reeled and my vision dipped and dived. I held on to the window frame until my head cleared. My first impulse was to run after him and scream to his friends what a bastard he was. But would they understand? Musoke had not bothered to ring Sarah – alone at home with their children and probably keeping his dinner warm – to tell her he was eating here. And Byron had a stable of girlfriends whom he treated like dirt.

There was a knock. It was Musoke. He stood in the doorway awkwardly.

'Come to inspect the damage?' I said. 'A pity you didn't think to arrive in time to stop it.'

He told me they were all sorry it had ended like this, and asked me to join them. He said Joe was upset and couldn't eat.

'Let the bugger starve then!'

'Please. Come out and have a drink with us and forget about everything.'

'As if a drink were the answer, Musoke!'

When he had gone I wandered over to the mirror. My face looked hard and angular, my eyes glittered stonily.

So this is what hatchet-faced means!

The light on the mirror glowed dispiritedly on my head, unable to impart a single spark of life to my dark cropped hair. 'Oh that shit-brown hair!' I cried and threw my brush and cracked the mirror.

It was very late when I heard him get into bed beside me.

'Heather?' I feigned sleep. His hand caressed my face with surprising gentleness. 'I'm sorry, my darling,' he whispered in Luganda. 'I never meant to hurt you.'

Hurt, bitterness and love rose in me like a wave. I wanted to weep out my soul on his chest, let him see and feel and taste my despair, let him know how shut out of his life I was.

In all things you do or say or feel I want to be first, first, first. . . .

But I knew I might as well cry for the moon.

Eva rang in panic as I was leaving for work the following morning.

'Icing sugar, you forgot icing sugar! We need tons of it!'

I stopped off at the post office and wrote out a telegram. 'Please bring tons of icing sugar,' I hesitated, thinking of my cracked mirror, then added, 'and tons of hair bleach' and sent it off to Mum's hotel in London.

Chapter 24

Mum and Dad flew into Entebbe that night, relaxed, suntanned, overjoyed to be with us. We laughed and talked and ate Swiss chocolates until well after midnight. They had bought presents for everyone and in a box on the table was the icing sugar and several packets of hair bleach. Tanya, overexcited by the company and her new toys and clothes, refused to settle until we all went to bed. She was up again at the crack of dawn to help Ernest and Abby take the breakfast trays to the guesthouse.

Dad had been plagued by constipation all through his holiday and Ernest, at my request, had piled the trays with fresh fruit, some of it picked that very morning by Kerasese. Dad, who opened at their knock, was to rave forever more about the tropical breakfast that came that morning, and every morning thereafter. Hearing activity, I jumped out of bed, threw a shawl over my nightdress and hurried barefoot across the dew-spattered lawn. Feeling happier than I had in ages I burst through the door to join them, perching on the end of Dad's bed with Tanya and chatting about plans for their stay. Mum was sitting up in bed in a pink bed-jacket and a hairnet, with her tray across her knees. Noticing her corsets on the chair, I hid a smile.

'I've taken the day off today, so I thought that once you're up you could watch Joseph's bathtime – he's so gorgeous – and then we'll do some sightseeing around Kampala. In the afternoon we could swim or take a walk down to the lake with the kids.'

For the next two days they were kept fairly busy. Mum and Dad bought carvings at curio shops and visited my school, and Joe took them to his club where they drank waragi. They adored the grandchildren, wheeling them in pushchairs and swinging them in swings. Their cameras, never off their necks for very long, went through rolls of film.

Unfortunately Mum came down with phlebitis on the third day – 'something to do with the varicose veins in her leg,' I whispered to Joe – and she remained ill for more than a week. While Mum languished, Dad and I continued sightseeing. I showed him Makarere University, the two great cathedrals and the Kasubi Tombs where the Kabakas are buried. Joe took him to the local Rotary Club where Dad was made guest speaker on the spot.

While Mum was sick, Dad organised Ernest and Kerasese to help fence in the pool. They erected a local type of fence – poles and wirenetting – that made the area a much safer place. It took less than a day to make and I wondered why Joe had found it so difficult to arrange.

On our drives Dad filled me in on the Kirk government and the prevailing social issues in New Zealand, while I explained aspects of Uganda's history that were all around us in the buildings, the names of the streets and the many different places of worship. Sometimes, around Mum's bed, we would discuss such issues as tribalism, the legacy of colonialism and, inevitably, Amin. Joe and I tried hard to downplay the current situation to keep them from worrying. It was fortunate that, for the three weeks they were with us, relative calm prevailed.

Mum's leg had flared up several times on their travels through Europe but never as badly as it did now. She was feverish and her leg so painful that she couldn't walk, but had to remain in bed. It was fortunate that Dad had stocked up on medicines before he came – he would have been pushing his luck to find the right medication in the local pharmacies. With good care and rest the leg slowly began to heal and Mum was able to sit under a tree overlooking the lake. Once she was better there was no stopping her. She fussed over the children, toured the town for craftwork and limped down to the jetty where she chatted to the fishermen, who did not understand her. In the evenings she helped me plan for the christening and wrote out recipes.

We took Mum and Dad to Jinja to show them the source of the Nile, stopping at Owen Falls Dam with its nearby hydro-electric station. Mum wanted to get out of the car to take photos.

'You'd better not,' said Joe, knowing it was a favourite dumping ground for bodies. But Mum, determined, was striding uphill across the grass before we could stop her.

'Come back, Mum! There may be soldiers!' I panted as I struggled after her. There was a sign expressly forbidding entry beyond this point but Mum, unaware and waving her camera, pressed on looking for a good picture. Two soldiers appeared and barred her way. Mum asked if she could take their photo. While they were gathering their incredulous wits I grabbed her by the arm and hurried her downhill, expecting at the very least to be ordered back. Joe stepped on the accelerator and the car leapt away before I had time to shut the door.

Mum, refusing to believe that she could have caused an international incident, set about looking for a sugar field to photograph.

Towards the end of their stay we took them to Masaka to meet Joe's family. Joe's mother bustled forward to take charge, welcoming them, showing them round, offering them refreshments and pointing out the various relatives. The cooking hut was a hive of activity and at midday food was brought out under the trees. Lunch was a typical village spread and I was pleased to observe my parents trying some of the more unfamiliar food.

'It's an unusual taste,' said Mum diplomatically to Joe's father as she tried the dried fish in groundnut sauce. 'Back home I cook boiled cod in parsley sauce.'

'I'm sure it is delicious,' said Joe's father politely, turning to the gawping, toothless uncle beside him and sending him off for home-brew.

After lunch Joe's family presented my parents with mats and basketware. Mary came over to show us her new baby, while Nakalo, her four-year-old daughter, claimed Tanya and they ran to the plantains to play. Then Mum insisted on assembling everyone in front of the house for a photograph. One of the aunties grumbled because she was wearing a plain basuti and felt that, if she was to be seen in New Zealand, she should be wearing her best one. The toothless uncle, determined to look distinguished, made everyone wait while he rushed home to collect his spectacles, and Joe's mother confused everyone by carefully positioning them for the photo and then changing her mind. The finished picture showed everyone looking somewhat out of sorts.

After the photo, people sat about drinking and gossiping. Dad, whose bowels had become pleasantly fluid as a result of his fruit breakfasts, wandered away with Mum to find the toilet. I wondered how Mum, in her corsets, would manage to straddle the deep narrow slit in the ground that served as a long-drop latrine. In the late afternoon we said our goodbyes and set off back to Kampala. My parents, overwhelmed by their reception, sat quietly in the back reflecting on their day. Joe told them they had been a hit.

On the last day of my parents' stay we had the party. It started off with the christening service at the Church of Christ the King, where seven other babies were also being baptised. By the time we got back to Lake Drive the local caterers had already set their food to cook on charcoal and paraffin cookers at the bottom of the garden. The smell that greeted us was tantalising. Mum and I went inside to put the finishing touches to our salads, while Joe and Kerasese set up the bar outside.

Agnes, Rose and Mary, the ayahs from my school, arrived to help and began carrying the cutlery and plates out to the main table. In the kitchen Ernest's face sweated as he turned the haunch of beef in the oven. As guests began to wander up the drive, Joe and I went out to meet them. Agnes, Rose and Mary picked up the trays of drinks and began to circulate. Eva arrived with the christening cake – an enormous, beautifully decorated affair crowned with snow-white icing.

'It's beautiful, Eva,' I gasped. We took it to the dessert table on the verandah, placing it among the fruit salads, trifles and meringues under a nylon net. A portable fan and bowls of ice kept everything cool.

More and more people arrived. Children played among the trees while their parents greeted old friends and ensconced themselves at tables. Handing Mum a gin and lemon, I took her round to meet my friends. Over by the pool Father was conversing with a group of businessmen. Nearby, in the shade of a tree, stood Miss Mubiru with Mrs Ssali, the latter resplendent in a tight sheath dress and a sweeping white hat that resembled an albatross in full flight. I noticed Tanya climbing trees with the children, her white christening dress getting dirtier by the minute.

Leaving Mum with Sarah Musoke, I made my way down to the caterers at the bottom of the garden. Two women were unwrapping vegetables from the steaming banana leaves while the chief cook ladled chicken into a large bowl. Kerasese sat near him, his eyes alert for tit-bits. One or two curious Europeans wandered over to watch.

'That's ebiyenda,' I said to a Dutch colleague of Joe's who was staring into a bubbling stew full of enigmatic shapes. 'Goat intestines.' The man made his way rather quickly to the bar.

Joe tapped me on the shoulder. 'Your father's a bit off colour,' he said.

Dad was in my bedroom looking rather seedy. 'Too many fruit breakfasts, I'm afraid,' he said. 'I've got a dose of diarrhoea. I'll have to lie down for a bit.'

Settling him on the bed, I gave him two tablets from his travelling pharmacopoeia. He looked jaded under the quilt and I suggested to him that they postpone their departure that evening and catch a flight later in the week. I went out to consult with Mum.

'He has temperamental bowels,' explained Mum to Sarah.

'Stay a few extra days,' I begged. 'Neither of you is quite up to par. It'd do you good.'

But Mum was adamant that they would be fit to travel, although she agreed to leave the final decision to Dad.

Lunch was set out. When everyone was served, Mum and I filled our plates and sat with friends on the verandah. I found I was not hungry.

It's been wonderful having them both here, having that feeling of belonging, that feeling that I matter, knowing they're interested in what I do and what I feel. Oh God, I'll be so lonely when they go.

I looked across the crowded lawn and wondered how it was possible to be lonely with so many friends and relatives. As I toyed with my meal, the understanding slowly came to me.

I'm not lonely for company, I'm lonely for him, *for that two-thirds of him which he keeps from me.*

Foreseeing endless years of marital starkness ahead of me, I suddenly longed to fly away with Mum and Dad.

After lunch the guests sat about with drinks, coffee and christening cake. I fed Joseph and he lay in my arms Buddha-like as I wandered around. By the swing Clarice and her daughters posed in front of Mum's busy camera. There was a scream as a breeze uplifted Mrs Ssali's hat and landed it in the pool. An elderly uncle with gout had to fish it out with his cane. Watching amusedly as Byron edged closer to Miss Mubiru, his spectacles radiating lust, I almost collided with Kerasese clutching a plate heaped high with a revolting mixture of goat stew and trifle.

In the middle of the afternoon Dad got up, looking a little better. After a cup of tea with a small piece of bread, he assured me he would be well enough to fly out that night. My heart sank. Dumping Joseph on Abby, I went inside. The kitchen was empty and I stared forlornly out the window. Clarice entered, putting an arm around my shoulders.

'What do you see out there, girl?'

'I see the wet glistening pavements of Lambton Quay on a Friday night. I see my cat washing himself on the doorstep in the early morning sun . . . and Vegemite on the breakfast table.' I felt tears sliding down my cheeks. 'I don't want them to go, Clarice.'

She handed me a teatowel and I wiped my eyes.

'You should tell them about your problems with Joe. They'd probably show far more understanding than you give them credit for.'

I thought of our family which, on both sides, had always been remarkably devoid of marital disharmony, and shook my head. 'Marriage is as sacrosanct to them as it is a farce to you.'

'And where does that leave *you*, girl?'

The shadows lengthened, the last guests had departed, and the servants were clearing up. It was almost dark when we drove out the gates to take my parents to Entebbe. The grass mats strapped to their expensive suitcases looked pathetically incongruous.

At the airport the luggage was checked in and the tickets confirmed. The lump in my throat threatened to choke me. We said our goodbyes and Joe and I hurried upstairs to wave them off. We watched them cross the tarmac – one still drooping from diarrhoea, the other still limping from phlebitis.

'Joe,' I said in a small voice as we drove back. 'I'm only in this country because of you.'

'Why do you say that?'

I told him how fearful I was for our marriage, how we were losing the ability to communicate with each other, how we needed to respect and consider each other as we used to in New Zealand.

'I think you're just miserable about your parents' departure.'

'No. I'm much more miserable about the state of our marriage.'

'You've got a great marriage. You have your own business, a nice home, two lovely kids, a car and servants. That's more than most people have – here or in New Zealand.'

'Funny, I didn't hear the word husband.'

'Clarice has filled your head with nonsense. You know that I treat you better than most husbands.'

Animals are treated, humans are cared for.

'Why can't that be enough for you?' he said, puzzled.

'Dear Joe, if you have to ask a question like that, there's no way you're going to understand the answer.'

He pulled my head on to his shoulder and we drove home in silence.

Chapter 25

Immediately after my parents had left, Joan came over and set to work on my hair with the bleach.

'Are you sure now?' said the ever-cautious Eva.

'Yes. To hell with being careful. I refuse to walk around looking as if a cow shitted on my head.'

Joan applied the lighteners and within hours I was fair again. I felt a lot happier.

'Keep it short,' advised Eva. 'Don't go looking for trouble.'

We took orange drinks to the poolside and began discussing Christmas. The three of us were all planning to go to our respective homes and we were saving in earnest. Eva was taking in dressmaking and Joan was doing the hair of expatriates since there were no longer any European hairdressing salons in town. I budgeted carefully and gradually our savings grew.

Around us, as we scrimped and saved, life went on in its usual unpredictable way. Amin sent a cable to President Nixon wishing him a speedy recovery from Watergate. When the Yom Kippur War exploded Amin mobilised his troops to fight in the Middle East but the Arabs politely turned him down. Amin jetted to the front anyway where he tongue-lashed captured Israeli soldiers. I wondered if David was among them. I longed for more news about the war but since all foreign newspapers were now banned in Uganda and BBC broadcasts were often jammed, it was almost impossible. The few local newspapers were state microphones and reported categorically that Israel had lost the war. It was with immense relief that I was able to lay my hands on a *Newsweek* magazine smuggled in from Kenya and learn the real outcome of the war.

Meanwhile an anti-Amin guerrilla movement made up of exiled Ugandans had sprung up outside the country. It called itself the Front for National Salvation – Fronasa – but, because of strict media censorship, hardly anyone in Uganda knew of its existence. The government, however, was fully aware of the movement, which provided an excuse for the army to engage in more indiscriminate looting, raping and murdering of civilians.

One morning hundreds of leaflets, presumably printed by Fronasa, were air-dropped along the main road of Kampala. The leaflet, which said that Amin would not last much longer and that help was on the way, listed the atrocities that had so far been inflicted and promised that the President would be brought to justice. It was the first organised openly defiant event in Amin's Uganda. The boost to morale was unbelievable; although no one dared pocket a single leaflet, its message of support was carried around in every heart.

'We're no longer alone,' a perfect stranger whispered to me as I stood on the pavement staring at my leaflet. All over Kampala people were smiling that morning, even when the army arrived in trucks to sweep up the leaflets.

A few days after the leaflet drop I returned home for lunch alone – Joe was at a business lunch – to find Abby beside herself with worry about Joseph, who was vomiting and feverish. Panicking, I took his temperature which was way above normal.

Malaria, meningitis, elephantiasis!

Leaving Tanya with Ernest, I rushed him to Nsambya Hospital, with Abby cradling him in the front seat. Outpatients was overcrowded. It was ages before the doctor, a cheerful Irish nun, called us in. I was so worried that my head ached and I could hardly talk.

The doctor examined Joseph while keeping up a friendly patter, mostly about Dublin. She suspected malaria, a blood sample was taken and we were sent back to the overcrowded waiting room to wait for the results. We waited for hours. The test eventually came back positive so we then had to queue up for an injection. Dr Dublin – I could not remember her real name – gave us medication and sent us on our way.

It was dark when we arrived home. Joseph was already much better, although he refused to drink. I tucked him up in his cot, fed and bathed Tanya and waited in the darkened living room for Joe. I had not eaten since breakfast, my head ached and my breasts were hard and painful from unreleased milk, so I lay on the couch like an invalid. I hoped Joe would not be too late. I checked up once more on Joseph before dozing off on the couch.

It was after midnight when I awoke to the dogs' barking and the sound of our car coming up the drive. Propelling myself sleepily and angrily off the couch, I unlocked the front door. Joe stood there, his face seemingly paralysed, his eyes glazed with shock.

'Good God. What is it?' I pulled him inside and shut the door.

'Oh Jesus, Jesus.' He was dazed and I helped him to the couch where he sank, shivering as if from cold.

'Musoke,' he whispered. 'They've got Musoke.'

'Oh God!'

'They took him from his office this afternoon . . . They beat him up on the road . . . They bundled him into the boot . . .'

'Oh God, no!'

His arms reached up for me and he drew me down and we wept together on the couch.

Musoke was one of several accountants who disappeared that week. No one knew why this group was singled out. It was just another senseless atrocity. After Joe and Byron had learned of his abduction they had spent the rest of the afternoon and half the night contacting go-betweens and body-hunters, intermediaries who, for a fee, used army contacts to glean information about abducted people. It was to no avail and his body was never found. Sarah and the children immediately left Kampala to live in the comparative safety of her parents' village. We barely got to say goodbye to them.

The shock and grief over Musoke's death was profound. Relatives gathered in Kampala for a memorial service and then for a traditional one in his home village. Death without a burial was a violation of traditional ways and the people were left with a sense of uneasiness and dissatisfaction instead of the peace and finality that follow a funeral.

For weeks after Musoke's abduction Joe came home straight after work to spend time with the children and me. We would sit on the verandah, listening to our blues music and playing with the children. Many times I thought about the kindly man whose life had come to such a violent end and my heart would swell with grief. I remembered how he, along with James and Byron, had been at the airport to welcome me when, as a nervous bride, I had first arrived in Uganda. He had been part of my Ugandan life from the beginning, a dear family friend who, in spite of our occasional differences, had always occupied a warm place in my heart.

After Musoke's death Joe and I again thought carefully about our future in this unpredictable country, but in the end we decided to stay. We planned the entire course of action that one of us should take if the other was suddenly arrested. We kept a low profile. We checked our wills. Musoke's death had struck very close to home.

The only ray of light in those dark bleak weeks leading up to Christmas was the knowledge that I was going home.

Tanya and I arrived in New Zealand ten days before Christmas. As we flew in over Cook Strait and I saw the sun sparkling on the sea, the heavy mantle of Musoke's death began to lift from my shoulders. It was wonderful to see my parents and my two brothers at Wellington Airport.

Dad had taken up a new position in a psychiatric hospital a few miles out of Marton. The house they now occupied was surrounded by farmlands, a good place in which to heal my wounds. In the paddock behind the house loomed the enormous skeleton of what appeared to be Noah's Ark. This was Dad's latest venture, a six-berth, forty-foot, ocean-going yacht.

'Shee-yit!' I gasped as I got out of the car.

'I was hoping your language had improved,' said Mum sadly as she led me into the house.

178

Janet was now married with two little boys and the next day we had a noisy reunion and a large lunch on the back lawn. Robin flew in from Australia a few days later and for the first time in years the entire family and most of its latest little additions sat down to Christmas dinner.

After Christmas there was the excitement of a cousin's wedding in Wellington. At the reception I had a great time meeting up with all my relatives and showing off Tanya who, at two-and-a-half, almost eclipsed the bride. Even the aunts, who had travelled up from Dunedin, unbent enough to smile at her as she pattered about in her lacy dress.

After the wedding, Tanya and I stayed on in Wellington with Paul for a few days. On the beach at Scorching Bay I told him about Makindye and Henry and Musoke, feeling relief as the awful memories poured out.

'You and Joe should leave that place,' he said quietly. On the shoreline some distance away Tanya was building sandcastles. 'You could both get jobs anywhere.'

'Only one thing would make me leave – and that's Joe.' He looked puzzled and I rushed on, begging him not to tell anyone. 'Paul, I know he's your friend, but he's changed. You'd hardly know him now.'

I told him of our quarrels, of the nights he left me on my own, of the way he refused to share responsibility for the running of the household.

'He expects me to accept the imbalance in our marriage without grumbling. And he shuts me right out of his life. We do things quite separately. We shop separately, entertain ourselves separately, even eat dinner separately. He doesn't seem to be interested in sharing much of himself at all. He knows it hurts me but he just won't stop.'

Paul sat up, his profile sharp against the sun. 'Have you considered . . . could there be another woman?'

'Of course not!' I was shocked.

'You're still very naive, still very idealistic, particularly about love.'

I sat up and looked far out to sea. 'I know there are always temptations. But couples who really love each other don't succumb to them.'

'You would know, of course.' His voice was amused. I watched a wavelet curl upon the shore, leaving a rim of white froth before it pulled away.

'There was an Israeli soldier once,' I said quietly. 'I came very close to loving him.' I hesitated. 'I think perhaps I did love him.'

Paul looked at me but said nothing.

'But I loved Joe more and there was no affair. So, you see, I do know about temptations. And I do know that Joe and I would never be unfaithful to each other.'

'Even so, you're not happy with him. For God's sake, remember you can always come home.'

I thought of the tight-lipped aunts – 'We knew this would happen' – and my parents, once shocked and embarrassed at the thought of our marrying, upset and bewildered at the thought our divorcing. And me – broke, disillusioned, guilty, struggling with two kids, and still in love with Joe.

Paul began to tell me about the new domestic purposes benefit for single mothers.

'Oh, shut up! I'd never leave Joe. Let's go and get a hokey pokey ice cream.'

I had been away four years. There were newer, faster cars on the roads. People were now eating yoghurt and muesli for breakfast and my sisters spoke of kiwifruit and tamarillos when they meant Chinese gooseberries and tree tomatoes. There were still the same social issues – Vietnam, the environment and so on – but they didn't seem very important to me now when I put them alongside Chief Justice Kiwanuka's murder, fatherless Nsubuga or the death of Musoke. I was impatient when I heard customers in supermarkets fussing over brands and prices of soap powder.

'In Uganda you have no choice. If you're lucky enough to see soap you grab it,' I said to whoever was shopping with me, but no one seemed particularly interested. I sometimes felt as if I had come in from another planet.

For the rest of the holidays we swam, shopped, reminisced and ate gallons of ice cream and strawberries on the back lawn. The days flew by in happy succession and my holiday soon drew to an end. I was ready to go, for I was missing Joe and Joseph terribly, but nonetheless it was a tearful farewell that took place at Wellington Airport.

I got back to Uganda with a few days to spare before school resumed. Joseph, now nine months old, had grown two new teeth in my absence. I showered him with kisses, toys and lots of love to alleviate the guilt I felt at having left him behind. I was deeply grateful to Abby who I knew had cared for him well beyond the call of duty. The presents I brought back for her could never repay the debt I owed her.

'It's good to have you back,' said Joe, his arm creeping around my waist. 'I missed you.'

'Poor Joe,' I said, but I was glad.

Chapter 26

Eva and Joan arrived back in Uganda from their holidays shortly after I did. We sat at Lutembe Beach discussing our Christmases while the sunlight poured down on the endless green vegetation and the vast silver-blue lake.

'I nearly didn't come back,' said Eva through her date loaf. 'Switzerland seemed so orderly and sensible.'

'But wouldn't you miss all this?' I looked around the peaceful bay.

'Not really. What's a view if there's no water in your bathroom tap and no milk for your children.'

'Back home I wore hot-pants and went roller-skating,' said Joan wistfully. 'My workmates in the salon say there's always a job for me.'

'God, don't all leave me!' I said in mock alarm. 'Don't you like it here at all? The people, your relatives, the country?'

They shook their heads and began a litany of Uganda's faults. When I leapt to the country's defence, Eva became cross.

'Just listen to you! You go round speaking their language and allowing your kids to speak it and you even let them eat God knows what with Abby in the servants' quarters. They could pick up horrible germs. You forget that you're a New Zealander.'

'I've never forgotten that. Nor have I forgotten that my children are half African.'

'They can't be half anything. They're either one or the other.' When Eva got a bee in her bonnet it was best to ignore her. I asked Joan about the American reaction to the Cambodian bombings.

'I dunno. I never asked.' She helped herself to date loaf. 'They have this dreamy caramel-flavoured lipstick back home. There's a nail polish to match although it's not caramel-flavoured or people'd be tempted to bite it. Cambodia, did you say? I thought we were bombing Vietnam.' The baby-blue eyes looked puzzled.

We are all so different, I thought. Would we have been friends under other circumstances?

Amin went on air to condemn women. He was having domestic problems with his three senior wives and he now lashed out at women in general, implying that they were all prostitutes at heart. With immediate effect women were banned from wearing trousers, wigs, mini-skirts, shorts, maxi-skirts with slits, cosmetics and rubber jandals.

'Rubber jandals! Since when have jandals been a symbol of licentiousness?'

'Maybe it's to discourage foot fetishism,' said Joe.

Official enforcers of the clothing edict were sent out on the streets with tape measures. Girls whose skirts were more than an inch above mid-knee were to be arrested. The enforcers found problems. Girls obediently lowered their hems but, by rolling their skirts over at the waistband, they could still hike them up to a fashionable length later. The enforcers also found that fat girls hindered their work because their knees were hard to find.

Mrs Ssali appeared more put out than anyone else in Kampala over the banning announcement. She owned at least half a dozen wigs and, to my knowledge, had never been seen without one. Her ready laugh became a thing of the past.

'Where is the justice?' she asked glumly as she sat at my desk, a picture of abject misery in a demure skirt and hair that was tufted and singed where she had tried to straighten it with a hot comb. Miss Mubiru suggested she try a scarf. Mrs Ssali brightened immediately and went on a shopping spree. Thereafter she arrived in scarves which, as she began to experiment, rose like towers or spread like mushrooms. Mrs Ssali began to smile again.

Amin smiled a lot in those days too. He was well pleased with himself. He had set up a Save Britain Fund to help Britain through her economic doldrums. He had experienced the excitement of being at the front in the Yom Kippur War. He had publicly supported Scottish nationalists, Welsh separatists and black American extremists. As Big Daddy of the world it was now time for his reward. He had already promoted himself to general and he now awarded himself the VC, the DSO and the MC, all of which had to follow his name. Beaming happily, he appeared on television to reassure people that his good works would continue, for a Ghanaian spiritualist – known around Kampala as a charlatan – had prophesied that he, Amin, was to rule Uganda for the next twenty years. The spiritualist became a favourite in the Amin entourage until one day, in a sudden change of mood, Amin had him deported on the grounds that he was a CIA spy.

The military regime moved into its fourth year. In early March, as Amin's Foreign Minister Odongo was dropping his children off at school, he was dragged from his car and rammed, shouting for help, into the boot of a State Research vehicle. His abduction was witnessed by his own terrified children, by passers-by on their way to work and by at least one foreign diplomat, but nothing could be done to save him. His body, almost unrecognisably mutilated, was found six days later in the Nile.

Odongo was a Christian Lugbara and his murder was seen to be the beginning of a new purge against that tribe and Christians. Tension within the army grew. It came to a head on 23 March in a revolt led by Chief of Staff, Brigadier Arube, a Christian. There was a six-hour tank battle in Kampala, but the attempted coup was unsuccessful and Arube, along with many supporters, was killed. Amin came to the mortuary where, in front of the staff, he chastised Arube's corpse for half an hour.

The Odongo murder and the Arube uprising unleashed another wave of terror. Personnel from the three special units – the Makindye Military Prison, the Public Safety Unit and the State Research Bureau – swept across the country in a merciless drag-net, taking their victims from all walks of life and disposing of the bodies in pits, swamps and lakes. Villagers, fearful of reprisals, dared not raise their voices.

Expatriates on the whole found the accounts of the slaughters difficult to believe.

'Thousands and thousands have died,' I insisted to a disbelieving Briton at an afternoon tea in Kololo. 'You don't know about the atrocities because you don't mix with the local people. Corpses are found in pits and rivers and forests and mass graves in the forests. The victims are known only to their relatives who dare not complain to the authorities.'

'Hearsay, dear lady,' boomed the man. 'Hearsay.'

'That's what you British said when Hitler was annihilating the Jews.'

No one spoke and the all-expatriate gathering looked a little uncomfortable. The hostess rushed into the silence with tennis cake and comments on the weather. She never invited me to her house again.

Joe bought a Range Rover off a departing American and we went on safari to Kabalega National Park, where we stayed at the visitors' lodge.

Joseph had his first birthday and, as food was scarce, we celebrated it with the lodge's usual menu of stringy chicken and rice, followed by bread without butter and tea without milk. But we didn't mind because everything else was so lovely.

Our days were spent exploring the countryside, marvelling at the animals – giraffes, elephants and lions – and revelling in the unspoilt beauty. In the evenings we sat outside the lodge with the children listening to the distant night calls of the animals and watching the sinking sun set fire to the western sky. We learned to identify wildebeest, kob, impala and the little dikdik, and we laughed at the antics of the monkeys.

'There's simply no place on earth to compare with this,' I said one day as we surveyed the savannah that stretched unbounded to the four horizons.

'I'm glad you share my love for this country,' said Joe, coming to stand beside me. 'How awful it is to see it suffer so. Even out here they come and slaughter the animals. I wonder if Uganda will ever fully recover.'

'It will, but it will need good nursing. Lots of love. Lots of patience.'

'I love you, Heather.' He pulled me against him and kissed me deeply on the lips. The unexpected passion was straight from our student days and for a few minutes there was only Joe and me and the empty savannah around us. The two children tumbled about at our feet, forgotten. I pulled away and, feeling rather shy, said, 'Jozefu, I'm having another baby. I'm three months gone.'

A smile lit up his face and he took me in his arms again.

On our last day we took a boat ride up the Nile to Murchison Falls. We passed crocodile, water buffalo and families of hippopotami. Joseph, in a sunhat and nappies, sat on my knee, babbling in delight. Egrets, herons and stilt birds fossicked in the shallows and high above in the treetops I could see fish eagles and cormorants.

It was a long trip back to Kampala, and the children slept for most of it. I lay my head on Joe's shoulder, reflecting that the few days I had spent at Kabalega with him and the children were the most perfect of my life.

We arrived home to the news that Amin had divorced his three senior wives, Malyamu, Kay and Nora. They had been banished after challenging Amin over his favouritism towards his new young wife, Medina. A few days later Amin had Malyamu arrested and thrown into prison on trumped-up smuggling charges.

The day Malyamu was arrested was also the day I began to haemorrhage and Joe had to take me into hospital where I subsequently miscarried.

'You've lost a lot of blood,' said Dr Dublin at my bedside. 'You'll need to take it easy for a while.'

I was still weak and miserable the next day when Joe turned up at the hospital to announce that he had quarrelled with the company hierarchy and had left his job. 'We'll have to vacate the Luzira house immediately since we're renting it from the company,' he said.

I asked him about the quarrel, but he hedged and made excuses to hurry away. I left the hospital a day later, still disconsolate over the loss of my baby. I hardly saw Joe who, although jobless, was as busy as ever. I was looked after by Abby and Ernest, and grieved alone into my pillow.

186

The next evening Joe told me he had bought a house in Lubowa and that we were to move there in the next few days. 'How could you buy a house without showing me first?' I said, shocked and hurt at his peremptoriness. 'What if I don't like it?'

Joe, impatient, refused to be drawn and dashed away the following morning to attend to his spare parts business. Although I was still weak I was once again left to cope with the packing. I never saw the house until the day we moved in with our belongings. Depressed and exhausted, I was prepared to hate it on sight.

Lubowa was situated in gently rolling hills some seven miles from Kampala. I guided the Mercedes along the narrow rural road that wound through a tea plantation and thick natural bush. Ahead of me Joe and the suitcases bounced in the Range Rover. The road turned suddenly, unexpectedly into Lubowa – a small cluster of bungalows almost buried beneath a profusion of beautiful trees, hedgerows and wild climbing flowers.

'Right in the middle of nowhere,' I said in surprise. In the back seat Abby and the children stared out the windows. I followed Joe's right-hand turn into a narrow shingled lane bordered by hedges and brilliant masses of scarlet bougainvillea. In front of me Joe slowed and stuck his head out the window.

'Ours is the last house on this road,' he shouted. I nodded and as we proceeded I looked about me with rising spirits. Unlike the staid perfection of the Luzira settlement, Lubowa seemed rustic and untamed, its tangled creepers and brilliant flowers growing in exuberant disarray. We drove through gates at the end of the road, down a tree-canopied drive and on to our newly purchased property.

It was large and gently sloping, with a house situated a third of the way down. The lawn was overgrown, as were the flowerbeds and the purple and red bougainvillea that trailed the fence and wrapped around the eaves of the garage and the servants' quarters at the end of the drive. There were avocado trees, pawpaw and hibiscus and several grand old trees with spreading branches, all standing knee-deep in the grass. The house itself was large and low, sprawling contentedly amid the unruly growth. Blue and pink flowers climbed to the windowsills and the sound of cicadas filled the air.

The reddish tiled roof looked good and strong; the stout cream walls glowed softly in the sun. It was empty and waiting. It cried out for a family.

And it's ours!

'Welcome home,' said Joe.

We settled in quickly. It was a rambling old house, completely different from the immaculate home at Luzira, with wide halls, spacious rooms and a big fireplace in the living room. The kitchen had scrubbed wooden benches and a huge old-fashioned pantry.

We discovered a creeper-covered children's playhouse at the bottom of the shamba, pulled down the growth and gave it a coat of paint. Kerasese's task of bringing some order to the garden seemed gargantuan and he muttered and moaned as he slashed at the bush and ripped out the weeds. Gradually he began to gain the upper hand but not before he had mangled several blind-worms with the hand mower and cut open his leg with a slasher.

Joe now had an office in town with a go-down, or cellar, which he shared with a colleague. Besides importing spare parts for a variety of vehicles, he was also involved in buying and selling cars, and retailing a variety of motor accessories. He had contacts in England, Germany and Japan. As shortages increased, he began to import sidelines such as sugar, tinned goods and agricultural tools. His business prospered.

I got to know some of the neighbours, pleasant, friendly people from a variety of ethnic backgrounds – Ugandan, Kenyan, British, Italian, Dutch, Somali. Most had young families and Tanya and Joseph began to make friends. There was a government cattle research farm some way beyond the settlement, and in the evenings Abby and the children and I, carrying buckets, took the track through the bushes to the milking sheds where, on most occasions, we could buy milk. I was never quite sure if it was being sold to us illegally and I didn't ask. The milking was done by Rwandese youths who, Kerasese told me, were full of intestinal worms. Worms or not, I was grateful for this secret supply since milk was no longer available in Kampala.

Around the corner from us lived the Kalule family. Stanley Kalule had been a schoolmate of Joe's and now he and one or two other Lubowa men began to join up with Joe and Byron for drinks after work. Stanley's wife, Rosina, was a serene soul with a happy lift to her mouth as if she were permanently about to smile. Joe told me that her placid disposition came from the waragi bottle, but I found this difficult to believe.

Nakalo, Mary and Ted's daughter, came to live with us shortly after we moved in, as Mary was having trouble managing all the children on her own. Nakalo, at five, was two years older than Tanya and she came to school with me each day, quickly picking up English and other skills. Joseph was now running about the house, a stocky, easy-going toddler. Nakalo and Tanya used to take him to the playhouse where they dressed him in strange fashions and wheeled him about in the pushchair. Sometimes the Rwandese children from the cattle station joined them and their laughter and chatter drifted in through the windows as I prepared my school work in the afternoons. Eva, when she visited, clucked disapprovingly since they spoke Luganda all the time, reverting to English only when my European friends came.

'They behave like village children,' she said crossly as she brushed the red dirt off Andrea's hand-smocked dress.

Early in August, Kay became the second of Amin's former wives to be arrested.

'It was claimed that she had a gun in her possession,' said Miss Mubiru at school. 'Trumped-up charge, I'd say.'

'They say she's been living a whirlwind social life since Amin divorced her,' said Mrs Ssali. 'Maybe he didn't like that.'

Whatever her foibles, Kay Amin did not deserve the fate that awaited her. Some weeks after her release from prison her body was found, its arms and legs completely severed from the torso, in a bloody sack in the boot of a civilian's car. The news hit Kampala like a bomb. What made the event even more sensational was that the owner of the car, a well-known doctor, and his wife and children were found in their house dying from massive overdoses of sleeping pills. All over Kampala, in offices, on the streets, in cars, in beds, the topic of conversation was the same – Kay Amin. Spiritualists and traditional soothsayers offered explanations for the gruesome death. The city hummed with speculation and the horror was relived again and again.

It was a grisly business and one that was never to be resolved. It was, however, universally believed that Amin, like some latterday Bluebeard, was involved in Kay's death. And he, never one to miss an opportunity to pontificate, took Kay's children to the mortuary to view the awful remains of their mother.

'This,' he shouted at the terrified children, 'is what happens to bad women!'

Chapter 27

'I love Lubowa,' I once told Clarice. 'It fits me like a comfortable old sweater.' But I could never really explain what I meant. It had something to do with the peace that slowly descended on me as I drove back along the winding rural road after a busy day at work. It had something to do with the joy I felt as I turned the last bend and caught sight of our house nestling in the bushy wilderness.

With enthusiasm I weeded the flowerbeds and whitewashed the trellis, and Kerasese dug up a plot for a vegetable garden. We planted maize and cabbages, tomatoes and beans. I bought a deep freezer from a departing European family and within months I was freezing vegetables from the garden. Kerasese made a bird table for Tanya which they erected under the trees. They placed scraps of food on it and he taught her the names of the birds that came to feed. I began to collect local art – we hung pictures on the walls, bought pottery and carvings for the mantelpieces.

'Everything we like seems to suit this house,' I said to Joe. 'It was truly meant for us.'

Joe sometimes had to go to Kenya on business trips and each time he went through an elaborate procedure to obtain air tickets and an exit visa.

'As long as you and the kids remain behind they're willing to let me go,' he explained. 'You're a sort of human bail.'

I hated these absences, but at least he was able to bring back unavailable foods such as sugar and cheese as well as equipment for my school, and clothes, lightbulbs and batteries. But it was flour that we valued most. It was rarely available now in Uganda and therefore there was no bread. We hoarded our supplies until there was enough for Ernest or Abby to make batches of bread which we then stored in the freezer.

I sometimes tried my hand at baking but my attempts were always unsuccessful – things didn't rise or they burned and Ernest's spotless kitchen got into a mess. I noticed that whenever I decided to bake Ernest went out and got drunk. Once, as I was about to throw out my burnt offerings, Kerasese intervened and said he would sell them at a Luo settlement nearby.

'But why should they want my baking?' I asked in amazement.

'Jaluos eat anything,' he said contemptuously.

'I wonder how he does it,' I said to Ernest when Kerasese returned jingling the money in his pockets.

'Huh!' grunted Ernest, 'that one could sell his own grand-mother.'

In the tranquillity of Lubowa I slowly began to accept things I once could not accept. I no longer quarrelled with Joe when he came in late. I came to terms with the fact that his participation in our family life would always be minimal, and on his terms. Only occasionally a small voice within me asked if I were not compromising my life away but I ignored it and our home remained a contented, happy one. It was hardly surprising that, in this peaceful climate, I found myself pregnant again.

Joan's husband William was sent to Britain at his firm's expense on a short management course. A few days after he left Joan rang me in great agitation and asked me to come over immediately. On my arrival she told me that she had been warned by one of William's colleagues that State Research men had turned up at work looking for William. The colleague had made discreet enquiries and found that William was on the death list for drinking with 'subversives'.

'We don't know any subversives! I don't even know what it means!'

William had somehow been warned not to return and Joan was advised to leave Uganda as soon as she could. 'You've got to help me. Our embassy's closed down and I'm really scared.'

I was uneasy. It was a potentially dangerous situation, as Joan could be used as bait to force William to return. We drove straight to town and organised an air ticket for Kenya the following day. As an American, she did not have to go through the rigmarole of applying for an exit visa. On the way back to her house I told her what to do.

'Don't tell anyone you're leaving. You're just going to have to walk out. Don't go giving away all your belongings or people will know you're leaving. Your relatives can come and collect all your stuff when you've gone. Only take one suitcase or it will be obvious to airport security you're going for good and they might ask questions.'

I agreed to take her to Entebbe the next day but I was nervous about it and didn't sleep well. In the morning I toyed with the idea of asking an American expatriate to take her but the only one I knew was upcountry. When I arrived at her house in the afternoon she was barely articulate, fretting about food in the fridge and what to do with the keys. Without listening to a word she said I picked up her suitcase and took it out to the car. She followed me out, locked the door and got into the car. The next door's housegirl stared at us as she hung out the washing. As we picked up speed on the Entebbe Road I began to relax.

'Lord, I'll miss you, Joan.'

'And I'll miss you, too. I wish I'd said goodbye to Eva and Clarice. Say goodbye to them for me, won't you? We had some good times, didn't we?'

'Yep, we sure did.'

'Everything happened so quickly . . .' Her voice faded. 'I still don't understand . . .'

'Who does, Joanie? It's a mad country.' I looked sideways at the tense, miserable face beside me and wondered why this harmless little hairdresser from Pittsburgh should be fleeing from Amin's murder machine.

At the airport the usual army security lounged about, armed

to the teeth, gossiping together, eyes flicking about for distraction. We waited almost wordlessly until Joan's East African Airways flight was announced.

'You're okay now.' I felt relief flooding over me. 'Off you go now. Goodbye. Good luck. Write.' I watched her disappear after the other passengers and then I turned to go.

'You, Muzungu! Stop!' A soldier with the feared temple tattoos strolled towards me. My heart somersaulted.

'Why are you here?'

'I've seen off a friend.'

'Where's she going?'

'America.'

'Hah! She must be rich! You have a watch?'

I wasn't wearing one and I felt helpless. Two airline personnel walked by and I wondered if I should call for assistance.

'You got Americani dollars?'

'No.'

'Sigara?'

'Hapana.'

He grimaced. The gap in his front teeth made him look monstrous. 'See!' he called in Swahili to a group of his friends. 'A poor Muzungu! Why do they come to this country? We only want the rich ones.' He slouched off, disgruntled, while the others stared at me with contempt. Shaking with relief, I left the airport.

Life became fraught with problems for urban Ugandans. Petrol was scarce. Roads were no longer maintained. Buses and public transport could barely function. People queued for hours for scarce commodities. The water pumps at the main reservoir had long since broken down, one by one, and most domestic water supplies were either cut off or rationed. At Lubowa water was rationed, trickling through the taps for only two hours a day. We had to fill every available container to tide us over to the following day.

Television transmission had become abysmal and subject to frequent breakdowns. Programmes were almost exclusively interminably repeated footage of Amin and the army, Amin and visiting dignitaries, Amin and his speeches, Amin and the Moslem Supreme Council. Many of the old newsreaders and personalities were gone – either dead, exiled or sacked – and their replacements were often untrained, incompetent and sloppily dressed. There were also chronic telephone breakdowns, constant power failures, sudden government directives over the radio – 'Anyone found hoarding cooking oil or salt will be shot', 'Everyone is to pray for the army' – and shortages of medical and educational equipment.

Institutions suffered badly. Many teachers, lecturers and professors had fled or been killed and schools, teachers' colleges and the university were chronically short-staffed. Similarly, technicians, pharmacists, doctors and nursing staff kept vanishing from hospitals.

Mulago Hospital, the biggest in Uganda, had immense problems with lack of water, equipment, food, funds and, of course, staff. Attached to the medical school of Makerere University, it was the finest hospital in black Africa, attracting doctors and scientists from all over the world. It had enjoyed an international reputation based on its research into tropical diseases, its training facilities for doctors and nurses, and its good, free medical services. But now, four years into the Amin regime, with its professional staff severely depleted, it was in dire straits. The floors, often unwashed because of lack of water, were soiled with blood and grime; the laundry, sterilisation and kitchen services were plagued with water shortages; and the army tramped in at any time of day or night, pushing aside waiting patients and demanding immediate attention. If an army patient died, the doctor treating him would, quite literally, have to flee for his or her life.

Kampala, city of crisp white buildings and rolling green hills, now sustained a life that was, at best, merely tolerable. Daily, the endless search for commodities continued. People queued for services, thumped reluctant telephones, were bullied by soldiers, or tripped in the growing numbers of potholes – and always, everywhere, cruised the dreaded State Research in their shining cars of death.

At home in Lubowa, far from the troubles of Kampala, I watched with satisfaction as my maize grew straight and tall.

Joe finalised plans for a huge consignment of car tyres to be railed into Uganda. We were both excited as it was the culmination of half a year's hard work.

'They'll go like hotcakes,' he said.

The go-down beneath his office was emptied to make room for the tyres, and trucks were hired to transport the load from the railway station.

'I feel uneasy about it,' I said over breakfast on the morning that the consignment was due.

'Why? Nothing can go wrong.'

But we both knew it could. And it did. As the last truckload of tyres was leaving the station a group of army officers surrounded Joe and led him away. The entire consignment was confiscated. At lunchtime a colleague of Joe's rang to give me the news.

'We're pulling strings for him. Please pray.'

We should have left Uganda years ago!

The children and Abby stood about me, sensing trouble.

'Mama, kibadde ki?' Nakalo patted my arm.

'There is kolele, Mummy?' said Abby uneasily.

I told her what had happened. She gasped, gathered the children and bustled them away. I moved over to the window and stared out at the garden.

Death has followed us even out here.

I tried to think who could help us. Pig Face, our Makindye saviour, had been transferred to Mbarara for three months and I knew the British High Commission would not intervene on Joe's behalf. I sank on to the arm of a chair wondering if this were, finally, the end for Joe and me.

There was a roar followed by a screech of brakes as Byron, Henry and Stanley Kalule arrived in Stanley's car. Having bribed an officer to work on Joe's release, they had come to keep me company. Rosina Kalule, having seen the men drive past her house, came over full of curiosity and needed brandy when she heard what had happened. We waited until evening for the phone to ring with news of Joe, but it remained silent. Abby fed and bathed the children and at six o'clock Rosina floated home with several double brandies under her belt. The rest of us settled down for a long wait. I reflected that I spent a good part of my life waiting for Joe.

At seven, I tucked the children into bed and wondered if they were now fatherless. There was a lump in my throat as I switched off the light.

At eleven o'clock we began to give up hope. I hovered on the verge of hysterical tears.

He'll never even see the new baby.

The phone shrilled into the silence. Henry leapt to answer it. It was their contact. Joe had been released and was on his way home. He arrived twenty minutes later, shaken and subdued. I clung to him with relief. He told us the price for his freedom was the consignment of tyres.

Nineteen seventy-four was drawing to a close. Amin had replaced the dead Chief of Staff, Brigadier Arube, with Mustafa Adrisi, a Moslem who had been a sergeant for most of his army career. I had once seen the face of a cretinous child in one of Dad's medical books. Adrisi had such a face. The vacant adenoidal expression was now to be seen in newspapers or on television, leering moronically at Amin's side.

Amin and Adrisi, twin souls, collaborated on many schemes, particularly bans. They banned certain radio programmes. They banned nudity among the freewheeling Karamajong. They banned a host of foreign books and foreign personnel, including David Martin, a journalist whom Amin intimated he would eat for dinner if he came to Uganda. They banned Henry's soccer club, Express – now nicknamed the 'Club of the Dead' because so many of its members and supporters had been murdered. They even tried to ban the word Israel from all written and spoken communication, and had to be dissuaded from rewriting the Bible.

Then a ban was announced on all Christian denominations other than the enormous Roman Catholic and Church of Uganda (Anglican) congregations. Even these were not safe from Amin, and priests and bishops were urged to flee for their lives, but most stayed on in Uganda to be harassed, bullied and some-times killed.

Hard on the heels of all the bannings, Amin dismissed his very able, very beautiful Minister of Foreign Affairs, Elizabeth Bagaya.

A lawyer and a member of the Toro royal family, she was rumoured to have consistently resisted Amin's advances. Infuriated, Amin publicly sacked and arrested her. He then went on television to announce that she had disgraced Uganda by having sex with a stranger in an airport toilet in Paris on her way back from a United Nations meeting. No one, of course, believed him, and the country was relieved when Bagaya later escaped to Kenya.

Just after the Bagaya affair Joe went on a two-day business trip to Kenya. I was almost four months pregnant by this time and looking forward to another baby. On the afternoon of Joe's intended return, a little tired from a busy morning at school, I kicked off my shoes and curled up on the couch with a Hemingway novel. Joseph was sleeping in the next room and outside Nakalo and Tanya were playing schools with assorted dolls under the trees.

Rosina Kalule, in search of a drink, came in through the double doors to wreck my life.

Chapter 28

They say misery loves company. Perhaps that is why Rosina told
me. Or perhaps she had a malicious streak within her, well
hidden beneath her guileless face. Whatever the reason, I lay
there on that late November afternoon listening to her catalogue
the behaviour of Joe, Byron and Kalule and their respective girlfriends. She presented me with the dates and times of their
liaisons. She described the deceit and lies involved. She sipped
her drink, sighed, shook her head a lot and said, 'Kino kitalo.'

Some part of me, deep down beneath the shock, knew
instantly, unequivocally, that all she said was true. 'This is
unbelievable,' I whispered as I felt my world sliding away.
Hemingway crashed to the floor.

Rosina divulged her informant – her niece who was at university with the three girlfriends. The niece had felt duty-bound to
tell her aunt. Rosina gave me the location of their trysts and
again the dates and times. Even as my brain spiralled downwards
it snatched at the details, matched the times and dates with Joe's
absences and excuses. There were signposts, there were warnings
but I hadn't seen them.

He's betrayed me! He's betrayed the children!

Anger, panic and bitter, bitter hurt crashed through me.

'Ah well, that is life,' Rosina was saying, 'although sometimes
it is better to be mwebafu.'

Mwebafu! Ten minutes ago I was *mwebafu* and utterly content.

Rosina's mouth kept moving, talking, killing me, always with that not-quite-smile at its corners. I hardly heard her.

How could he! He's always loved me. What was wrong with me that he had to creep off with someone else?

I turned to Rosina in agony. 'Here I am with a baby inside me! What can I do? I can't fight back.'

Oh Joe, how could you?

I thought of the times he had said he was working late, the perfume he brought back from Nairobi that he said was for his aunt, the female caller who had rung several times for him.

'What's the name of Joe's bitch?'

Rosina told me her name was Gloria and that she came from Toro.

'The whore! She's wrecked it all – my home, my family, my happiness, all of this around me, the trees and birds, my vegetable garden!' The tears fell fast and furiously. Rosina offered me a handkerchief. I looked into her calm face. 'And look at you! How can you sit there so unconcerned while Kalule's screwing around?'

She told me that she was used to it and I called her apathetic. 'I think I'll go,' she said and left, a vision of tranquillity.

The pain and injustice of it all bore down on me, making me cry with new intensity.

I'm only twenty-seven. I'm not fat or toothless or bald or smelly. I tried the best way I knew how. What did I do wrong?

There was no bottom to my grief, no bounds to my despair. The lynchpin of my carefully built-up life had been savagely ripped out and everything I believed in had hurtled down and smashed.

I can never trust anyone again.

Afterwards I was never sure how I got through that afternoon. I cried and cried until I was sick in the toilet. Abby wisely took the children away to fetch milk while I lay on my bed weeping.

My bed and my bedspread. I bought them for us when I was mwebafu!

Towards evening I heard Abby feeding and bathing the children and later putting them to bed. I heard her switch off the lights and go off duty. Nakalo and Tanya cried for me from their beds, aware that something was wrong.

200

I heaved myself off the bed. I felt hot and feverish from crying and I wondered if I would lose the baby. Abby had left water in a jug in the bathroom. Splashing my face, I looked in the mirror. A gargoyle with swollen blotchy features stared back at me through eyelids puffed up from continuous weeping.

You bitch, Gloria!

The children's voices were urgent. I could tell they were frightened by my absence. I hurried to calm them.

'You've been crying, Mummy,' said Tanya accusingly.

I nodded.

'Why did you cry, Mama?' asked Nakalo.

When I told them I was upset about something, Tanya said that Daddy would look after me when he got home. It almost set me off again.

I kissed them goodnight and went out. I washed, slipped on a nightgown and crawled into bed. I lay there, jealousy twisting in me like a knife. Was she beautiful? Did he whisper words of endearment to her as he loved her? Did they, in their sweetest moment of union, declare undying love for each other? And what if – I sat bolt upright – what if Gloria had a baby?

Joe arrived home from Nairobi at ten o'clock bearing a very heavy suitcase.

More perfume for Gloria?

He switched on the light and dropped the case on the floor, greeting me jovially and saying he was dying of thirst. He loosened his tie, took off his jacket and shoes and padded out to the kitchen for a beer.

My heart pounded with unexploded rage. I sat up, grabbed his jacket and rifled the pockets, ready to break any bottle of perfume I found. There was no perfume, but my fingers closed over a sheet of paper. It was the hotel receipt. And there it was in black and white. Meals for two, drinks for two, a room for two. The room was booked in both their names. For a second I could scarcely catch my breath. She had gone to Nairobi with him!

I leapt out of bed, screaming. I opened the suitcase and began flinging the contents around the room. Bags of flour and sugar hit the walls, bursting open and spilling all over the floor. Soap, butter, bacon and cheese – things we hadn't seen for months – struck the walls and ceiling like misguided missiles.

Joe rushed in, a bottle of beer clutched in his hand.

'You rooting, fucking pig!' A packet of biscuits hit him in the mouth. I hurled clothes, bath towels and tins of jam at him, and finally the empty suitcase.

'How could you? How could you?' Sobbing, I told him all I knew. 'You even took that bitch Gloria to Nairobi with you!'

He stood, shocked, motionless in the doorway. I thought I had seen Joe in every conceivable mood, but now an entirely new emotion superimposed itself on the still face. Guilt. There was a certain ugliness about it.

'It's not true,' he whispered.

'Even now you lie! I'll never believe you again.'

Joe put down his bottle and came towards me, straining to control his shock, trying to sound rational. 'Look, Heather. It's all simply untrue.'

'It's here in black and white!' I screamed, flinging the hotel account at him. He explained that it was a clerk's error, probably a mixing of two bills.

'Bullshit, Joe! Your names are on it. I'm not stupid.' The ease with which he lied took my breath away.

Tanya wandered sleepily into the shambles, blinking and looking bewildered.

'You've upset the baby,' said Joe, relieved at the distraction.

'*I've* upset her? That's good coming from you. You've wrecked her life, mine and Joseph's. And the new baby's.' I dissolved into tears. 'You didn't consider your unborn child when you fucked Gloria, did you!'

Tanya, wailing, tramped through the flour to reach me. I gathered her up and sat her on the chest of drawers out of harm's way.

Joe, rapidly returning to normal, announced I was hysterical and he would not stay in the house a minute longer.

'Off you go then, off to Gloria's bed!'

His hand came up and caught me across the face. I spun around, cradling my cheek. He picked up a tin of jam and flung it with all his might across the room. It hit the windows and the glass exploded in a crystal shower, hovering in slow motion for a second before tinkling to the floor. The curtain billowed in the sudden wind and I noticed with some surprise that it was raining.

The rain hissed in, spraying the floor and walls. Tanya stood up on the drawers, crying in fright. I told her to sit down.

'You've believed an entirely unsubstantiated story.' Joe put on his shoes and stood up to go, but I clung to his arm, gasping and furious, determined that he stay and suffer with me.

Behind the anger there's fear in his eyes. Oh, those eyes! Do they soften for her as they once softened for me when he wanted me? And his lips – my lips – so fine and firm and sweet to kiss. Oh God, did he kiss her, gently opening her mouth as he used to mine? And these hands that now hit at me, did he caress her with them as he once did me?

'Oh God, Joe!' I screamed in pain. 'You've wrecked our lives.'

'The baby!' cried Joe in horror.

I turned in time to see Tanya, crying uncontrollably, her feet slippery with flour, teeter for a second on the chest of drawers before pitching forward head first. Her face struck the corner of a small wooden footstool with a sickening thud before she landed in a heap on the floor. She lay silent, spreadeagled, face down. We rushed to her.

I turned her over, her head rolling into my lap. A wound, a chasm, widening like a slowly yawning mouth, ran from her forehead through the eyebrow, almost into the eye. The edges twitched and jumped and I was sure I glimpsed bone before the wound filled up with thick red blood. Horrified, I pressed the bottom of my nightgown against it. Within seconds it was saturated with blood. Joe handed me a towel.

'She'll need tons of stitches,' I said shakily. 'We'll have to get her to hospital.'

Joe gently bent over Tanya and removed the towel. 'Oh God in heaven!' he whispered as the awful mouth-gash dribbled dark blood into her eye and down her cheek. He hastily replaced the towel. Rushing for Abby, he told me to meet him at the Range Rover with Tanya. Abby arrived in a minute or two, drenched and staring as she surveyed the room. She asked no questions but immediately took Tanya from me so I could dress.

'Bless you, Abby.' I struggled into jeans. 'Just wait with the children until we get back.' I wrapped Tanya in a rug, ran through the rain with her and within seconds we were speeding to the hospital.

For a while neither Joe nor I spoke. The only noise was the driving rain, the windscreen wipers and an occasional whimper from Tanya. The towel was heavy with blood. I could hardly find a dry portion to cover the wound.

'It's a hell of a cut!' I finally burst out. 'Gloria has a lot to answer for.'

'Don't be ridiculous.'

'Look at you sticking up for your whore!'

'I barely know her. That's the truth. She's a cousin of a friend of mine. Your informant should get the facts right.'

'My informant didn't write out that hotel bill.'

We turned right at the clock tower on the outskirts of town and took the road to the hospital. It was almost midnight when we drove up to the deserted casualty department, where we were admitted by a plump, pink-uniformed nurse who took one look at the wound and hurriedly went for the duty doctor. She turned out to be my obstetrician – the cheerful nun from Dublin.

'We're very short-staffed,' she told us. 'I'll need you to come in and hold the child.'

She led us into the surgery and I deposited Tanya on the bed. 'Oh my goodness, little girlie,' gasped Dr Dublin as she removed the towel. The nurse in pink washed the wound. It was gaping and hideous and I knew Tanya would bear the scar for life.

We did this to her, Joe and I.

I turned away guiltily.

'Hold her firmly while nurse shaves the eyebrow,' said the doctor. Tanya struggled and screamed as the razor carefully removed the eyebrow. On the other side of the table Joe, holding an arm and a leg, began to sway. I felt a pang of concern for him. The doctor, who was drawing anaesthetic into a syringe, sent him out with the pink nurse. The nurse's body undulated beneath her uniform and my concern evaporated instantly.

I, too, swayed as the long anaesthetising needle sank again and again into the wound. As the doctor began stitching and the gaping lips slowly came together, I began to relax. When the last stitch had been put in place I felt all my energy had drained from me. I leaned against the wall in tears.

'There, there,' said Dr Dublin, applying a dressing. 'It was only a few stitches, that's all.'

Oh, if only it were, doctor.

'You're looking pale. Are you taking your folic acid? You have to be careful. You've miscarried once this year.'

I would have died for him, I loved him so.

'Are you sure you're all right now, dearie?'

I nodded.

I'm too ashamed to tell you.

We rewrapped Tanya in the rug. She looked a different child and was almost smiling again. The stitched cut ran like a miniature railway track under the dressing.

'Oh, that's much better,' Joe said in vast relief when he saw her. As he took her from me his eyes held mine for a second, pleading. I turned from him, suddenly longing for him to take me in his arms and convince me it wasn't true, soothe away all the hurt and misery.

It was still pouring as we drove back to Lubowa. Lightning flashed across the sky.

I hope it hits her right between the legs.

The wipers swished lugubriously.

'I'm going to tell your mother,' I said, tight-lipped, unable to leave the situation alone. Joe said nothing.

Once home we put Tanya to bed and Abby went back to her quarters. Joe and I stood at Tanya's bed in the semi-darkness, staring down at her as she dropped off to sleep.

'If . . . if you would just tell me why, I'd try to understand.'

'There's nothing to tell. I've never been unfaithful to you.'

'We both know that's a lie.' I felt my heart break within me.

I left him at Tanya's bedside and went to my bedroom. I had forgotten about the shambles. The floor was awash with sugar, flour, broken glass and Tanya's blood. Joe's bottle of beer had been upturned in the fracas, spreading brown rivulets among the groceries. On the bed lay my nightgown, rumpled and blood-soaked. The rain hissed and spattered through the broken window and the wet curtain flapped like a giant moth. I picked my way over to the wardrobe and brought out an overnight bag. I packed a few things into it, then took the Mercedes keys from the dresser. Tears flowed.

This lovely room! Everything in it I bought with love.

I went outside into the cold, wet night. Bella and Mengo

bounded up to me joyfully, splattering me with their muddy paws. I was soaked before I reached the garage and the askaris sheltering inside stared at me in amazement. I drove away, hardly able to see through the tears and rain, reliving the terrible hurt and weeping over the steering wheel. I grieved for my shattered dreams and the end of blind innocence. I found myself driving through the wet streets of Kampala. The Apolo Hotel, now named the International, glowed high above the city. I turned the car towards the lights and spent what was left of the night in the hotel.

Chapter 29

The rain had stopped by morning and from my seventh floor room the city looked laundered and sparkling. I had to descend several floors – the only place where there was water in the taps – to use the bathroom. Returning to my room, I sat on my bed dejectedly, recalling the events of the night before. When I had arrived at the hotel the sleepy desk clerk had jerked into wakeful ness at the sight of me, wet, distraught, my clothes splotched with Tanya's blood. He had asked if I needed a doctor, and I felt sure he was discussing me with the curious night porter as I went up to my room.

I took clean clothes from my bag and slowly dressed. My stomach threatened to erupt with morning sickness. I felt guilty for leaving the children, especially Tanya, but I had had to get away from the house where my wrecked marriage lay scattered across the bedroom floor.

I went downstairs to the dining room, which was swarming with breakfasting security men. The hum of voices subsided at my entry, sleek black heads swivelling to watch me from behind large sunglasses. I felt I had walked into a roomful of giant flies. I sat down among them, too wretched to be afraid. My breakfast arrived but I couldn't eat. I sat staring forlornly at my scrambled eggs, which turned fuzzy through my welling tears.

I loved him so much. Why wasn't that enough for him?

207

I paid my bill and walked outside into the brilliant sunshine. Everything – the flawless blue of the sky, the lines of early morning traffic, the lilting cries of the mendazi sellers – seemed callously unaffected by my plight. I got into the Mercedes and drove to school. Life had to go on.

'You look pale,' said Mrs Ssali in concern. 'Are you feeling all right?'

I nodded, wondering if her husband screwed around like mine.

I tried to carry on as usual, dispensing my wisdom among the children in monosyllabic despair. 'If you mix blue and yellow you get green,' I advised a budding Goya at the paint table.

Such lack of self-control! Imagine if I'd taken up with every person that waggled an arse before my eyes.

'Wipe your brushes carefully. That's the way.'

If it was a one-night stand, a hurried, furtive, sordid indiscretion, maybe I could understand. But this is the real McCoy.

At lunchtime I drove back to Lubowa consumed with misery. I turned the corner into our road and my spirits lifted at the prospect of seeing the children. For the hundredth time since the day before tears filled my eyes. They were playing with toys on the living room floor when I entered. Looking up, they shrieked with joy and ran towards me. Their utter spontaneity, their complete absence of grudge at my deserting them, moved me deeply and I tried to embrace them all at once. We all squashed up together, laughing.

I looked at Tanya's face. The swelling extended across her nose and down one cheek. 'Goodness, what interesting colours. Every colour of the rainbow in that bruise.' I sat her on my knee. 'Is it very sore?'

'No. Where have you been?' It was normal curiosity.

'I stayed in a hotel because I was upset last night, but I got lonely and came home.'

'Why did you go?' asked Nakalo, her head on my shoulder.

'Were you cross with Daddy?' Tanya looked worried.

'Yes. You heard us. Can I have a peek at your stitches?'

'No. It'll hurt!' She slid off my knees, her hands clasped over the dressing and glared at me. She looked like her father. Joseph climbed onto my lap and smiled happily up at me. I felt my reserves break down.

'Oh I love you, Jo-jo,' I whispered, rubbing my face in his curls. Tears slid from my eyes and fell into his hair. Nakalo and Tanya put their arms about me protectively. We clung together, the children bewildered and uncertain. After a while I left them and went to my room. Abby was washing the floor on her hands and knees. Someone, Kerasese perhaps, had boarded up the broken window.

'Thanks for cleaning up the mess, Abby.'

She smiled, but there was concern in her eyes. 'Are you okay, Mummy? Would you like tea?'

'Not yet, thanks.'

This unassuming, uneducated woman has more dignity in her little finger than he has in his whole body.

I watched as Abby completed her work and gathered up the bucket and cloths. 'We're lucky to have you around,' I said.

When she had gone, I went over to the far window and wondered what Gloria looked like with her clothes off. How did it happen the first time with them? Was it as beautiful, as breathless, as it had been for us the first time in Joe's room above the harbour?

He told me then he would love me forever.

The memories wrenched at my insides. Restlessly I wandered over to the wardrobe. Almost without thinking I opened it and stared at the row of trousers and sports coats hanging there. And I began to go through the pockets.

I had never done this sort of thing before and, feeling guilty, I ferreted through business cards, old papers, and forgotten handkerchiefs, expecting at any moment to be struck by a bolt of lightning. There was a tattered receipt, six months old, for a meal for two at the Grand Hotel.

Rosina had mentioned the Grand as one of their meeting places. The other place she had mentioned was a Rubaga address, the house of a bachelor friend of Joe, Kalule and Byron.

I found several more Grand Hotel receipts, then a crumpled piece of paper with a local phone number on it and the name Gloria written beneath it, presumably in her handwriting – a bold scrawl. I stared down at it, mesmerised. Then, driven by anger and something close to fear, I went to the dining room and dialled the number. An elderly man claiming to be her father told me Gloria now lived in a certain university hall of residence. Impelled by anger, my words rushed out.

'Since you're her father perhaps you could tell her to keep away from other people's husbands. Mine in particular.' There was a shocked silence. I slammed down the phone, ashamed at upsetting what appeared to be a decent old man.

I then put a call through to Joe's hotel in Nairobi. The Asian receptionist confirmed beyond a doubt that Joe and his 'wife' had spent two nights there. I went to the toilet and was sick.

Joe arrived home for lunch, looking for trouble. 'How dare you leave the children the way you did! What sort of mother are you?' He stood, hands on hips, glaring at me.

'And what sort of father are you?'

He turned his back on me.

'I thought you were honourable. I buried my own life to support yours. And you betrayed me. I'm going to leave you. And take the kids.'

'You can go, but you won't take my children!'

'*Your* children! Who reads them stories? Who feeds and clothes them? Who tucks them up in bed at night? You do nothing for them except skite about them to your friends!'

'At least I didn't desert my daughter when she nearly lost an eye.'

'You and Gloria were as much to blame for that cut as if you'd taken a knife and carved her up yourself.'

Ernest came in to tell us lunch was ready. We sat at the table in silence, the children regarding us with apprehensive stares. I could eat nothing. I looked up at Joe's hard, stony face and was suddenly overcome with panic.

I still love you. I could never really leave you.

'What did I do wrong?' I whispered, choking on my tears.

'You listened to lies,' he retorted, pushing back his chair. Four pairs of eyes watched him get up. 'I don't want to eat. I'm going back to work.' Without a backward glance, he strode out of the room.

'No, don't go!' I cried, suddenly terrified at being alone with my misery, desperately wanting him to stay and console me. I ran outside after him. 'Please Joe, don't go!'

He had already started up the Range Rover when I caught up

with him. I leaned through the window crying, gasping, begging.

'Please, don't leave me! I'm sorry! Stay and talk. Please, Joe!' The car began to move and I hung on at the window. 'Don't go! Please don't leave me, please!' The Range Rover gathered speed and I fell to the ground, weeping.

Abby brought me back to the house and took me down to my bedroom. I lay on the bed exhausted as Abby pulled up the quilt and drew the curtains.

'You sleep now, Mummy. Don't worry about anything.' She went out, closing the door softly behind her. I curled up and slept a deep dreamless sleep.

It was four o'clock when I awoke, my eyes thick and burning from tears. I pulled back the curtains to expose the brilliant, sun-drenched garden. The sudden intensity of light hurt my eyes and I remembered longingly the soft grey skies of a Rangitikei spring. I let the curtain drop.

I wandered thoughtfully through the house, seeing everything as if for the first time. I loved it all – the solid white walls, the pictures, the wide halls, the lovely old fireplace. I loved the warm-toned hand-woven rugs on the floor and the strange little alcove in the dining room which I had filled with polished makonde carvings.

This is my home. She will not drive me from it!

The days passed in a vacuum of silent bitterness and Joe moved into the spare room. Devastated, drained, mired in misery, I simply existed, as useless, as directionless as a satellite without its planet. Tears came easily to my eyes and I wondered if the children would remember their mother as a woman who always cried. At times I tried to convince myself that I had made a colossal mistake about Joe's infidelity; at other times I tried to comfort myself with the thought that even if he had slept with Gloria, it was simply a biological activity and what the hell!, he always came home to me.

One day, nagged by doubt – or hope – I extracted the Rubaga bachelor's address from Rosina and drove there. The house was a neat little brick building set well back from the road among banana plantains. The houseboy opened at my knocking and told me that the owner was out.

211

I asked if he knew Joe.

'Yes.'

'Does he come here often?'

'From time to time.'

'Who does he come with?'

The houseboy looked uneasy, although he could not possibly have connected me with Joe. 'He comes with a . . . a lady.'

'What for?'

The houseboy moved from one foot to the other uncomfortably. I took a bank note from my wallet. 'The lady is from Toro. They stay here maybe an hour . . . maybe two. When they go they leave me with money to wash the sheets.'

I handed him the money and stumbled back to the car.

'I was such a fool to go there!' I raged to Eva and Clarice the next day. 'I only hurt myself more. I knew deep down that it was true.'

Their reactions were the opposite to what I expected. Eva, conservative, arch-defender of the nuclear family, told me that I should leave him at once. 'You should not have to put up with that,' she declared.

Clarice, strong, independent, scathing of all males, advised me to hang on. 'Don't give everything up because *he's* unfaithful. Why should *you* do penance?'

But I remained in a quandary. In spite of everything part of me wanted to stay with him, wanted to win back his love and try to recapture our happier times. But another part of me howled for vengeance. Angry and hurt beyond bearing, I wanted to punish him for his behaviour. But most of me felt helpless – trapped in a pregnancy that often made me sick.

'Pack up and leave him,' said Eva harshly. I looked at her with concern. There was a new tension about her and I knew things weren't going well in their household.

'We had everything going for us.' The tears that were never far away began to fall. 'Our beautiful kids, a pleasant lifestyle, our own businesses, a nice home, good friends. Why wasn't that enough?'

'They're all rooters at heart, girl,' said Clarice. 'Just accept that. Then give him another chance. I know Joe. You've always been special to him. This fling of his was just an ego-booster. Try again. But this time take off the rosy spectacles. Treat marriage as a battle of wits. It might turn out to be fun for both of you.' Her eyes sparkled and she reached over and grasped my shoulder. 'Try it.'

That night I waited for Joe to come in.

'I want to talk about us,' I said, breaking weeks of virtual silence. 'I'm willing to put all the shit of the last few weeks behind me if you're honest with me in the future. I . . . I only ever wanted one thing from marriage.'

'What's that?' His voice was subdued.

'A husband – one that I don't share with anyone else.'

'I never meant to hurt you. I love you. I love the kids.'

'What about Gloria?'

'Gloria, Gloria! She's just a name!'

'Not to me she isn't.'

He looked at me with heavy eyes, and then turned away. 'I've been to hell and back. You needn't worry about me any longer. I . . . I'm sorry about everything.'

It was the closest he ever came to admitting his liaison with Gloria. Communication resumed, we all moved back to our bedrooms and our marriage hung together by a thread.

Departure restrictions had relaxed so Joe took us to Mombasa for the Christmas break but I did not enjoy it as I had Kabalega. Gloria had changed everything. Women were now a threat. The coastal Swahili women swayed as they moved, smiling from exotic faces and I would glance at Joe as they passed to see if he were watching. Gloria was everywhere – strolling the beach with us, eating with us, in bed with us. She simply would not go away. I was relieved when we gathered up the children and boarded the plane for Uganda. I would no longer have to pretend to be enjoying myself.

As soon as we returned, I reported to Nsambya Hospital for my ante-natal check-up.

'You've put on very little weight,' said Dr Dublin. 'And you've become thin in the face and arms. Are you eating sensibly?'

I tried to eat more for the baby's sake, but it nauseated me and I often vomited.

'You're to blame for this, Gloria,' I said aloud one evening after I had lost my dinner down the toilet and, feeling angry and miserable, I telephoned her at her university residence. My heart thumped as she was called to the phone.

'Hello,' she said. I was amazed that her voice sounded quite pleasant. I began to shake.

'I understand you had an affair with my husband . . .' My voice rose as I poured out my spleen. Halfway through she hung up on me. I felt much better.

'You lost your dignity,' chided Eva when I told her.

'Who cares? I'll torment her as she has tormented me.'

And from then on, whenever I was down, determined that the cause of my suffering should suffer too, I telephoned her and told her what I thought of her. It never failed to lift my spirits.

As the weeks went by Dr Dublin continued to worry over my failure to gain weight. I was given extra medication, tests and exhorted to eat more.

'I really try to eat,' I said. 'But I so often seem to throw it up.'

'Are you fretting about something?' she asked.

'No,' I lied, knowing that the ghost of Gloria would always haunt me. Sagging with despair, I drove home in tears.

Moira was born in the early hours of an April morning, welcomed into the world by me, a midwife and a fat junior nurse. She was a small, frail baby and I cried until daybreak as I nursed the tiny scrap of humanity, worrying about her future when her mother and father's relationship was so precarious. I worried, too, that Joe would have easy access to Gloria now that I was out of the way.

'My baby seems weak,' I said to the ward sister later that week when Moira fell asleep at my breast. 'She's hardly able to suck. She just falls asleep.'

But she told me Moira was fine.

'I'm worried about this baby,' I said to Joe when he visited. 'She's so . . . so . . . listless.'

Joe, anxious to get to his office, told me I worried too much, kissed me and left. Even kind Dr Dublin, who chatted on my bed each night, did not understand my concern.

'A fine little girl,' she declared after checking her over. 'A bit small, a bit sleepy, but nothing to worry about.'

214

Back home I continued to worry. The baby drank very little and gained weight only slowly. She seemed perpetually tired and slept for hours on end. Even in the bath she seemed sleepy. Over the weeks she progressed reluctantly, never attaining the robust energetic ways of the other two.

'I wish Dad was here to check her over!'

'All babies are different,' said Joe. He took her from me and held her up gently, a tiny bird in his huge hands. Blinking at him she gave a charming little smile. Joe laughed. Moira trembled at the sudden sound, her head nodding as it often did.

You're small and weak and unco-ordinated because of us.

Chapter 30

Armed security men burst into Eva's house one night, accusing her of hoarding scarce commodities. Her husband Alex was out with friends in a bar. The men pushed Eva around, threatening to kill her, demanding the hoarded goods and ransacking the kitchen. Eva was terrified and Andrea woke up screaming. When they eventually found that she had nothing to hide, the men belted her across the bottom with a gun before leaving.

I viewed with shock the fiery purple-red welt across her buttocks.

'They took my radio when they left,' she said. 'I suppose I should be thankful they didn't take my life.'

Alex, shocked, promised to come home early every night thereafter. For two weeks he co-operated magnificently, after that mildly, and then not at all.

'What did you expect?' said Clarice caustically.

Gone were the days when Eva's house ran like clockwork.

By now the rest of the world knew that Amin was a murderous megalomaniac intent on creating a Moslem state in Uganda and that, under his reign of terror, twelve million Ugandans were ruled by a handful of Nubian thugs.

'Why then,' people whispered to each other, 'does the world not save us?'

Namanve Forest became the graveyard of Uganda. Skeletons, newly dead carcasses and bloodstained clothing could be found on casual excursions into the forest. It was whispered that there were cannibal camps deep in its heart. The rumour became fact when a schoolteacher miraculously escaped from one of these camps and, on reaching Kenya, told such tales of barbarity that they could scarcely be believed.

Later, another man, who had been left for dead among a pile of corpses in the forest, struggled out from the tangle of limbs and, with a bullet lodged in his head, found his way to a mission hospital where he was operated on and nursed back to health. Gradually other accounts of these camps emerged and by the end of 1974 people had learned not to enter the silent forest of death.

In spite of these reports, Uganda's plight went unheeded. Embassies, trade missions and foreign corporations still had amicable relations with Amin's government, treating the President like an amiable clown and raising not a voice in protest at the slaughter around them.

'Look at the French Embassy! Right next door to the State Research Bureau!' said Henry angrily. 'They must be able to hear the screaming but they carry on as if nothing were amiss.'

'It's worse than a nightmare,' said Sarah Musoke when we visited her once. 'You can wake from a nightmare, but from Amin there is no respite.'

It was not surprising, therefore, that there was little local sympathy over the arrest of Dennis Hills, an erstwhile English lecturer at the local teachers' college. The Hills affair burst onto the international scene shortly after Moira was born. Hills had committed the crime of referring to Amin as a 'village tyrant' in a book he was writing.

'What a blatantly stupid thing to do,' said the African people, most of whom had had relatives killed for less.

'It puts all us white people in danger,' said Eva as anti-European sentiments began to blare forth from Radio Uganda.

Hills was put on trial before a kangaroo court composed of army officers. After much publicity he was sentenced to death. The world reacted quickly. There were appeals for clemency from many heads of state, including a personal appeal from Queen Elizabeth. Old British Army pals of Amin, friendly Moslem leaders, Christian groups and individuals from a variety of countries bombarded Amin with pleas for mercy. James Callaghan himself, the British Foreign Secretary, flew to Uganda to plead with Amin. The foreign press focused unwaveringly on the situation until Hills was released.

'Where was the international furore over the thousands of innocent deaths before this?' said Joe witheringly. 'As Head of the Commonwealth the Queen never once intervened on behalf of the thousands of black Ugandans being slaughtered, yet here she is appealing for a single white man who practically asked for his plight. It's utterly racist.' I remembered Musoke, savagely eliminated, just one victim among hundreds of thousands whose deaths had gone virtually unremarked, and I knew that Joe was right.

When Moira was three months old, a waif of a baby, we took her to the village to receive her traditional name. During the afternoon I developed an ache in my lower abdomen. I went to the latrine and found I was bleeding.

Uterine cancer!

'Don't be silly,' said Joe when I told him. 'It's just an irregular period.'

On the way back to Kampala I huddled miserably in the seat with Moira in my arms.

If I died you'd have Gloria and the kids all to yourself.

The symptoms did not improve over the next few days and I went to see Dr Dublin, who told me I needed a D and C and scheduled me for surgery the following week. During the operation the uterine wall was accidentally perforated. It was thought to be relatively minor and I was sent back to the ward to recover. As the day wore on I felt increasingly fatigued and by evening even sitting up became an effort. Dr Dublin checked me over. In all my association with her I had never seen her look really worried until that moment. It seemed that I was haemorrhaging internally through the tear in my uterus.

'You'll have to go back to theatre, dearie. I'm sorry but we've got to stop that bleeding.'

Too weak to care, I was doped up and rushed back to theatre

and woke to find myself with a drip in my arm and a drain in my stomach. On top of this I contracted a bacterial infection and then malaria.

'You never do things by half now, do you?' smiled Dr Dublin as I presented one side of my bottom for a malaria shot and the other for an antibiotic. I lay back on my pillow hot and exhausted, too sick to care whether I lived or died. I remained in hospital for nearly three weeks.

One day as I was recovering Joe brought in an exquisite gold Swiss watch for me.

'Oh, it's beautiful!' I slipped it on.

'You look so pale and thin, Heather.' He took my hand. 'Please get well quickly. I can't bear to see you like this.' His eyes filled with tears and he turned away. It had been a long time since I had seen such caring in him.

Maybe . . . maybe everything will be all right.

'Joe, I want to come home. I miss the babies. I miss you all.'

Eye to eye, hand in hand, we sat there, he worried and loving, me longing to hope. I felt the ghost of Gloria leaving us and a blessed peace descended on me.

I was discharged from hospital just as the OAU conference was about to take place in Kampala. Amin promoted himself to field marshal for the occasion. His title now ran: His Excellency, Al Haj, Field Marshal Dr Idi Amin Dada, VC, DSO, MC, Life President of Uganda, Conqueror of the British Empire.

An Amin directive ordered everyone to wear costumes made of specially produced patriotic material for the duration of the conference. The material showed bullfroggish Amin faces against red, yellow and black Ugandan flags. The directive further stated that everyone was to look happy.

'On pain of death,' I said to Joe and we began to laugh.

His directive was obeyed and during the conference I went to school in my long patriotic skirt. Mrs Ssali's turbans often showed Amin's face beaming down like the man in the moon. On streets all over Kampala people in their ridiculous outfits greeted each other with hilarity so that Amin's order for everyone to look happy was unwittingly fulfilled.

Amin married his fifth wife, Sarah, during the conference. He had arranged the murder of her boyfriend – Sarah was later to find his severed head in a locked refrigerator – and made her undergo the marriage ceremony three times. The first wedding was in accordance with the Moslem tradition; the second was held a few days later for the benefit of the OAU visitors, with Amin decked out like a peacock in his new blue field marshal's uniform and heavily weighted with scores of self-awarded medals; and the third was for the television cameras so that the whole country could see the wedding – again and again and again. I felt sorry for the eighteen-year-old bride on Amin's arm who looked very, very scared.

One evening, shortly after the OAU conference had finished, Rosina Kalule, harbinger of doom, wandered in as once before to assuage her thirst. After a couple of waragis she told me she had been talking with her niece at Makerere who knew Gloria. I wondered if I imagined a trace of malice in her soft voice.

'I'm not interested, Rosina,' I said hastily, my heart thumping in dreadful anticipation.

'Oh, it's nothing to worry about,' and she told me about the gold watch Joe had recently given Gloria. In every detail the watch was like mine. 'It's nothing to worry about,' she repeated smoothly, 'I'm told the watch was his parting present to her.'

'Parting present! A kick in the arse would have been a better parting present!' The agonising feeling of betrayal rose within me again. I looked down at the watch on my wrist ticking away like a little time bomb.

'Maybe Joe got two for the price of one,' she said as she examined my watch. 'It's so pretty.'

'I'll never wear it again!' I flung it off.

Oh God, it's no use trying any more.

I had allowed the watch to signal in a new start for us. Through it, somehow, I had dared to hope again, dared to trust again.

'Oh God! How could he?'

'Now, now. What are you upset for? That watch was like a golden handshake. A farewell. An inducement to get lost.' There was a smile on her lips as she poured herself more waragi.

'Bullshit! It was a token of appreciation, a memento of him. In other words, a return ticket.'

I knew beyond all doubt that everything was over. Whether he sincerely meant to break with Gloria was irrelevant. Whether in fact he even gave her a watch was irrelevant. I had lost – he had taken from me – the ability to trust. We would end up destroying each other if we stayed together.

Rosina belched. Anger and bitterness rose within me. 'Get out,' I said quietly. 'You've had your kicks, you sadistic bitch.'

'Ah, you Bazungu are so difficult.' She got up, shaking her head sadly. A little smile hovered in the corners of her mouth.

After she had gone I sat on the arm of the chair staring numbly into the gathering darkness beyond the window. I knew it was the end – I would have to leave Uganda.

Chapter 31

I confronted Joe about the watch when he came in that evening. The unattractive look of guilt came over his face and his eyes flicked away from mine. I told him, feeling surprisingly calm, how I felt about having my services ranked equally with Gloria's and thereby getting an identical reward.

Joe admitted that there had been two watches and that Gloria had been given hers, not by him but by Byron, as a parting gesture to make sure she stayed away.

'Why should she have a parting gift at all?' He didn't answer, but it didn't matter.

Nothing matters when trust has gone.

I told him of the hurt I was feeling, how I had lost the ability to trust, the grief I felt at losing that trust. I put his food down before him and joined him at the table. He ate rapidly as if it would disappear.

'I . . . I don't think I can ever fully trust anyone again.'

'That's your problem. I can't help it if you're an emotional cripple.'

'You gave that whore a watch and you expect me to applaud!'

He rose angrily to throw his dinner into the bin. Then he turned on me and slapped my face. Stunned, I sat motionless at the table, my ears ringing. When I had gathered my wits I said quietly that the children and I would be leaving him.

'*You* leave, then! *You* get out of my life! But I tell you one thing.' He pulled me off the chair by the shoulders. 'You'll never take my children with you! *Never!* They're mine! They stay in Uganda!'

'You're not fit to be their father. You only want them as proof of your virility. Have some more with Gloria and leave me with mine.'

'Don't delude yourself! You won't get custody of them. They're Ugandans. You'll need my written consent before these children can travel abroad and I'll never give that.'

'I'll get ambassadorial help. They'll be given dual nationality and I'll get them out that way.'

He laughed. 'That's good! You try. Ugandans can't have dual nationality. It was stopped during the Asian business.' He walked out of the room. I stood there in mounting panic, knowing he was right.

We were at Clarice's.

'The only thing I can do is to win back his trust and dupe him into allowing the kids and me to holiday in New Zealand at Christmas. Once there, we simply won't come back.'

I had explored every possibility, including visits to two different lawyers, and the New Zealand holiday seemed the only option that would work. I knew it would take time to gain Joe's confidence after the row about the watch but I had nearly five months until Christmas in which to be a model wife.

'I don't think he'll fall for it,' said Eva. 'He's not stupid.'

'Is it fair?' said Clarice. 'He really does love those kids, you know.'

I felt a pang of conscience.

'You'd have to live such a lie,' said Eva.

'I can. He did.'

Clarice's dark eyes flashed. 'You'd be depriving the kids of a father forever.'

'Not necessarily,' I said. 'He might see the light and join us. We could be so happy in New Zealand.'

'The incurable romantic!' hooted Clarice. 'These men don't crawl after women.'

223

'The tragedy is leaving your home open for Gloria,' said Eva. 'If you intend to trick him, you'll have to leave everything behind.'

This had occurred to me, too. Now that the scales were falling from my eyes I had begun to tally up the contribution I had made to the household. Joe had bought the house and the cars, but practically everything in the house – the freezer, the stove, the beds and bedding, the furniture and paintings as well as the children's clothes, all the food and the servants' wages – were paid for by me. The thought of Gloria and Joe enjoying the spoils of my labour made my blood boil.

'I feel like ringing her. Can I?'

Clarice nodded, smiling broadly. For the last time I dialled Makerere and asked for Gloria.

'Hello,' I said as she replied. 'How's your watch?'

'Pardon me?'

Clarice grabbed the phone from me. 'That watch is a cheap and nasty piece of works! Just like you! You both belong in the garbage!'

Snatching back the receiver, I told her she was a homebreaker and a disgrace to womankind.

'I'll get the law on you,' came the breathless reply and she slammed down the phone in my ear.

'The cheap and nasty piece of works!' mimicked Eva and we all began to laugh.

'I'm going to miss you both so much,' I said when we had all quietened down. They sat across the table from me, suddenly serious, their eyes bright with tears, but whether from mirth or sadness I couldn't tell.

'Dear Paul, Don't die of shock at this letter out of the blue. I want to know more about this Domestic Purpose Benefit thing you were talking about that day at Scorching Bay. Sad things have happened since I last saw you . . .'

I scribbled on for fifteen minutes before putting the letter in an envelope to post the following day. Then, humming, I picked Moira out of the playpen to change her nappy. 'Hello, little Moi-moi! Shall we go outside and see the others?' She smiled and kicked as I changed her. Outside we sat on a grass mat under the trees, watching Nakalo, Tanya and Joseph raking up leaves with twig brooms. I smiled as they became too enthusiastic in their help and upset Kerasese's piles of leaves. He shouted at them, waving the rake in his skinny hand. Nakalo and Joseph ran off screaming, leaving Tanya behind sweeping stoically. She had never been afraid of the old man. He had taught her how to transplant seedlings and to recognise the shoots of the carrots, spring onions and sweet potatoes that grew in rows in the vegetable garden.

Ernest brought out afternoon tea – orange juice and fruit for the children and a pot of tea for me. Nakalo told me she had seen a monkey in the avocado tree.

'I think he's very lonely,' she said. 'He has a sad face, Mama, like you when you're thinking.'

'Oh dear. Do look like a monkey?' I pulled a face, made monkey noises and got them to laugh.

As we sat there chatting and drinking in the warm afternoon sun I realised with a little shock that these distinctively African afternoons were numbered. I settled Moira in the crook of my arm, knowing how deeply I would miss this way of life.

Joe and I were back on our former footing. At first it had been an effort not to question his lateness or comment on his little acts of thoughtlessness, but gradually I had slipped into the easy acquiescence of our early Lubowa days and a sense of stability prevailed. It was a relief to experience the tranquillity after the weeks of storminess. As I used to do when I was mwebafu, I kept his dinner warm and his beer cold, almost enjoying seeing to his comforts because of the peaceful companionship that followed.

After he had eaten his dinner, we would sit in the darkened living room discussing politics, mutual friends or snippets of news we had heard on overseas broadcasts. As we laughed about the children, or made plans for renovating some part of the house, I almost forgot that I was soon to leave. The knowledge would return with a short, sharp stab.

One night he came in at ten o'clock with a bottle of wine and a bag of ensenene. We drank as we prepared the grasshoppers, discarding the wings and limbs, and tossing the plump bodies into a buttered frying pan.

'Dinner is served,' sang Joe, as he tipped the food into a bowl.

'You clot,' I giggled. 'You'll wake the kids.'

Tiptoeing into the lounge, giggling a bit from the wine, we feasted on ensenene and then made love on the couch. Afterwards I wondered why on earth I wanted to leave. I lay beside Joe reminding myself sternly that there was more to marriage than a ten o'clock fry-up and a roll on the couch. I had to dredge up the whole litany of his sins – the way he kept me shut out of his social life, how in six years of marriage he had never offered me housekeeping money, the way he spent most weekends drinking with his friends, my lonely evenings waiting for him to come home, his irresponsibility as a parent, the way he took me for granted and, of course, Gloria – before I was once more sure in my mind that to save my soul I had to leave him.

Tonight, however, had been fun. I stirred beside him.

'Jozefu?'

'Darling?'

'It'd be so nice for all of us to go home for Christmas.' Joe wasn't keen on the idea for himself but agreed that I should go with one of the children, perhaps Moira since I was so worried about her health. 'My family would be terribly disappointed if you and the other kids didn't come. Can't we all go together?'

Oh, if only you would come. Our lives would be so much better over there.

'Perhaps take Joseph as well. He missed out last time.'

'But what about Tanya?'

'I can't let you all go. I'd lose you all if the plane crashes. Anyway, Tanya's already been – I'd like her to stay back and keep me and Nakalo company.'

I didn't want to arouse his suspicions by pleading. I consoled myself that there was plenty of time to make him change his mind.

There were two problems to solve before my departure – Nakalo and my school. Nakalo had been with us for a year. We all loved her and I was plagued with guilt at the thought of abandoning her. I toyed with the idea of sending her back to her mother in the village, although I knew Mary already had her hands full. I finally decided that she should go to Henry and Violet, who already had a young niece living with them who would be good company for Nakalo. I planned to ask them nearer the time if they would have her while we were away. I knew they would agree and would be happy to keep her when we failed to return.

With Nakalo taken care of, I turned to the question of the school. I tried for as long as I could to put off accepting what was the only real option, but finally I had to face up to it. The school had to be sold. It was sickening to contemplate. It was as much a part of my life as the children were. I had watched it develop and grow over the years, had slaved over it, shed tears over it, exulted over it as lovingly as any mother over a child, and the thought of handing over to someone else filled me with burning resentment.

There were only two people on earth that I considered worthy of the school. I offered it to them as the second term drew to an end.

'Katonda wange!' Mrs Ssali was incredulous. 'Why are you giving up?'

I told her it had been a strain since my operation and that I needed a break. 'It's taken me a long time to reach this decision. It's an ideal venture for you both. You both know the ropes.'

'We'll get the money somehow,' said Miss Mubiru excitedly, breathlessly, much as I had been when it was first offered to me nearly six years ago. I turned away as a wave of bitterness swept over me.

Fortuitously I was offered a position in the kindergarten of a small international primary school on Buganda Road. The job was available from the start of the third term in September.

'They'll pay in American dollars,' I told Joe with what I hoped passed for enthusiasm. 'It'll mean selling my school, of course, but the benefits are obvious. Less responsibility, fewer children, nice surroundings and money in an overseas account.'

He was surprised at first, as I knew he would be, but he thought it a sound move. 'It's also in a built-up part of town,' he said. 'Not as vulnerable as your school sitting out there on the swamp.'

My school was vulnerable only to you. It survived everything else.

'Your school was always a bit of a liability. You'll be a lot happier without it. Kiss it goodbye with no regrets.'

'Right,' I said, biting back the sharp retort that leapt to my lips, realising now that he could never, never have understood how much the school had meant to me.

There is so much he never understood.

Mrs Ssali and Miss Mubiru raised the money to buy the school. During those last days of my tenure I was consumed with sadness and found myself lingering around the children as they worked, talking with them more, listening to them more, wondering where life would take them.

I showed the two teachers the list of names in the back of the fees book and explained my welfare system of full fees, partial fees and no fees.

'What do you think?' said Miss Mubiru to Mrs Ssali. 'I'm willing if you are.'

'We'll continue in the same tradition,' she said firmly.

I urged them to keep up the mid-morning snacks and gave them the whereabouts of my secret milk supply. 'I'll make sure you get enough for your own use as well.' They were agreeable and I left them conferring about the appointment of another teacher to replace me. I wandered away heartsick.

Six years I ran this school and Gloria has deprived me of it. She's also deprived me of a husband and my children of a father.

'It's not wholly her,' said Eva, when I voiced this. 'Joe must bear half the blame.'

'If she wasn't such a slut, this never would have happened.'

'It would. With somebody else,' said Eva and I knew, deep down, she was probably right.

On my last day of school I poured out my concerns to Mrs Ssali and Miss Mubiru.

'Don't forget about the medication in the box for Deogratias's asthma attacks. If he gets too bad rush him across the road to the clinic.'

'We know,' said Mrs Ssali, smiling patiently.

'Now you're familiar with the rent and the Moslem Supreme Council, aren't you? For God's sake keep on the right side of them! That new boy Kibuka – I'm sure he's partially deaf. You'll need to talk with his parents. And can you occasionally pay visits to the nearby primary schools? I'm sure it helps our kids gain admission. Oh yes, if the toilets block up call Ronnie Lubega's father – he fixed them last time.'

They assured me they would.

'You will keep John and Agnes and Rose and Mary on, won't you?'

'We promise,' said Mrs Ssali, rolling her eyes heavenward. She brought out her basket and took out an enormous cake.

'Come on now. It's your farewell. Let's have a party!'

It was difficult to join in the spirit of the party. I looked about me, lost in thought.

There's Magdalene Mukasa with her withered polio arm. We have taught her to write and to paint. I know there is more potential in that arm. I hear John with his radio outside. Although he dresses in rags and lives in a room on a swamp, I've nothing but the highest regard for him. And those Masembe children – their father deserted them and the mother cooks for the army to support them. How they're enjoying the cake!

The children sang songs and played games and we passed around the cakes and drinks. I forced myself to be gay and hearty. When it became too much I went outside to the verandah, idly surveying the car-washers filling their buckets at the swamp.

Here I stand at the grand old age of twenty-eight! For ten years I've lived my life around Joe – six of them as his wife. They were years when I was young, enthusiastic and adaptable. All wasted! He stole from me the best years of my life!

'How sad you look, teacher.' John was at my side.

'It's difficult to say goodbye.'

'You were happy here, si bwe keri?'

I nodded.

'Is it really all over?'

'Yes.'

'Teacher, we're not just talking of school, are we?'

I said nothing. John, perceptive, compassionate, seemed to know.

Mrs Ssali's and Miss Mubiru's voices drifted out through the window. I supposed they were planning ahead for their school.

'*Their* school,' I said aloud.

'*Your* school. Wherever you go in this world your school will always be here, right opposite the mosque.'

'It's a comforting thought.'

'I too will always remember it as your school.'

'Thank you.' We shook hands sadly. 'Weraba, John.'

'Weraba.'

I turned and left him as the tears began to fall.

I rang my parents the next day, Saturday, while Joe was out with friends. For almost a year I had kept from them the business about Joe and Gloria but I felt now was the time to tell them. It was night in New Zealand and Dad's gruff sleepy voice answered. I burst into tears, pouring out all my misery – Joe's infidelity, giving up the school, the great cracks in our marriage, my worry over Moira. I told them of the difficulties of getting out of Uganda with the children and my plans to trick Joe into letting us return to New Zealand.

'I don't like your tricking him,' said Dad.

'Look what he did to me!'

'Have you tried talking with your parish priest?' Mum's voice chimed in on the extension.

'He fornicates too, Mum.'

'And what about Moira?' said Mum.

'It's nothing specific. She's just so . . . so . . . small and frail. I want her to see a specialist. I want to come home. I want to leave Joe.'

There was silence.

I told them about Gloria, the Rubaga house, the gold watch.

'She has a lot to answer for,' said Mum. 'You must hold your head up and pretend she doesn't exist.'

'Doesn't exist! She's forever in my mind.' I heard my voice rise. 'She just won't go away. Whenever I look at the kids I think of her. Whenever I look at Joe I'm reminded of her. Whenever I see an attractive woman on the street I wonder if it's her. I can't read or write or teach or sleep that she doesn't come into my mind. She just won't go away!'

'. . . a thoroughly nasty piece of baggage,' I heard Mum say, with unusual venom.

'You can come home right now,' said Dad. 'I'll send you the money.'

'Thanks, but I'd never get the kids out that way. I'll have to do it my way. Christmas isn't far off.'

'In the meantime think positively.' This was Mum. 'Do something with the family. Why don't you pack a picnic basket and take Joe and the children out for tea?'

'I don't fancy taking fish stew and boiled vegetables on a picnic.'

'How bitter you sound,' said Dad sadly.

'We'll look forward to seeing you at Christmas,' said Mum.

After we had hung up I stood motionless, drained and homesick. I supposed Mum and Dad would put on the kettle and sit together until dawn, consoling each other over cups of tea. I could almost see the silhouette of Noah's Ark and the shadowy browsing sheep in the paddocks as the sun crept up. How peaceful, how perfect a partnership they had. I wondered if they would ever fully understand the misery and devastation that went hand in hand with a splintering marriage.

I smiled through my tears as I recalled Mum's attempt to patch it up with a picnic basket.

Chapter 32

The kindergarten on Buganda Road was a far cry from my school in Nakivubo. A drive swept to the front door where quality cars deposited their children at eight-thirty each morning. The building was spacious and clean with an outdoor play area and infinite facilities. If I needed anything, I only had to mention it to the American principal and it was there on my desk the following morning.

In my charge I had no more than fifteen mostly expatriate little children. They were bright and confident, arriving each morning with scrubbed faces and brushed hair, their Disneyland schoolbags containing ham sandwiches, Barbie dolls and Superman figures with ray guns. They were nice children but I longed for my shy, raggedy, little totos by the swamp.

There was no great sense of personal satisfaction in my work at this kindergarten and I felt slightly guilty at being paid so much for doing what seemed so little. There was no formal teaching as such, since these children needed no preparation for primary school interviews. They simply walked into the first-grade classroom down the hall on their sixth birthday. Sometimes bored mothers with nothing else to do popped in to 'help' and I was drawn into chats about housegirls and where to find a good dentist. While we cut, pasted, sang and painted, my thoughts often wandered across town to my school and I longed to be there.

Uganda's economy continued to decline. Racketeering and the black market were now an established way of life. Prices rose almost daily. Had the land not been so fertile, widespread starvation would have decimated the population long ago, but while there were fruit on the trees, vegetables in the gardens and fish in the lakes, the people could get by without sugar, flour, soap, milk and almost everything else.

Amin had by this time found a new favourite, an eccentric Briton by the name of Bob Astles, who had drifted into Uganda years before. A scrawny man with a face that suggested a lifelong diet of sour lemons, Astles became Amin's chief adviser, sidekick, lap dog, court jester – and a feared man. There were rumours of his complicity in vast coffee-smuggling operations and in questionable land deals. He was believed to be an accomplice in many of Amin's gruesome activities and was loathed by Ugandans and his fellow Britons alike.

Amin, Adrisi and Astles were now the most hated names in Uganda. I once saw a newspaper picture of the three of them at a military parade in Entebbe. They sat together – bloated Amin, cretinous Adrisi and mean-faced Astles. 'God save Uganda,' I murmured, but God didn't.

A new shock wave hit the country when Amin tried to murder his former wife Malyamu. He had already had her arrested and imprisoned for 'smuggling' and when she was released he had her car rammed by his bodyguards as she drove through the outskirts of Kampala. Incredibly she survived the crash but remained in hospital for weeks. Amin, furious that his plans had been thwarted, ordered hospital authorities to transfer her from the private ward, for which she was paying, to the noisy over-crowded public ward. When she was discharged she had to flee for her life, leaving Uganda and her six children to the vagaries of Amin.

I used the plight of these six motherless children to again bring up the subject of taking all the children back with me for my Christmas 'visit' to New Zealand.

'Please change your mind, Joe. Let Tanya come. My parents are dying to see her.'

'It'll be her turn next time. Perhaps even I'll go too.'

And that was as far as it got.

By December I was ready to cancel our trip. Joe refused to change his mind and there was no way I would leave without Tanya.

'What the fuck do I do?' I demanded angrily of the walls as I sat alone one evening ten days before we were due to depart. The clock ticked into the still living room. The children were asleep, Abby and Ernest in their quarters, Kerasese was out wheeling and dealing among the Jaluos and Joe was not yet home. I was tempted to pile the kids into the Range Rover and head for Kenya but deep down I knew it would be courting fate to leave without the children's correct travel documents. With my head in my hands I allowed myself to dream that we were all free, thirty-two thousand feet above Entebbe on our way home. I also dreamed of making a big bonfire before I left, in which I would burn all my possessions so that Gloria couldn't have them.

The sound of distant ululating, the local call of alarm, penetrated my ruminating brain. I heard the guard dogs howl, one after the other, all along our road. There was shouting and a resounding crash. Kondos! I froze. One of the askaris knocked on the kitchen door and I rushed to open it. He stood in the shadows, bundled in his greatcoat, fingering a wooden club. All around us in the darkness dogs howled like fiends from hell.

'Memsahib, kondos up the road! At the Italian house!' He estimated that there were about ten of them, all well armed. I hurried back inside and tried to dial the police.

'Work, bugger you!' But the phone remained dead and no amount of abuse or thumping would cajole it into action.

Abby rushed in. 'Mummy, they are breaking into the Airplane Muzungu's!' The British airline representative's house bordered ours.

'Lord, we could be next!' In panic I thought of the sleeping children. Outside I heard Bella and Mengo barking viciously but, like our two askaris, they could not protect us from armed thugs.

'We'll go to your room, Abby! We'll leave the doors of the house open. Let them loot the place unhindered.'

We woke the children and, carrying the two smaller ones, with Tanya and Nakalo stumbling sleepily beside us, crossed the lawn to the servants' quarters. Once in Abby's room we bundled them up on the narrow bed and Abby settled on a small wooden stool with Moira in her arms. I crouched at the end of the bed, thinking how frightened and vulnerable we all looked and feeling intense anger at Joe for leaving us on our own so much when he knew this could happen at any time.

Ernest passed the door on his way to the gates. I went with him. Through the iron bars we could see the kondos regrouping outside the airline man's house. It occurred to me, ridiculously, that if they looted our house I would not be needing the bonfire to get rid of my goods. I watched the road in fearful apprehension. The askaris had melted into the bushes, knowing that the slightest opposition from them would mean a swift death. The kondos were talking together, their loot in piles at their feet. They were carrying guns and pangas.

Suddenly from the direction of Entebbe Road came the distant blaring of police sirens. Obviously some one's phonecall had got through. The kondos dispersed quickly, picking up their booty and piling themselves into two station wagons parked a little further up the road.

'Thank God!' I felt limp with relief.

The first car surged forward, its lights illuminating the darkness ahead and lighting up a lone drunken figure zigzagging down the road. The car made no attempt to avoid the swaying pedestrian, who was struck with a loud crack and catapulted several yards into the bushes. The two cars roared into top speed, turned the corner and were lost to sight.

The residents now swarmed onto the road. The Italian man, badly beaten, was being helped into a neighbour's car. I could hear his wife's shrill voice as she got in beside him. I hurried up the road with Ernest to see if I could help but the neighbours had everything under control. The car moved off slowly, the Italian man holding a blood-soaked cloth to his face. People stood around in hushed groups, talking. I joined them for a few minutes but I was anxious to get back to the children and went home. Down the road several askaris were searching the bushes for the injured pedestrian. The police arrived, sirens blaring, as I reached our driveway.

'The police are here. We can go back to bed,' I told Abby.

'What good are the police if it was the army?' said Abby grimly.

As we wrapped the children in blankets and prepared to return to the house, two policemen appeared at the door. I jumped and clutched the sleeping Moira to me. They informed me that they had recovered the body of the pedestrian from the bushes. It was Kerasese. He had been killed outright.

'Oh God, no!' I gasped.

There was a scream from behind me, followed by an eerie wailing. 'I want Kerasese! Make him come home. I want him now.'

Tanya, screaming, was tugging my arm, her face contorted with fear. Before any of us could move she had pushed past us, dodged the men at the door and had run screaming into the night. Handing the baby to Abby, I rushed after her. I caught up with her at the gates where she was kicking and screaming in an effort to get through the bars. I drew the frantic, shuddering little body to me but she escaped, squeezed through the bars and ran down the road to where Kerasese was lying in the midst of a knot of people.

By the time I had opened the gate and rushed after her she had seen the broken body and Ernest was bringing her home. She was sobbing inconsolably as I carried her into the house and down to her bedroom. I had to let her cry it out. Abby, herself in tears, was comforting a frightened Nakalo. The two little ones were asleep and Abby and I sat with Tanya and Nakalo until they finally dozed off.

It seemed ages before Joe arrived. By that time Lubowa was calm and Kerasese's body had gone with the police. Only when I felt his arms about me did I feel my reserves break down.

'The poor old man! Oh God, it was awful!' I burst into tears.

'I'm sorry,' he whispered, stroking my hair. 'I'm truly sorry.'

I cried into his shirt front, reliving our fear of the kondos, Kerasese's death, Tanya's anguished reaction.

'There, there. In a few days you'll be home in New Zealand.'

'I'm not going home! Don't you see! I can't leave Tanya after this.' All hopes of my trip home vanished.

'There, there. Sirika wo.'

'I never really knew Kerasese, never bothered to find out much about him. I never even knew how fond Tanya was of him. Life floats blindly past me. I didn't even know the Vietnam War was over.'

'Don't cry. I think you should go home, darling. You really need the break.'

I shook my head.

He was silent for a while and then he said, 'What if Tanya were to go with you?'

It took a few seconds for the implication to sink in. 'You must come, too. Please, Joe!' I heard the desperation in my voice but I couldn't stop. 'I can't bear to leave you! I love you so much! Come back with us and things will be all right.'

'Ssh . . . ssh . . .'

I clung to him, never wanting to let him go.

Whatever happens, wherever I end up, I'll go to my grave loving you.

The beaten Italian man returned to Lubowa with a faceful of stitches and a pin in his jaw. The airline man bought a Dobermann and our askaris added more bows and arrows to their arsenal. Lubowa hummed with the aftermath of its night of violence and Kerasese, universally disliked in life, became a hero in death.

I couldn't bear to engage another shamba man. The sweeping garden in its wild and colourful profusion was a memorial to Kerasese and while I remained in Uganda I wanted to keep it that way. It was because of him, after all, that I had got my chance to leave.

It was a sombre household that prepared for our departure. Ernest brought out the suitcases from the back of the garage and dusted them down, his face quiet and sorrowful. Abby, red-eyed, washed and ironed the children's clothes and laid them out to be packed. Joe, full of remorse over his absence on the fateful night, tried to compensate by presenting us with first-class air tickets. Such extravagance succeeded only in making me guiltier than ever, knowing that I would never use the return portion.

I brooded over all sorts of things in those last days. Had Kerasese been happy with us? Would the children adjust easily to New Zealand society, different as they were from both Maori and Pakeha? Would Joe follow us to New Zealand when we failed to return? Was I being unfair to the children by taking them away?

The children sensed the brooding atmosphere and kept out of the adults' way, passing very little comment on the suitcases appearing in the hall. Sometimes Tanya would come to me and bury her head in my lap for a few seconds. I tried to get her to talk about Kerasese but she said very little and her face became clouded and sad. She never again swept the yard with the twig broom or put scraps on the bird table.

The day to leave arrived. Nakalo had been taken to Henry and Violet's the previous morning. She had asked me to bring her back a doll. Her eyes regarded me trustingly as she stood with Violet on the doorstep clutching her suitcase.

'I'll . . . I'll try,' I had said but could not meet her eyes. I had scooped her up suddenly, kissed her hard and then run quickly back to the car.

Ernest and Joe finished loading up the Mercedes. I gathered up the children and we got in. Joe started up the car and we waved to Ernest and Abby as we moved off. They stood together on the driveway – dear, dependable Abby, short and stocky in a blue dress and scarf, smiling and waving, and Ernest in his bare feet, white apron and shorts. I felt my throat constrict and I had to turn away.

The drive to Entebbe seemed endless. I dared not cry, I almost dared not speak. I nuzzled Moira's curls as she sat on my knee. I looked up at Joe, imprinting in my mind the soft dark curves of his cheek and jaw, features repeated in miniature in the faces of the children.

Forgive me, Joe.

Through the window the evergreen foliage flashed by. We passed vegetable stalls, elderly white-gowned men on bicycles and groups of sturdy women carrying produce on their heads.

Goodbye, Uganda.

We talked, or rather Joe did. Overcome with feelings of guilt and grief, I could only answer in monosyllables through a throat that was thick and tear-clogged.

Eventually we came to Entebbe. Armed soldiers stared at us as we all got out. Moira fretted and wanted a bottle. Her baby things were in one of the cabin bags. 'Shh . . . sh . . .' I whispered and longed for Abby.

As if in a dream I followed Joe into the building. He had a child on each hand and I hung back a little, reflecting that this would be the last time I would see them thus linked. Tears dripped on to Moira. I stopped and hastily wiped them away on her dress. It was an effort to get myself back under control.

We checked in, Joe joking with the children about the sheep and ice creams they would find in New Zealand. My whole body felt tight and nervy and I gasped when our flight was finally called.

'Hey, Jozefu!' He swung Joseph up to him. 'You'll look after Mummy and your sisters on the plane, won't you?' Joseph beamed with pleasure.

It was time to leave. I turned to Joe, my heart beating very fast. 'Goodbye . . . Have a great Christmas . . . I love you, Joe . . . goodbye, darling . . .'

He put Joseph down and kissed me for the last time. Then he bent and kissed each of the children. He finally took my hand and kissed that too.

'Goodbye, Heather. I'll miss you, darling. Have a safe trip.' He kissed my hand again. 'Weraba.'

'Weraba.'

I could still feel his warmth on my mouth as we climbed the stairway into the aircraft. I could still smell him in my nostrils. I could still even see my eyes in his as we said goodbye. I wanted to huddle in my seat, retaining him in my senses for as long as I could.

'Welcome! Do come in!' The effusive freckled-armed hostess pounced on us at the doorway and bustled us to our seats, flushing Joe from my senses forever. She seated the children and buckled us all in, prattling. 'You must be so glad to leave that awful place! We hear such terrible things about Uganda!'

I remembered Abby in her blue dress waving from the driveway. 'It's a wonderful country with wonderful people,' I said churlishly. She looked at me rather strangely and closed my curtain against the sun before trying again.

'Do you enjoy nannying?'

'They are *my* children,' I said tiredly, wondering how often in the future I would have to say this.

The hostess left us and I pulled back the curtain to stare out of the window. Beside me Tanya and Joseph examined half-sucked sweets in sticky fingers. The plane shuddered to life and moved along the runway. I leaned my head against the window, too tired even for tears.

Goodbye, Joe. Goodbye, everything.

We took off as smoothly as a bird. Lake Victoria unfolded beneath us, sparkling and silver-blue, and as we climbed higher the great carpet of Uganda, lush-green and opulent, spread out like a gift at our feet. From here there was no Amin, no Makindye, just the soft, shimmering contours of a country they called the Pearl of Africa.

Glossary of (mainly) Luganda Words

askari (Swahili) — guard, caretaker
ayah (Swahili) — child-carer, nanny
Baba Saidi! (Swahili) — father of Saidi!
Baganda (singular, Muganda) — the largest tribal group in Uganda; the 3.5 million inhabitants of the traditional kingdom of Buganda
basuti — long gown of Baganda women
berali fulu (from English) — bloody fool
Buganda — the largest traditional kingdom in Uganda, lying on the western shores of Lake Victoria
Bayindi (singular, Muyindi) — Indians (Asians)
bwana kidogo (Swahili) — little master
dukka (Swahili) — small trading store found all over East Africa
ebiyenda — local stew of goat intestines
ensenene — edible grasshopper
fitina (Swahili) — jealousy, malice

241

fuluma mangu! (Swahili)	get out!
fundi (Swahili)	workman
hapana (Swahili)	no
jambo (Swahili)	hello
Kabaka	hereditary king of Buganda
kanzu	gown worn by Baganda men
kale	okay, all right
Katonda wange!	my God!
kibadde-ki?	what's the matter?
Kiganda	pertaining to the Baganda
kino kitalo	it is sad
kolele (Swahili)	noise, trouble
kondo (Swahili)	armed robber
kulika yo!	welcome
leeta Jozefu	bring Joseph
Luganda	language of the Baganda
matoke	cooking banana, a staple food of the Baganda
mendazi	a sweet cake
mubi	thief
Muganda	a person of the Baganda group
Muyindi	Indian (Asian)
Muzungu	European
mwebafu	naive, unknowing
nnabe	small ant
ni malaika wewe? (Swahili)	are you an angel?
ni mimi! Mwalimu! (Swahili)	It's me! Teacher!
oli lubito?	are you pregnant?
oli mulwadde?	are you sick?
samosa (Swahili)	pastry stuffed with meat or vegetables
sirika wo	hush, quiet (a term of comfort)
shamba (Swahili)	yard, property, garden
shauri yako (Swahili)	your problem
si bwe keri?	is it (not) so?
sigara (Swahili)	cigarettes
sigili (Swahili)	small charcoal stove

sufuria (Swahili)	big cooking pot
totos (coll. from Swahili)	children
Wabenzi (from Benz)	member of Mercedes Benz tribe, i.e. an owner of such a car
weraba	goodbye